HITLER'S WINTER

OSPREY
PUBLISHING

HITLER'S WINTER

THE GERMAN BATTLE OF THE BULGE

ANTHONY TUCKER-JONES

OSPREY PUBLISHING
Bloomsbury Publishing Plc
Kemp House, Chawley Park, Cumnor Hill, Oxford OX2 9PH, UK
29 Earlsfort Terrace, Dublin 2, Ireland
1385 Broadway, 5th Floor, New York, NY 10018, USA
E-mail: info@ospreypublishing.com
www.ospreypublishing.com

OSPREY is a trademark of Osprey Publishing Ltd

First published in Great Britain in 2022

ISBN: HB 978 1 4728 4739 3; PB 978 1 4728 4740 9; eBook 978 1 4728 4738 6;
ePDF 978 1 4728 4741 6; XML 978 1 4728 4737 9

22 23 24 25 26   10 9 8 7 6 5 4 3 2 1

Foreword © Peter Caddick-Adams, 2022

Plate section image credits are given in full in the List of Illustrations (pp. 20–22).

Maps by www.bounford.com
Index by Alan Rutter

Typeset by Deanta Global Publishing Services, Chennai, India
Printed and bound in Great Britain by CPI (Group) UK Ltd, Croydon CR0 4YY

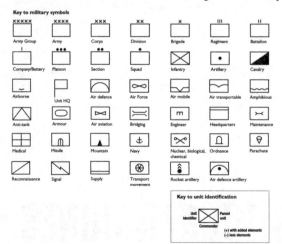

Contents

13 The Losheim Gap   139
14 Falcon Takes Flight   147

    PART FIVE: RACE AGAINST TIME   157

15 Victory at St Vith   159
16 Stalled at Bastogne   168
17 Clear Skies   177

    PART SIX: HERE COME THE AMERICANS   187

18 Almost to the Meuse   189
19 American Counter-attack   197

    PART SEVEN: TOO LATE TO HELP   207

20 Rockets to Antwerp   209
21 Battle of the Airfields   215
22 Alsace Diversion   224

    PART EIGHT: COMPLETE FAILURE   239

23 Back Where They Started   241
24 Where Did It All Go Wrong?   252

    Appendix   263
    Notes and References   288
    Bibliography   305
    Index   313

Foreword

By Professor Peter Caddick-Adams

The last winter of World War II was not only bitter but presented the Western Allies with the most unpleasant of surprises. Seemingly from nowhere, on 16 December 1944, German forces erupted out of the Ardennes regions of Belgium and Luxemburg in what became the Battle of the Bulge. At the end of the month, United Press International reporter Larry Newman was in Bastogne to interview the US 3rd Army's commander in Bastogne. 'It was cold as hell', he recalled. 'Patton was calm, cool, collected. It was war to him. What he had been brought up to expect – he had served in World War I, and his grandfather and great uncle had been Confederate lieutenant colonels, killed in the Civil War'.

Using his maps and reports, Patton described to Newman how the Germans had penetrated deep into Belgium, torn open a huge dent in the Allied lines, threatened to break through to the North Belgian plain and seize Antwerp. Several papers had already referred to the Axis salient in the Allied lines, but no one knew exactly what to call it. Although the battle was two weeks old, Newman, new on the scene, was about to file his first despatch about it. He needed a new angle. He began to toy with the words Patton had given him on his notepad, etched with his memories of battlegrounds, stories of heroism and sacrifice, flecked with grime and blood from other conflicts.

The phenomenon had been around for as long as military history itself. A precedent had been set already during World War I when the German front lines had curved in a giant arc around the Belgian city of Ypres throughout 1914–18, leaving an eastwards-facing fist, protruding from the British lines. In that war the Ypres area had been known as 'The Salient'. Newman wanted something different, less formal, and more American. 'I named it the Battle of the Bulge', he remembered modestly.

Within a short space of time, Newman's term had become widely accepted shorthand for the battle. The very next day the US Army's newspaper, *The Stars and Stripes* echoed Newman's UPI report with its own banner headline: 'Retake 1/3 of Bulge'. Larry Newman had made his enduring contribution to military history. However, as the Ardennes campaign was dying and the ink drying on Newman's headline, on 31 December, a second Nazi offensive was launched named *Nordwind* ('North Wind'). This was partly an attempt to exploit an American sector further south the Germans knew had been weakened in sending extra manpower to Bastogne. Less well-known than it should be, this second thrust from the Reich was likewise stalled by American units. In initiating not one, but two, major assaults, December 1944 to January 1945 was, indeed, Hitler's winter. Today, the US Army recognizes both attacks with their 'Ardennes-Alsace' campaign streamer.

That 32 US divisions fought in the Ardennes, where the daily battle strength of US Army units averaged 26 divisions and 610,000 men, indicates the Battle of the Bulge was a far larger commitment for the US Army than Normandy, where 19 divisions fought, and much greater than the Pacific. Altogether, the US Army Ground Forces activated 91 divisions during World War II: of which all but three entered combat. The vast majority of these (61 divisions) deployed to Europe, including Italy, as opposed to the remainder, which deployed to the Pacific, to which should be added six US Marine divisions. In fact, we should not get carried away by the infantry, armored and airborne divisions: far more important in the isolating terrain of the Ardennes were the endless non-divisional units, cavalry groups and independent tank destroyer, artillery, tank, and anti-aircraft battalions, who played their role alongside the badged divisional units, swelling US numbers and firepower greatly.

This, then, was the largest battle fought by American forces during the war. It has been related many times from the Allied point of view, in print and by movie. The earliest volumes included Colonel S.L.A. Marshall's *Bastogne* (1946), Robert E. Merriam's *Dark December* (1947), Charles B. MacDonald's *Company Commander* of the same year and his later memoir, *A Time for Trumpets* (1985). Later analysis of the Bulge included John Toland's *Battle* of 1959, other works by the US official historians Forrest C. Pogue and Hugh M. Cole, John D. Eisenhower's *The Bitter Woods* of 1969 and Gerald Astor's *A Blood-Dimmed Tide* (1992). The legacy of these statistics, authors and several good movies (plus the incredibly bad *Battle of the Bulge*, premiered in 1965 and denounced by Eisenhower personally), was that the Ardennes has since become American shorthand for the whole ground campaign in Europe. Although General Brian Horrocks' British 30th Corps provided an important backstop along the River Meuse and later helped close the Bulge, the campaign represented the American achievement in World War II in a way no other single battle ever could.

The observant reader will note no German contributions to the above post-war recounting of the Ardennes or Alsace campaigns, which is where this important study, *Hitler's Winter*, fits in. For the first ten years after VE Day, the Wehrmacht and particularly the Waffen-SS were under a cloud in the way they had fought, and various war crimes trials were brought against their ranks. You will read about the massacres of American prisoners and Belgian civilians in and around Malmedy and elsewhere in these pages. In 1946 75 former Waffen-SS men were assembled and tried en masse before a military court of senior US officers between May and July in the former Dachau concentration camp. Despite the overwhelming desire for justice, it started to emerge that in their enthusiasm, investigators and prosecutors had overstepped the mark in conducting mock trials, using false death sentences, beatings and abuse to extort confessions. By December 1956 all 73 of the convicted had been released, partly because the international situation had moved on.

Internationally, the successful Berlin Air Lift of June 1948–May 1949 had cemented Western antipathy towards the Eastern *bloc* and had resulted in the foundation of NATO on 4 April 1949, in the words of its first Secretary-General, Lord Ismay, 'to keep the Americans in, the Russians out and the Germans down'. With the formation of the Federal Republic of Germany the following month, 23 May 1949, it was inevitable that the new West German state would join and become a cornerstone of NATO. It took five years to navigate the hostility of France, with the result that the Federal Republic of Germany was admitted to the North Atlantic Treaty Organisation on 23 October 1954. This triggered the defensive alliance of the USSR and seven other Eastern European countries, signed on 14 May 1955, known thereafter as the Warsaw Pact. The establishment of the Bundeswehr, the West German armed forces, followed on 12 November 1955. The name Bundeswehr was appropriately proposed by General Hasso von Manteuffel, whose part in the Ardennes you will encounter shortly. He was, by then, enjoying a post-war carer as a defence advisor and liberal politician in Bonn.

Thus, it was only from 1955 that the Germans began to relate their own memories of the events. Many senior commanders took part in the US Army Historical Division's Foreign Military Studies Program. This amounted to nearly 2,500 papers, devoid of politics and purely military in scope, written from 1945 to 1959, which covered most aspects of the Reich's war effort. They were influential because at the operational level they concentrated on German successes, in logistics, the handling of armour, command and control, security, deception and surprise. They helped rebuild German military self-confidence – vital to NATO – and forge the reputation of the new Bundeswehr. Some studies – in the era of the Cold War – examined the methodology of defeating the Soviets in battle, but many focused on Germany's last big campaign in the West – the Battle of the Bulge. The program, devised with considerable forethought, included the invaluable 'ETHINT' (European Theater Historical Interrogations) series of interviews, conducted immediately after the war. Just about every senior German commander in the Bulge alive after the war, and in Western custody, took part. As many were conducted within a year of the events of the Bulge, they provide a particularly rich seam of primary source material, which Anthony Tucker-Jones has mined to profitable effect in *Hitler's Winter*.

German assistance in remembering and analysing the Bulge, and to a lesser extent, Alsace, also came from walking the ground. Doctrine for offensive activity in any potential NATO-Warsaw Pact encounter emphasized, as had been learned in the Ardennes, vast numbers of tanks and mechanized infantry, employed under conditions of surprise, shock and moving at high speed, advancing as far as possible before a reaction was triggered. From the late 1940s, strategists of both sides focussed on the tank-friendly terrain of the Fulda Gap, an area between the East German border and Frankfurt-am-Main that was the most obvious route for any Soviet tank attack on West Germany from Soviet-occupied Europe. Attacking forces instinctively search for geological 'gaps', manoeuvre corridors which lead to objectives such as river lines, cities or ports. It is no coincidence that Napoleon withdrew along the Fulda Gap after the Battle of Leipzig in 1813, and US 12th Corps advanced eastwards through it in March–April 1945.

The region round the village of Fulda is very similar to the Ardennes, and characterized by deeply scoured glacial valleys, separated by steep-sided hills, surmounted by forests. Off-road the 'going' for armour is almost impossible. As a consequence, the US and West German forces in the area envisaged a defence by holding road junctions and towns, stationing guns and armour on the hilltops. Soviet doctrine foresaw combined arms assaults, the frequent use of chemical weapons against built up areas and attempts to bypass NATO roadblocks wherever possible. The concept of a major tank battle in the vicinity of the Fulda Gap was a predominant element of NATO war planning throughout the Cold War, and weapons (such as Apache attack helicopters and A-10 tank-busters) were developed specifically to counter it.

Thus, in preparing for World War III, the template that both East and West used was the German breakthrough into the Ardennes of both 1940 and 1944 via the smaller Losheim Gap, where Kampfgruppe Peiper made their breakthrough. Many NATO groups conducted terrain walks and battlefield tours of the Ardennes and Alsace battlefields, where possible accompanied by the original participants. In places, the ground is little changed; foxholes remain, as do battle-scarred buildings, which help the mind roll back the years to Hitler's winter. The enduring relevance of the Ardennes campaign meant that, throughout the Cold War, NATO drilled its troops in the Losheim Gap battlefield, in rehearsal for what might occur in the Fulda. In the event of war, NATO forces would be supplied via Antwerp – just as in 1944, the same port remained the Allied logistics centre, and a Soviet objective.

If you, the reader, is impatient to get on with the battle, and wonder why the author spends the first two-fifths of this splendid volume setting the scene beforehand, Anthony Tucker-Jones does so with very good reason. Anyone connected with the military business will recognize that only 5 per cent of wartime revolves around doing battle. The remaining 95 per cent, the boring bit, involves soldiers, sailors and airmen preparing their kit, and endlessly training. Yet it is the 5 per cent that military historians pounce on. *Hitler's Winter* goes some way to correcting the balance. By the autumn of 1944, haemorrhaging military manpower in the East and West and narrowly surviving assassination by some of his own staff, Hitler had come to interpret loyal dissent as treason and refused to let his plan be altered in any way. Furthermore, as you will read, his paranoia for secrecy imposed unreasonable restrictions on his own forces to prepare for their Ardennes adventure. There would be no overt preparations, no rehearsals, no flights or reconnaissance. No junior commanders were admitted to the plan until literally hours beforehand. German intelligence of either the terrain or their opponents was lamentable. Through lack of training, the supporting parachute drop was an unmitigated disaster. Secrecy and lack of rehearsal meant the synchronized German air attack of New Year's Day irreparably broke the fighter arm of the Luftwaffe, many aircraft being brought down by their own side. The author helps us comprehend how, with the bare minimum of bridging and logistical support, a high degree of (very private) scepticism among his commanders and in his own obsessive behaviour, the German Führer almost set his grand attack up to fail.

Thus, there are many lessons relevant to modern leadership, logistics, intelligence and other aspects of war to be gained in studying the Ardennes and Alsace campaigns from the rarely heard German point of view. This is the reason why Anthony Tucker-Jones's study of these battles is timely and important. In understanding how the Third Reich planned and fought these 1944–45 battles, the author's analysis also hints at what underpinned NATO strategy in opposing the Soviet threat to Europe into the 1990s.

Professor Peter Caddick-Adams
Croatia

Prologue

The Pied Piper

SS-Lieutenant Colonel Jochen Peiper cut a dashing figure with his boyish good looks and dimpled chin. He had a warm smile and piercing eyes. This, though, masked a steely ambition. Peiper had served on Reichsführer Heinrich Himmler's staff as an adjutant at the age of 23 in the late 1930s. It was during his time with Himmler that he had met his wife Sigurd or 'Sigi' Hinrichsen, employed as one of the Reichsführer's secretaries. His bravery knew no limits, and he had seen combat with the 1st SS Leibstandarte SS Adolf Hitler in Poland and Russia. He took part in the dramatic recapture of Kharkov in early 1943 and by the end of the year had taken command of the division's tank regiment. In the New Year he gained the Oak Leaves to his Knight's Cross. After fighting against the Allies in the battle for Normandy, the much-depleted 1st SS Panzer Division had managed to escape the Falaise pocket through the hell of the St Lambert-sur-Dive corridor. By that time it had lost about 5,000 men.

Peiper departed Normandy sooner than his comrades, as he had reportedly been wounded during fighting with the Canadians around Caen. Or at least that was his version of events; in reality he had suffered a nervous breakdown and was relieved of command. Initially he had been sent to a hospital in Paris, but was then shipped to Tegernsee Reserve Hospital in Bavaria. This was ideal because it was not far from where Sigi and his children lived. Peiper did not re-join the 1st SS Panzer Regiment until early October 1944, by which time the division was in the Lübbecke, Minden, Osnabrück area. He found he had a new divisional commander as his previous commander, Theodor 'Teddy' Wisch, had lost a leg at Falaise and had been replaced by SS-Brigadier Wilhelm Mohnke.

After checking in with his regimental headquarters at Rahden, Peiper reported to Mohnke's headquarters at Lübbecke. Peiper found the brigadier was a tough veteran who, despite losing part of a foot in Yugoslavia, had gone on to fight with the 12th SS Panzer Division in Normandy. Mohnke explained the division was being brought back up to strength and that clearly some sort of operation was being planned. In November the 1st SS moved to the Cologne area and was involved in helping the civilian population clear up after Allied bomber attacks. The new recruits were appalled by the mashed and mangled bodies that they had to retrieve from the devastation. 'Their hatred for the enemy was such,' remarked Peiper, 'I swear it, I could not always keep it under control.'[1] When they were then sent to Düren to help after an air raid, Peiper confessed he wanted 'to castrate the swine who did this with a broken glass bottle'.[2] Peiper and his men wanted revenge.

Mohnke and Peiper found themselves coming under the command of SS-General Josef 'Sepp' Dietrich's new 6th Panzer Army. This was reassuring as they knew him from their days in Normandy. Their presence near Cologne seemed to make sense as it indicated they were preparing to counter any Allied attempts on the Rhine. Unbeknown to Peiper, on 10 December Dietrich issued orders announcing that SS-Major General Hermann Priess' 1st SS Panzer Corps was to break through the Hollerath-Krewinkel sector using its infantry divisions. It was then to thrust over the river Meuse in the Liège-Huy sector with the 1st SS on the left and 12th SS on the right. Furthermore, these orders stated, 'Bridges on the Meuse will be taken in undamaged condition by ruthless and rapid penetration. This will be accomplished by specially organised forward detachments, under the command of suitable officers.'[3]

Priess was horrified when he saw these orders:

... the area assigned to the corps for the attack was unfavourable. It was broken and heavily wooded. At this time of year and in the prevailing weather conditions, the area was barely negotiable. Few roads were available ... these were single track, in many cases woodland and field tracks.[4]

He immediately contacted SS-General Fritz Krämer, Dietrich's chief of staff, and requested that his line of attack be shifted south where the roads were better. Krämer's response was a firm no and Priess was told to follow orders. Furthermore, Krämer then decided to go behind Priess' back.

The following day, 11 December, Peiper found himself having a very interesting conversation with Krämer. The latter canvassed his views on a possible attack from the mountainous Eifel region into the forested hills of the Ardennes. In particular, he was keen to know how long it would take a panzer regiment to cover 50 miles (80km). Peiper was intrigued. 'Feeling that it was not a good idea to decide the answer to such a question merely by looking at a map,' recalled Peiper, 'I made a test run of 80km with a Panther [tank] myself, driving down a route Euskirchen-Müstereifel-Blankenheim.'[5] His findings were promising, though this test was conducted under controlled conditions without any resistance. 'I replied that if I had a free road to myself, I could make 80km in one night; of course, with an entire division, that was a different question.'[6] Peiper realized that this was not just a hypothetical conversation when, two nights later, he received orders to move his regiment south. He soon discovered that the entire division was conducting the same manoeuvre. Something was clearly afoot, but the question was, what?

Peiper and the other regimental commanders arrived at Mohnke's Tondorf headquarters at 1100 hours on 14 December full of anticipation. Mohnke, pointing at a map, told them that in 42 hours they were to strike the American infantry divisions deployed in the Ardennes and cut their way to Antwerp. Peiper shifted uneasily and wondered how on earth they were going to prepare in such a short time. Mohnke explained that in order to take their objectives the division would have to be divided into four battle groups. Looking at Peiper, he said his would be the most important as it would be formed round elements of the 1st SS Panzer Regiment. The second would be formed using SS-Lieutenant Colonel Max Hansen's 1st SS Panzergrenadier Regiment. SS-Lieutenant Colonel Rudolf Sandig's 2nd SS Panzergrenadier Regiment would form the third and SS-Major Gustav Knittel's 1st SS Reconnaissance Battalion the fourth. The way for both the 1st SS and 12th SS Panzer Divisions would be secured by Otto Skorzeny's newly created panzer brigade divided into three battle groups. The American lines in the

Losheim Gap would first be breached by the 12th Volksgrenadier and 3rd Parachute Divisions to open the way.

Mohnke told Peiper his battle group was to be strengthened by the addition of the 501st Heavy SS Panzer Battalion equipped with Tiger II tanks plus the Luftwaffe's 84th Flak Battalion. His panzer forces would amount to a weak panzer regiment equipped with about 35 Panzer IVs, 35 Panthers and 20 Tiger IIs. The latter, although impressive looking and well armed, were far too heavy to be of much help. It was simply not suitable for fighting in the close confines of the Ardennes, but Peiper had to make do with what he was offered. How times had changed; back in the summer during the fighting in France his regiment had received 175 panzers. By the time it had escaped Normandy in late August it had no combat-ready tanks or artillery. Battle Group Peiper numbered about 5,000 men, which seemed hardly enough to slice their way through the Americans.

Peiper looked open-mouthed at the map marking the five routes to be taken by the battle groups. These had been selected by Krämer. Just two to the south were assigned to 1st SS, while the 12th SS to the north had three. Peiper, followed by Sandig, was to use Rollbahn D, which would take his men through Stavelot, Trois-Ponts on to Harzé and then the Meuse to the south-west of Liège. Hansen and Knittel were to use Rollbahn E. All the routes were fairly close to each other, which meant any bottlenecks would immediately cause a log jam amongst the units using them. It was clear to Peiper that even trying to reach the start point of Rollbahn D was going to be a problem. During the German retreat earlier in the year they had blown up the bridge over the railway cutting a mile or so east of Losheimergraben. This would have to be replaced for the vehicles of the 1st SS, 3rd Parachute Division and the 12th Volksgrenadier Division to cross. Otherwise, the road from Scheid to Losheim would become an enormous traffic jam.

Peiper's eyes quickly traced the route he was to take westward through the village of Honsfeld to Baugnez. He was to pass Ligneuville and then head for Stavelot on the Amblève. Afterwards his men were to make for the village of Trois-Ponts and cross the Salm there. This looked like it could be trouble because the Amblève and Salm met at Trois-Ponts. There was a road and rail bridge over the former and two road bridges over the latter. In addition, there was a road bridge over the Bodeux, a tributary of the Salm. They then were to traverse the valleys of the Ardennes to reach Werbomont. Only then could Peiper find a good road that would speed up his dash for the Meuse at Huy. To get there, they would have to first cross the Ourthe River. Hitler was sending them on a magical mystery tour and, like all good Nazis, they would follow his orders. Surprisingly, though, despite being a highly decorated officer in an SS division, Peiper claimed he was not actually a member of the Nazi Party.

Peiper was alarmed by the tight schedule. They had three days to get to the Meuse, one to penetrate American defences, one to get the armour through the Ardennes and one to reach the river. They were to be over the Meuse by day four. Peiper felt that everything rested on his shoulders and it was a heavy burden. This was confirmed when he was told to report to Dietrich's chief of staff. 'I don't care how and what you do,' said Krämer firmly. 'Just make it to the Meuse. Even if you've only got one tank left when you get there. The Meuse with one tank – that's all I ask of you.'⁷ Peiper stirred uneasily; what of Antwerp? Did this mean that Dietrich and Krämer did not believe they could reach the port? The implication was that if they at least reached the Meuse then honour would have been served with Hitler. Krämer saw Peiper's expression and said, 'Drive hard, Peiper, and hold the reins loose.'⁸

The next day, 15 December 1944, in a damp forester's hut not far from Blankenheim, Peiper briefed his commanders. His two companies of Panzer IVs would lead the way, followed by the two Panther companies. Both were to be supported by panzergrenadiers transported in armoured half-tracks. The Tiger IIs would be kept back in reserve ready for once his battle group reached the open countryside near the Meuse. Peiper was sceptical they would ever get there. He noted that the road from Ligneuville to Stavelot was suitable for little more than bicycles. Furthermore, if the Americans blew the bridges over the Amblève and Salm, the Tigers would be stuck. There was more bad news: two trains carrying fuel for 1st SS Panzer Corps had gone missing, which meant they would have to refuel during the advance.

Peiper's battalion commanders, SS-Majors Werner Pötschke and Josef Diefenthal as well as SS-Captain Schlett, stood scratching their heads. They, like everyone else, knew that an attack on the Americans was imminent, but how were they supposed to prepare with less than a day's notice? They were doubtful that the forecasted bad weather would keep the Allied fighter-bombers off them for very long. The commander of their combat engineers, SS-Captain Rumpf, did not relish the idea of trying to cross the rivers while under air attack. SS-Lieutenant Vögler, in charge of Battle Group Peiper's self-propelled anti-aircraft guns, appreciated that speed would be vital before the sun reappeared through the clouds. It seemed as if their boss wanted them to follow him blindly as if he were the Pied Piper of Hamelin. What they did not know was that Peiper was determined to make Hitler's winter offensive of 1944/45 a success, no matter the cost.

List of Maps

List of Illustrations

atrocity. (Photo by: Photo12/Universal Images Group via Getty Images)

A Panther knocked out in La Gleize. Battle Group Peiper made its last stand there before abandoning all its equipment and withdrawing. (Photo by Popperfoto via Getty Images/Getty Images)

A German assault gun lost during the fighting for the road junction at St Vith. (Photo © CORBIS/Corbis via Getty Images)

Although the Germans successfully took St Vith, Allied bombers pounded it into oblivion. This photo was taken after the snow melted. (Photo by Popperfoto via Getty Images/Getty Image)

Cold looking German prisoners captured in the Bastogne area. General von Manteuffel's failure to secure the vital road junction there severely derailed Hitler's plans. (Photo by Authenticated News/Archive Photos/Getty Images)

Death and destruction wrought on the streets of Antwerp by a V-2. Hitler wanted to wreck the port if he could not recapture it. (Photo by: Photo12/Universal Images Group via Getty Images)

Allied troops and Belgian civilians killed by an indiscriminate V-1 attack. The V-weapons' inaccuracy made them tactically useless. (Photo by Mondadori via Getty Images)

Germans killed in the last-ditch attempts to take Bastogne. The American garrison tied up elements of three divisions. (Bettmann via Getty Images)

German troops being rounded up by men of the US 4th Armored. This division cut its way through to besieged Bastogne on 26 December 1944. (Bettmann via Getty Images)

Frozen German soldiers in early January 1945. By this stage Hitler's Ardennes offensive had completely stalled. (Photo by ullstein bild/ullstein bild via Getty Images)

An abandoned Tiger II on the streets of Stavelot. This heavy breakthrough tank was not designed for urban warfare and it failed to help Battle Group Peiper. (Photo by Allan Jackson/Keystone/Hulton Archive/Getty Images)

German losses during the Battle of the Bulge included 50,000 captured. (Photo © CORBIS/Corbis via Getty Images)

The makeshift grave of a 'stubble hopper' from 5th Parachute Division found in the woods near Warnach. German dead numbered 13,000. (Photo by A. H. Herz/Hulton Archive/Getty Images)

PART ONE

A Daring Plan

Scarface

Otto Skorzeny was feeling rather pleased with himself as he stood before Adolf Hitler in Berlin on 21 October 1944. He had been granted a private audience with the Führer. His right arm shot out as he conducted the required Nazi salute. Skorzeny's jaw was firmly clenched but a small smile flickered at the side of his mouth. He was a chancer who had just pulled off another propaganda coup for the beleaguered Third Reich. Through a combination of willpower and bravado he had made himself into Hitler's indispensable 'Mr Fixit'.[1]

His slicked-back hair almost made him look like some sort of Austrian matinee idol. However, the most striking thing about him was the appalling scar on the left side of Skorzeny's face. It ran from his chin up to his ear. The scar tissue showed that at some point a flap of skin had been almost completely severed from the jaw bone. Skorzeny wore this disfigurement with pride because it was a duelling scar from his student days in Vienna. Such a mark was considered the height of fashion. His self-confidence in the presence of the Führer was well founded. Hitler had grandly dubbed him 'the most dangerous man in Europe'.[2] In truth Skorzeny's achievements were nowhere near as dashing as Nazi propaganda claimed. However, Skorzeny did have the luck of the Devil.

Hitler's Nazi 'fixer' had served the early part of the war with the 2nd SS and then the 1st SS Panzer Divisions. In April 1943 he had been appointed to command the Waffen-SS special forces, known as the Amt VI-S, which were designed to rival the army's covert

Brandenburg regiment. Skorzeny, setting up base in Friedenthal Castle near Oranienburg, found himself in charge of the SS-Jagdverbande and the 500th SS Parachute Battalion supported by the Luftwaffe's Kampfgeschwader 200. From then on there had been no looking back for the Führer's wunderkind.

Hitler smiled and stretched out his arms. 'Well done, Skorzeny! I've promoted you to SS-Lieutenant-Colonel with effect from the 16th October,' said the Führer with genuine gratitude, 'and awarded you the German Cross in gold. ... Now tell me all about it.'³ In his role as Hitler's special operations fixer over the last two years, Skorzeny had pulled off two remarkable feats that had greatly helped slow the war against Germany. He was fresh from the beautiful city of Budapest on the Danube where he had conducted an audacious coup to prevent the Hungarians from defecting to the Russians. At the head of a column of massive Tiger tanks, he had seized Castle Hill and brow beat the wavering Hungarian government back into line. Budapest's garrison, confused by the action of their ally, had simply laid down their arms.

The Hungarian fascist party took power and the crisis was averted, at least for the time being. The irony was that the Hungarian leader, Admiral Horthy, had acquiesced to Hitler's demands 30 minutes before Skorzeny's show of brute force. Luckily for Skorzeny and the SS division that had followed him into the city, the Hungarians chose not to resist, otherwise a bloodbath would have ensued. The SS did not realize Budapest would soon become their prison once the Red Army encircled it at the end of the year.

Skorzeny's other great success was that the previous year he had taken part in the rescue of deposed Italian dictator Benito Mussolini on 12 September 1944. Mussolini was under house arrest after his country defected to the Western Allies. Although it had been a Luftwaffe-run operation, Skorzeny shanghaied the mission and brazenly grabbed all the glory. Skorzeny was not supposed to join Mussolini, but he squeezed into the plane to German-occupied Rome anyway. He safely delivered Mussolini, leaving Luftwaffe General Kurt Student fuming. Skorzeny then flew Mussolini to Vienna and a few days later the fallen Italian dictator arrived at Rastenburg to see Hitler. This had enabled Hitler to put Mussolini in charge of the German puppet state established in northern Italy.

Hitler chose to have a selective memory, ignoring the failure of the 500th SS Parachute Battalion's attempts to kill Josip Tito, the Yugoslav resistance leader. This airborne operation on 24 May 1944 led by SS-Lieutenant Rybka had cost 1,138 German casualties and Tito had escaped. The few survivors were sent back to Skorzeny. He had sought to avoid being blamed for this debacle, which had witnessed the first wave of men jumping from their gliders massacred by alerted Yugoslav partisans. By the time the ground forces had reached them the battalion had almost been wiped out. Now, though, Skorzeny was firmly in favour with the Führer.

When Skorzeny finished briefing Hitler on the successful events in Hungary he stood ready to leave. 'Don't go Skorzeny,' said Hitler, motioning him to sit back down. 'I have perhaps the most important job in your life for you.'[4] Skorzeny could not help himself and scowled. 'What now?' he thought. 'In December,' explained Hitler, 'Germany will start a great offensive, which may well decide her fate.'[5] Skorzeny leant forward, intrigued, and Hitler proceeded to explain how he planned to strike the Allies just as he had done in 1940. Skorzeny struggled to follow what Hitler was proposing as the strategic scope of it all was well beyond his pay grade. 'One of the most important tasks in this offensive will be entrusted to you and the unit under your command,' said Hitler, 'which will have to go ahead and seize one or more of the bridges over the Meuse between Liège and Namur.'[6] Skorzeny nodded and Hitler added as an afterthought,' 'You will have to wear British and American uniforms.'[7] This was to be known as Operation *Griffin*.

It was clear that Hitler was not simply boasting about his 'great offensive'. Skorzeny recalled:

> He told me about the tremendous quantity of material which had been accumulated, and I recall that he stated we would have 6,000 artillery pieces in the Ardennes, and, in addition, the Luftwaffe would have about 2,000 planes, including many of the new jet planes. He then told me that I would lead a panzer brigade which would be trained to reach the Meuse bridges and capture them intact.[8]

Such an idea was nothing new. The German Army had masqueraded in foreign uniforms before, particularly in Poland, the Low Countries and Russia, but nothing had been tried on this scale. Hitler then told

Skorzeny that his preparations must be ready by 2 December. Skorzeny was not happy at the lack of time and pointed out that the attack on Fort Eben Emael in 1940 had been the culmination of six months of detailed planning. For the Ardennes operation he was being given just five weeks. Hitler sympathized and told him to do what he could. 'I am giving you unlimited power to set up your brigade,' responded Hitler. 'Use it, Colonel! Yes, I have promoted you to lieutenant-colonel.'

Skorzeny was then introduced to General Heinz Guderian, Chief of the General Staff. He was the senior German army officer; however, in light of Guderian only having responsibility for the Eastern Front there was little he could do to help Skorzeny. Furthermore, Guderian did not agree with the Ardennes offensive as he failed to understand Hitler's strategic logic. In his view the Russians posed a far greater threat than the Americans and the British.

Later Skorzeny was briefed by General Alfred Jodl, Chief of Operations for the Armed Forces, who told him the offensive was intended to recapture Antwerp. Skorzeny marvelled at the vast scale of what was going to happen:

> The forces employed were to form an Army Group under Field Marshal Model, and comprise of the 6th SS Armoured Army, under the command of General Sepp Dietrich, of the Waffen-SS, on the right, the 5th Armoured Army under General von Manteuffel, in the centre, and the 7th Army on the left.[9]

Jodl explained that his brigade would be assigned to 6th Panzer Army. Skorzeny, however, was not happy at the idea of masquerading as British or American troops, as he and his men, if caught, were liable to be shot as spies. The army legal department advised him that they should wear their German uniforms under the Allied ones, which they should remove before the shooting started. 'I need hardly add that I welcomed such advice,' noted Skorzeny gratefully.[10]

Despite Skorzeny's mission being top secret, he was alarmed to learn that the High Command had sent out an order to the entire army calling for English speakers for a special operation. When Skorzeny saw a copy of these orders he was flabbergasted because they explicitly named him and his headquarters at Friedenthal outside Berlin. His operational security was blown before he had even started. Skorzeny complained up the chain of command, recommending that his not-so-secret commando operation should be immediately cancelled. He even raised the matter personally with the head of the SS, Heinrich Himmler. The Reichsführer listened sympathetically to Skorzeny's concerns. 'It's idiotic, but it has been done,' said Himmler with an unhelpful shrug. 'We cannot hold up your operation now.'[11] When Skorzeny persisted Himmler held out his hands, adding, 'The stupidity has taken place. The action must be carried out notwithstanding.'[12] Skorzeny left with a mounting sense of doom and annoyed at Himmler's lack of backbone.

At the training ground located at Grafenwöhr, Skorzeny set about forming his brand-new unit dubbed the 150th Panzer Brigade. This was to number some 3,300 men. The key problems Skorzeny faced were to train his men and round up enough enemy uniforms, weapons and vehicles for them to pass themselves off as Allied troops. Skorzeny had less than 35 days to prepare and to equip his force. He moved swiftly to flesh out the panzer brigade with veterans from his Jagdverbände and the SS parachute battalion. Two battalions of Luftwaffe paratroops were also nominally assigned to his force, though they operated independently. Eventually his recruits comprised 1,000 men from the German Army, 500 Waffen-SS, 800 Luftwaffe and 200 personnel from the navy. This left Skorzeny some 800 men short.

To create an effective illusion that his brigade was indeed American he needed 15 Sherman tanks, 20 self-propelled guns, 20 armoured cars, 120 trucks, 100 jeeps and 40 motorcycles. This requirement should have been relatively easy to fulfil. However, despite the vast numbers of American military vehicles captured by the Germans in the preceding months, Skorzeny soon found that the hard-pressed front-line units were very reluctant to give up their precious booty. Furthermore, the Germans found it much harder to salvage captured tanks in north-west Europe than they did in North Africa because by this stage of the war their armed forces were under constant air attack by Allied fighter-bombers. By the summer of 1944 the 5th Parachute Division, 10th SS Panzer Division, 21st Panzer Division, 25th Panzergrenadier Division, 150th Panzer Brigade and 281st Captured Tank Company could muster a total of just 39 operational Shermans between them. Many other panzer units also employed individual tanks and armoured fighting vehicles. Most were swiftly lost in action or through lack of spares.

Under Operation *Raven Hill*, Commander-in-Chief West divided the requisition of equipment for Skorzeny's mission between his three army groups. Army Group G was ordered to provide eight American tanks and 20 trucks; H was to provide two tanks and 50 jeeps; and B five tanks and 30 jeeps, which were to be delivered to Skorzeny's training ground at Grafenwöhr. In the event only 74 trucks and 57 cars arrived, along with just two Sherman tanks and two American armoured cars. Skorzeny discovered he was the recipient of much worn out rubbish, as 30 per cent of the vehicles needed repairs and both the Shermans were inoperable. To make matters worse the brigade was flooded with Polish and Russian equipment, provided by units who had little idea of the role to be played by the 150th Panzer Brigade. None of the Shermans captured in the summer materialized, and the 5th Parachute Division, which committed captured Shermans to the Ardennes offensive, did not give any up either.

Despite Skorzeny's repeated complaints, he found himself being supplied with German equipment rather than American. Skorzeny grumbled that he had to make up the difference with German vehicles. 'The only common feature of these vehicles was that they were all painted green, like American military vehicles.'[13] Initially his unit was equipped with five Panther tanks, five Sturmgeschütz or StuG assault guns, six German armoured cars and six armoured personnel carriers.

The brigade also lacked 1,500 American steel helmets, and what uniforms that had been gathered were summer issue, clearly unsuitable for winter warfare. American speakers were also found to be in short supply. When Skorzeny surveyed his linguists, he discovered he had just ten men who could convincingly pass themselves off as American and another 40 or so who spoke fluent English but had no slang. Most of the fluent English speakers were German merchant sailors. There were another 150 who could speak English reasonably well and another 200 with some schoolboy English. Short of men, Skorzeny had little choice but to scale back the brigade from three to two battalions and gather 150 of the best linguists into a commando unit called Einheit Stielau. This was named after the captain placed in charge. There were just enough captured American uniforms and small arms to equip them.

Sergeant Heinz Rohde, who had been seriously wounded and was serving as a signals instructor in Hamburg, found himself amongst the commando volunteers. 'We were led into the quartermaster's clothing store,' he recalled, 'which was piled high with all types of American uniform and told to kit ourselves out, from underpants on upwards.'[14] Rohde was transformed into Sergeant Morris Woodahl of the US Army. The men were uncomfortable wearing these captured uniforms and quickly concealed them beneath German para-overalls and German side caps. It was very clear that the commando recruits were hardly elite, as Rohde found himself alongside Luftwaffe and naval personnel who had been drafted in. Corporal Wilhelm Schmidt recalled, 'Our training consisted of studying the organisation of the American army, identification of American insignia, American drill and linguistic exercises.'[15]

The commandos were to spearhead Skorzeny's attack, cause chaos and throw the Americans off the scent as his main force sped towards the vital bridges. The commandos, though, had no experience of demolition or covert operations and there was little time to train them properly. Nonetheless, they were assigned three different tasks: demolition, reconnaissance and disruption. 'In the few weeks at our disposal,' said Skorzeny, 'we could hardly hope to teach them their job properly. They knew the perils of their missions and that a man caught fighting in enemy uniform could be executed as a spy.'[16] However, he was impressed by their enthusiasm, adding, 'They were clearly animated by the most glowing patriotism.'[17] In the event, the Americans would be further confused by regular army and Waffen-SS units wearing captured American winter clothing gathered from the battlefield. This was prized for keeping the bitter cold out but wearing it carried the risk of being shot as a spy on capture, and this happened to German prisoners of war on several occasions.

Skorzeny's staff officers were drawn from the 108th Panzer Brigade and those for his two battalions' headquarters from the 10th and 113th Panzer Brigades. The latter had been newly raised along with five other panzer brigades and thrown into the fight against General George S. Patton Jr's US 3rd Army in the Lorraine in September and subsequently cut to pieces. The remains of the 113th had been reassigned to the 15th Panzergrenadier Division. Skorzeny's brigade was supposed to include two companies of panzers and by late November had been supplied 22 Panther tanks and 14 StuG assault guns. The tank crews were provided by the 6th Panzer Division and the assault gun crews came from the 655th Heavy Panzerjäger Battalion. Armoured car crews were supplied by the reconnaissance battalions of the 2nd Panzer Division and 90th Panzergrenadier Division. When they finally went into battle, they only seem to have deployed ten Panthers and just five StuGs. The implication was that most of the armour supplied to Skorzeny was unwanted, broken-down cast-offs.

There was simply no way to make a Panther look like a Sherman, as its shape and size were completely different. Instead Skorzeny's men ingeniously opted to make them look like the Sherman's tank destroyer cousin, the M10 Wolverine, based on the Sherman chassis but with a much more angular hull and turret. To do this the Panthers were disguised with sheet metal, painted olive green and given prominent white five-pointed American recognition stars. These Skorzeny cynically noted were only sufficient to 'deceive very young American troops seeing them at night from very far away'.[18]

His American vehicles were very thin on the ground, comprising four American scout cars, 15 trucks and 30 jeeps, plus a single Sherman which was up and running on the eve of the attack. All the vehicles were likewise painted olive green and given Allied white recognition stars. To avoid friendly fire, Skorzeny's men were instructed to wear various field signs including blue or pink scarves, and the rear of each vehicle was painted with a small yellow triangle. The under-strength brigade had little choice but to become three battle groups designated rather unimaginatively X, Y and Z.

Rumours began to circulate that this odd assortment of armoured fighting and motor vehicles had been assembled to dash across France to relieve the German garrisons still holding out in some of the French ports. Perhaps they were going to Brest or Lorient. Another arose to the effect that the Einheit Stielau commandos were headed for Paris to seize the Supreme Allied Commander General Dwight D. Eisenhower. This rumour was started by an eager lieutenant in the commando company who approached Skorzeny with the idea.[19] He suggested they could enter the city disguised as escorts for a prisoner of war convoy and captured German armour being taken to an Allied exhibition. Skorzeny encouraged him to work out the details and even suggested the Café de la Paix in Paris as a rendezvous for the commandos. 'We'll have a further talk,' said Skorzeny, 'but mind you, keep as silent as the grave.'[20] Skorzeny also considered plans for sabotaging Allied fuel pipelines running from Boulogne and Le Havre. 'We calculated that enemy intelligence would simply not know what to make of the medley of lurid and conflicting information which reached their ears,' said Skorzeny.[21] It was only on 10 December 1944 that his men found out that their true mission was far less glamorous and did not involve quite so much travel.

Big or Small Solution

Hitler, desperate to stop the rot following the German collapse in France, wanted to counter-attack as soon as possible. On 6 September 1944 he reluctantly agreed with his armed forces operations staff that this would not be possible until 1 November. They first had to retrieve as many units as possible and re-equip them. Just ten days later Hitler broached the subject with his commanders. 'Special conference in small circle,' noted Luftwaffe General Werner Kreipe in his diary. 'Decision by the Führer, counterattack from the Ardennes, objective Antwerp. ... Rip open boundary between the English and the Americans, a new Dunkirk.'[1] Hitler also demanded 1,500 fighter aircraft be ready by 1 November. He then embarked on a war of wills with Field Marshal Gerd von Rundstedt, Commander-in-Chief West, and Field Marshal Walther Model, commander Army Group B, over his plans.

Looking at the map it was apparent to von Rundstedt and Model that the most obvious place to attack the Allies and reach Antwerp would be through the Netherlands. This could be conducted by the German 15th Army pushing south supported by the 1st Parachute Army. However, the open Dutch countryside, criss-crossed by canals and rivers, would make a concealed build-up by the panzers impossible, plus it was very poor tank country. Similarly, striking westward from Roermond and Aachen towards Antwerp offered a shorter distance, but once again the terrain was not very favourable. Furthermore, the attackers would meet strong opposition in this area, particularly around Aachen. General

Günther Blumentritt, who served as von Rundstedt's chief of staff, observed, 'We will meet powerful resistance there, for three battles have been fought in the area and strong enemy forces are concentrated there.'[2] Blumentritt agreed with Hitler that the best place to launch an attack was south of Aachen through the Eifel Mountains. 'Enemy forces are not strong there,' he noted. 'The wooded mountainous area offers cover and permits surprise.'[3]

In the meantime, Hitler needed to gather sufficient forces to strike in the Ardennes. Waffen-SS veteran SS-General Josef 'Sepp' Dietrich, former commander of the 1st SS Panzer Corps, 5th Panzer Army and 7th Army in Normandy, was summoned to see Hitler on 14 September. He assumed the Führer wanted to hear about what had gone wrong in Normandy; instead, he found himself being instructed to set up the headquarters of what was to become the brand-new 6th Panzer Army. He was not told why. Unknown to Dietrich, his new command was to spearhead Hitler's drive on the Meuse and Antwerp, with General Hasso von Manteuffel's 5th Panzer Army supporting the main thrust and General Erich Brandenberger's 7th Army protecting their southern flank.

Dietrich was unclear why, as an SS officer, he had been chosen for such a key role. He suspected his appointment was partly due to Hitler's growing distrust of the army following the assassination attempt on the Führer using a bomb on 20 July 1944. He certainly did not want the job. Dietrich was a corps commander through and through and knew he was being promoted far beyond his abilities. Despite briefly taking charge of the 5th and 7th Armies, these had only been temporary appointments due to the deteriorating situation in France. However, he was not in a position to refuse Hitler. 'What good is that?' he grumbled. 'I have never been trained to command an army. What they need is a person like [General] Gause who knows a lot more about it than myself.'[4] Ironically Gause would be appointed his chief of staff.

At the end of the month a disgruntled Dietrich set up shop at Bad Salzuflen near Herford with just ten staff officers. He did not get any troops until October. They were to come under Hermann Priess' 1st SS Panzer Corps (1st SS and 12th SS) and SS-Lieutenant General Willi Bittrich's 2nd SS Panzer Corps (2nd SS, 9th SS and Panzer Lehr). Bittrich was fresh from helping defeat the British at Arnhem. These corps would be concentrated around Minden and east of the Ruhr respectively. Unfortunately for

Dietrich 1st SS Panzer Corps was not free until 22 October and 2nd SS Panzer Corps until mid-November. The upshot of this was that his staff would have to initially oversee their component divisions.

Nazi power politics now came into play. In light of it being commanded by an SS-general and containing SS divisions, Himmler would have loved the idea of Dietrich's command being designated an SS army. Previously his Waffen-SS divisions had always fought under the control of the regular army. 'Headquarters in Berlin would not allow my Army to become an SS Army until Apr 45, when we were in Hungary,' Dietrich later explained, 'because I had both SS and Wehrmacht troops under my command.'[5] It may have been that Hitler was not prepared to pander to Himmler's ego, or the German Army would not tolerate such a development. SS-General Fritz Krämer, who would later replace Gause, noted, 'This Army was often called the Sixth SS Panzer Army. Its correct designation however, is Sixth Panzer Army, according to a written directive of the German High Command issued in the beginning of December, 1944.'[6] Nevertheless, this did not stop Himmler and many subsequent historians viewing it as the 6th SS Panzer Army. Indeed, von Manteuffel referred to it as such.

General Guderian, Chief of the Army General Staff, was very unhappy with Hitler's plans. On the Eastern Front things were going from bad to worse. In the Baltic Army, Group North was rapidly becoming trapped in a bridgehead around the port of Riga. To the south the Russians had reached Warsaw, and were fast approaching Budapest and Belgrade. Guderian warned that gathering their remaining forces for a blow against the Americans would leave the Eastern Front dangerously exposed. Guderian knew they faced a terrible race against time. Conducting a counter-attack in the west so late in the year would make it almost impossible to redeploy their troops in time to meet the inevitable Red Army offensive in the New Year. Hitler was furious. 'There's no need for you to try and teach me,' he ranted at Guderian. 'I've been commanding the German Army in the field for five years, and during that time I've had more practical experience than any gentleman of the General Staff could ever hope to have.'[7] Guderian was powerless, noting bitterly, 'the grotesque flattery of his [Nazi] Party comrades ... had given him the illusion that he was a great military commander.'[8]

General Kreipe noted on 18 September, 'OKH [Oberkommando des Heeres, or the Army High Command] has most serious concern about plan for the Ardennes.'[9] General Jodl, Chief of Operations at the Armed Forces High Command (Oberkommando der Wehrmacht – OKW), was not keen on Hitler's proposal for the Ardennes either. He felt it would be better to use their regenerating forces to buy time before the onset of winter. To that end he suggested five smaller options involving double envelopments ranging from the Belfort Gap in the south to Düsseldorf in the north. Hitler, though, was not receptive to such ideas.

By the end of the first week of October a chastised Jodl had prepared a draft plan for an assault towards Antwerp, which would be launched at the end of the following month. Notably von Rundstedt was not consulted. By then, Jodl claimed, the regenerating German armed forces would have gathered 32 divisions, consisting of 18 infantry, plus 12 panzer and panzergrenadier. These would come under the command of von Manteuffel's 5th Panzer, Dietrich's 6th Panzer and Brandenberger's 7th Armies. They would be supported by 1,400 bombers and fighters. Despite his junior rank, Skorzeny was made aware of Jodl's five options when he saw Hitler. 'Ultimately the offensive from northern Luxembourg,' he wrote, 'with the supplementary offensive from Aachen, had been selected and worked out.'[10] This suggests that Hitler was wed to this proposal from the very start.

Field Marshals von Rundstedt and Model were made privy to Hitler's intentions on 22 October. Their respective chiefs of staff, Siegfried Westphal and Hans Krebs, attended a briefing with Hitler at the Wolf's Lair that day. They had feared the worst from Hitler because the Americans had just captured the German city of Aachen. Instead he briefed them on Operation *Watch on the Rhine* (*Wacht am Rhein*) – named after a patriotic 19th-century song. This, said Hitler, was to be launched on 25 November and would drive a decisive wedge between Field Marshal Montgomery's British 21st Army Group and General Bradley's American 12th Army Group. After the chiefs of staff returned to their respective headquarters both von Rundstedt and Model were horrified by the news. Model was succinct in his condemnation: 'This damned thing hasn't a leg to stand on.'[11]

The field marshals' immediate response was that *Watch on the Rhine* was far too ambitious for the forces available. Even if they got to

Antwerp, which was highly unlikely, the British and Americans would rapidly counter-attack the exposed flanks of the long corridor created by the thrust. Furthermore, they would be better off using their reserves to respond to Allied attacks rather than squandering them all in one go. The situation on the Western and Eastern fronts was simply too precarious to risk an all-or-nothing gamble. 'The only hope,' said von Rundstedt to Model, 'was to wean Hitler from this fantastic aim by putting forward an alternative proposal that might appeal to him, and would be more practicable.'[12]

Both von Rundstedt and Model quickly came to a similar conclusion as Jodl. Something smaller could produce much better results. They felt they should restore the integrity of the Siegfried Line by pinching off the exposed American salient at Aachen. This would stop the American push on Cologne and the Rhine. They reasoned their best hope was to drive the Allies back from the Roer to the Meuse and take Liège, which was the Americans' main supply hub.

On 27 October the pair got together with Dietrich, von Manteuffel and General Erich Brandenberger at Fichtenhain near Krefeld. They discussed the feasibility of launching an attack from the Geilenkirchen area as well as the one in the Ardennes. This could catch the whole of the US 9th Army as well as elements of the US 1st and British 2nd Armies in a pocket bordered by Aachen, Liège and Maastricht. This would make Liège the goal and not Antwerp. To protect Dietrich's thrust it was proposed that 15th Army be redeployed from the Netherlands to launch an attack north and south of Aachen. It would link up with 6th Panzer Army around Maastricht. Once the panzers had encircled Liège, 15th Army would also assume responsibility for the defence of the River Vesdre to the south-east of the city. It was agreed by the gathered commanders that what was dubbed Operation *Autumn Mist*, or the 'small solution', should be put before Jodl. Major General von Mellenthin claimed, 'Such an attack might have "bagged" fifteen divisions and enabled us to transfer strong reserves to the East.'[13]

Although Hitler ordered preparations for the attack in the Ardennes should be made purely on a need-to-know basis, he could not help but inform his inner circle. Joseph Goebbels, the Nazi propaganda minister, received a phone call from the Führer on 28 October 1944 to wish him a happy birthday. 'Goebbels came out of the next room with a beaming face,' observed his personal assistant Rudolf Semmler.

'He said that Hitler wanted to speak with his wife as well.' She then appeared visibly elated and with tears in her eyes. Semmler noted, 'she told us there were great hopes for the future. By Christmas the outlook would have changed completely. For Christmas the German people would receive the present of a great military triumph. Then the turn of the tide would come.'[14] To Goebbels and Semmler it was obvious that the Führer was planning a major offensive. The big question, though, was, where? Dietrich met with Hitler and Martin Bormann, the Führer's highly influential private secretary, at the end of October. It is hard to imagine that while discussing 6th Panzer Army the subject of the Ardennes offensive was not touched upon.

Jodl outlined his 'basic thoughts' on the proposed Operation *Watch on the Rhine* on 1 November. The object of this was the destruction of enemy forces to the north of the line Antwerp-Brussels-Bastogne. However, he concluded rather chillingly, 'In our present situation, we must not be afraid to stake everything on one card.'[15] Jodl agreed to meet with von Rundstedt, Model and von Manteuffel at Model's headquarters on 3 November. He listened to their concerns and suggestions but was adamant Hitler's 'big solution' must be carried out. Even if Jodl was receptive to their 'small solution' there was nothing he could do. To help preparations the attack could slip from 25 November to 10 December.

Field Marshal von Rundstedt despaired at Jodl's 'basic thoughts'. He was not happy at all and later remarked, 'If we reached the Meuse we should have got down on our knees and thanked God – let alone try to reach Antwerp.'[16] However, he knew that if he did not cooperate then Hitler would simply sack him again. Ideally, for the Ardennes thrust to stand a chance, he wanted a second diversionary attack just north of Aachen, but knew they did not have the resources. The field marshal had little choice but to agree with Jodl's assessment. 'It is clear to me …' he forlornly wrote, 'that now we have to stake everything on one card. This is why I retract my concerns.'[17] General Westphal urged his boss von Rundstedt to see Hitler personally and try to dissuade him from his course of action. The despondent field marshal felt that such action would be a completely pointless exercise. Westphal noted, 'He considered that Hitler's stubbornness and his habit of conducting hour-long monologues preventing anyone else from speaking made such personal representations hopeless.'[18]

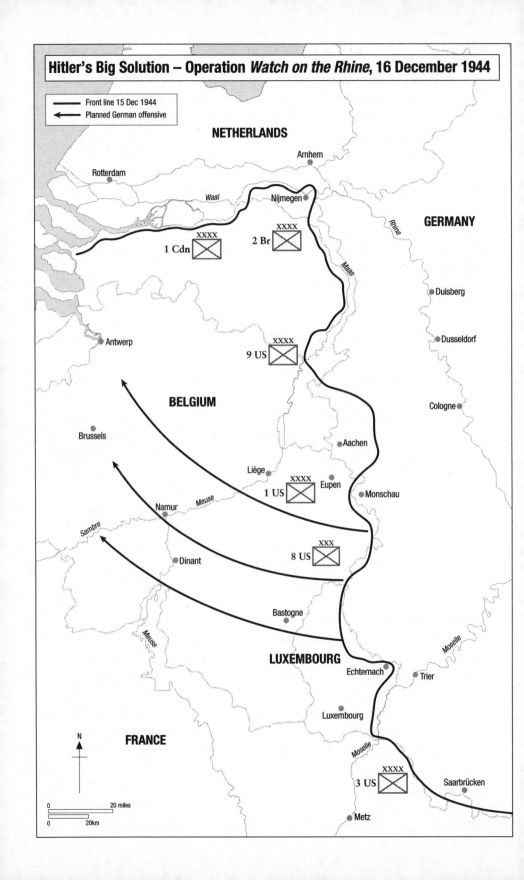

Hitler's Big Solution – Operation *Watch on the Rhine*, 16 December 1944

Front line 15 Dec 1944
Planned German offensive

NETHERLANDS

GERMANY

Arnhem

Rotterdam

Waal

Nijmegen

Rhine

1 Cdn XXXX

2 Br XXXX

Maas

Duisberg

Dusseldorf

Antwerp

9 US XXXX

BELGIUM

Cologne

Brussels

Aachen

Liège

1 US XXXX

Eupen

Monschau

Namur

Meuse

Dinant

8 US XXX

Sambre

Bastogne

LUXEMBOURG

Echternach

Moselle

Trier

Luxembourg

N

FRANCE

Moselle

3 US XXXX

Saarbrücken

0   20 miles
0   20km

Metz

Hitler issued the order for marshalling and preparation for the attack on 10 November. His only concession to von Rundstedt's concerns was to agree to a secondary attack at Aachen, though it would not be simultaneous. To facilitate this and the freeing up of 5th Panzer Army, Hitler authorized 15th Army to be moved from the Netherlands to the Aachen area. This was to be replaced by the newly created 25th Army under Friedrich Christiansen. In reality the latter was little more than a corps commanding a handful of divisions. It and the 1st Parachute Army were placed under the newly formed Army Group H, which came under General Kurt Student. Dubbed Operation *Late Vintage*, 15th Army's attack would be conducted four days after the main assault.[19]

General Blumentritt was sent to command the 12th SS Corps, which formed part of 15th Army. He was told to prepare to spearhead an attack north of Aachen with the objective of Maastricht. Setting up his headquarters near Rückelhoven on the Roer, he found Model a regular visitor. Model's attitude did not fill him with confidence. 'Since the offensive had been ordered,' noted Blumentritt, 'he wanted only the so-called "limited" solution at most; that is, a converging attack on Maastricht, and accordingly against the area around Aachen.'[20] It soon became apparent to Blumentritt and General Gustav-Adolf von Zangen, the commander of 15th Army, that their resources were such that they would never be able to support the Ardennes offensive. There was talk of them being reinforced by a panzer and panzergrenadier division, but if such mobile units were available they would inevitably be needed elsewhere. There was even fanciful talk of Christiansen's Army Group H pushing through the British and Canadians to unite with Dietrich at Antwerp. He had neither the manpower nor the equipment for such an operation.

Meantime Model continued to press for the 'small solution'. On 16 November he suggested in light of the 'unsuccessful' American breakthrough at Aachen that they counter-attack there instead; von Rundstedt forwarded this to the OKH. Again the 'small solution' was rejected by Hitler who called it 'pusillanimous'.[21] Hitler was aware that American operations at Aachen and in Lorraine were soaking up available reserves and did not want to become distracted. To make matters worse Army Group G's front far to the south was verging on collapse.

Also on 16 November, Hitler acted to remove General Gause, Sepp Dietrich's chief of staff. The suspicion is that this was done because he was an army officer and not from the Waffen-SS. In his place Hitler appointed SS-General Krämer, who had served as Dietrich's chief of staff with 1st SS Panzer Corps in Normandy. Krämer was very aware of the threat posed by Allied fighter-bombers to 6th Panzer Army, having witnessed the destruction wrought on the panzers in France.

A week later Hitler conducted another planning conference in Berlin. Those present included von Rundstedt, Model, Westphal, Krebs, Dietrich, von Manteuffel and Jodl. 'Everything was again explained to the generals,' said Jodl, 'who all had their maps with them.'[22] Dietrich was later to claim he had told his colleagues that 6th Panzer Army 'would not be ready in Dec 44'.[23] He was also to later grumble:

> I had merely to cross a river, capture Brussels and then go on and take the port of Antwerp ... through countryside where snow was waist deep and there wasn't room to deploy four tanks abreast, let alone six armoured divisions.[24]

Albert Speer, the Armaments Minister, likewise could not understand the logic of attacking across such inhospitable terrain. 'Most of the highways have rises and curves which make them as difficult to traverse as Alpine roads,' he observed. 'In all the planning the question of supplies seems to take second place ... But if supplying has not been properly calculated and provided for, the operation is doomed.'[25]

While all this was going on von Rundstedt and Model had to try to pre-empt the Allies' next moves. A major concern was that if the Americans reached the Rhine between Düsseldorf and Cologne they could break through into the industrial Ruhr region. To safeguard against this, Dietrich was ordered to move his 1st SS Panzer Corps to the north of Cologne and his 2nd SS Panzer Corps to the south-west. Dietrich was also obliged to send forward three of his divisions as reinforcements.

It was made very clear to von Rundstedt that Hitler was intent on micromanaging the Ardennes offensive when he received a 12-page assault tactics guide on 19 November. It came with orders from Hitler that all commanders were to be briefed on these tactics and he wanted copies of the briefings. 'When I saw Hitler's orders for the offensive,' said von Manteuffel, 'I was astonished to find that these even laid down the method and timing of the attack.'[26] Understandably the Commander-in-Chief (CinC) West was not happy at being told how to do his job. The following day Model sent him a message urging him to get the 'small solution' reconsidered. Model reasoned that the time was ripe to launch a two-pronged attack to catch the Allies in the Aachen area. When Model arrived at von Rundstedt's headquarters on 23 November, he continued to lobby for the 'small solution'. He also warned that the panzer divisions would not be ready before 15 December.

Three days later Jodl met with von Rundstedt and, although he was sympathetic, he pointed out it would be almost impossible to get Hitler to change his mind. Model, in a fit of anger, phoned Jodl and yelled down the phone, 'You can tell your Führer that Model will not carry out such an order.'[27] It proved to be a hollow threat. Pointedly Hitler also planned to move his headquarters from Rastenburg to the Eagle's Eyrie, just a kilometre south of von Rundstedt's headquarters at Ziegenberg Castle north of Frankfurt-am-Main. The CinC West knew that he was being made redundant. The Führer was intent on running the battle personally.

Hitler held yet another conference with Dietrich, von Manteuffel, Model and Westphal in Berlin on 2 December; von Rundstedt was conspicuous by his absence. Model was close to physical exhaustion; the task of trying to manage the Western Front and plan for Operation *Watch on the Rhine* was almost too much for him. Once again he argued for the 'small solution'. Hitler placated him by saying they could always implement this if the larger plan did not work. Westphal made no attempt to support Model, which indicated that Model did not have von Rundstedt's backing. Model wanted the offensive to commence at 0800 hours on the basis that the troops were not trained for night operations. Hitler decided to go for 0530 hours.

The generals, despite their ongoing reservations, were amazed at what Goebbels, Himmler and Speer had achieved creating new divisions and resurrecting old ones. Hitler had gathered his new reserve in secret and held it back despite predictions by his generals that the Western Front would collapse if it was not immediately reinforced. Just four of Himmler's new Volksgrenadier divisions had been committed to battle during November, and the refitting of four panzer divisions had only been delayed rather than derailed. That in itself constituted a small miracle. Although impressed by the massing forces, amongst von Manteuffel's many concerns was the issue of Reichsmarschall Hermann Göring's air force playing its part.

Model's briefing during the seven-hour conference clearly had an impact on Hitler and the others. When they were leaving both Dietrich and von Manteuffel felt moved to shake Model's hand and thank him for his efforts. 'Model stood up to Hitler in a way that hardly anyone else dared,' noted von Manteuffel, 'and even refused to carry out orders with which he did not agree.'[28] Nonetheless, Model did not resign in protest. Afterwards the Führer held talks with von Manteuffel during which he candidly admitted that his gathering forces were probably insufficient to reach Antwerp. However, Hitler made it clear he was prepared to gamble that the offensive's outcome would enable him to transfer troops to the east to counter the Red Army.

The Führer was not greatly concerned when von Manteuffel warned him that he felt the Americans were most likely to counter-attack from the Sedan region towards the key communications hub at Bastogne. 'I pointed out,' said von Manteuffel, 'the way that so many of the roads converged on Bastogne.'[29] It was clearly vital that von Manteuffel take and hold Bastogne, but he was worried that Brandenberger's weak 7th Army would be unable to protect his southern flank from counter-attack. That same day Dietrich's headquarters, under the direction of Bittrich, carried out a map exercise in order to familiarize his divisional commanders with *Watch on the Rhine*.

On 10 December Hitler summoned all his army-, corps-, divisional- and brigade-level commanders to the Reichs Chancellery to be briefed. An officer from the elite Führer Begleit Brigade observed that Hitler said the Ardennes offensive was to reach the Meuse within two days and Antwerp in three weeks. This would achieve three objectives: firstly, it would trap 48 Allied divisions or force a general Allied withdrawal; secondly, it would give German industries a four-week breathing space; and thirdly, it would split the Allies.[30] The following day Hitler agreed to postpone the attack until 15 December.

In the meantime, Dietrich and Krämer relocated their headquarters to Bad Münstereifel, south of Euskirchen. There they took stock of their preparations. On the assumption that vehicle fuel consumption would be twice that of normal in the winter conditions, 6th Panzer Army had amassed enough fuel for 125 miles. The only problem was that the bulk of this was held in depots east of the Rhine. This could only be brought forward if the weather kept Allied fighter-bombers grounded. Dietrich discovered that artillery commander General Walther Staudinger was not happy because many of the guns he had been supplied were a mix and match of calibres. This meant no standardization with the ammunition supplies, so even if shells reached his units there was no guarantee they could fire them.

Just four days before the Ardennes offensive was due to commence those senior army and Waffen-SS commanders involved were instructed to report to von Rundstedt's headquarters. 'There we were all stripped of our weapons and brief-cases,' recalled an alarmed General Fritz Bayerlein, 'and were then driven about the countryside in a bus for half an hour.'[31] The generals sat tight lipped wondering why they had been separated from their staff cars. 'When the bus stopped,' said Bayerlein, 'we were led between a double row of SS troops into a deep bunker.'[32] Unbeknown to the gathered generals they had been secretly taken to Hitler's headquarters at Ziegenberg. There they were met by Hitler and Generals Keitel and Jodl. Von Manteuffel was surprised by the physical deterioration of Hitler who he described as 'a stooped figure with a pale and puffy face, hunched in his chair, his hands trembling, his left arm subject to a violent twitching …'[33]

After the attempt on his life on 20 July the Führer was taking no chances. When the generals sat down, an SS guard appeared to take up position behind each of them. Bayerlein, conscious that he was being watched closely, said he was 'afraid even to reach for a handkerchief'.[34] Disturbing as this situation might seem, there was an explanation for the menacing guards. 'The seating accommodation was inadequate and the SS-generals politely left the chairs to their senior army colleagues, while they stood,' observed von Manteuffel. 'This created the impression on some of the army generals that an SS officer was posted behind each army officer's chair. This was certainly a misunderstanding.'[35]

Hitler surveyed the room before launching into a tirade about the coalition of 'ultra-capitalists' and 'ultra-Marxists' that was threatening Germany. Warming to his subject, he told his commanders that their enemies were at 'loggerheads' and that 'these antagonisms grow stronger and stronger from hour to hour'.[36] The generals were not convinced as they were well aware of what was happening on the Eastern and Western fronts. 'If now we can deliver a few more heavy blows,' said Hitler, 'then at any moment this artificially bolstered common front may suddenly collapse ...'[37] Hitler, looking each general in the eye, then added menacingly, 'provided always that there is no weakening on the part of Germany'.[38] More importantly Hitler had convinced himself that if he could give the British and Americans a sufficiently bloody nose, they would drop their demands for Germany's unconditional surrender. Looking round the room, Hitler told his generals 'to make it plain to the enemy that no matter what he does he can never count on a surrender, never, never'.[39]

General von Manteuffel made some tactical suggestions, which surprisingly Hitler accepted. Amongst these was his intention to light the way for the troops by creating artificial moonlight. This could be achieved by bouncing searchlight beams off low cloud. Hitler looked at him for a moment, then asked, 'How do you know there will be clouds? Herr Generaloberst?' The other generals waited expectantly for his answer. 'Because, mein Führer,' said von Manteuffel with a glint in his eye, 'you have decided there will be bad weather that morning.'[40] Hitler seemed to like this and gently wagged a finger at his cocky general.[41]

When Hitler had finished, he met each of his generals. He was not pleased by their attitude. Dietrich recalled, 'Hitler asked me, "Is your Army ready?" I answered, "Not for an offensive." To this Hitler replied, "You are never satisfied."'[42] Hitler's only concession was to agree to letting the attack slip another day from 15 December to the 16th due to fuel supply problems. Operation *Watch on the Rhine* had now lapsed almost six weeks. To Model it had all the hallmarks of Operation *Citadel* on the Eastern Front, which the previous year had kept slipping and failed as a consequence. Afterwards the generals gathered at von Rundstedt's house to celebrate his birthday. It was a sombre affair and no one discussed the coming offensive. 'The death penalty hovered over the secret,' said Dietrich gloomily, 'and it would have been to no avail to discuss it anyway.'[43] By midnight all the generals had bid von Rundstedt good night and were driving back to their commands.

Hitler was determined that his plan and his plan alone be carried out. Bypassing von Rundstedt's headquarters, he sent his final orders direct to Model. Under no circumstances was Model to strike north while still east of the Meuse. Model understood that this meant under no circumstances was he to try to implement the 'small solution' with an attack at Aachen. The fact that these orders had come direct from Hitler indicated that von Rundstedt had been side-lined.

The commanders below divisional level would not receive their orders until 14 December, a mere two days before kick-off. This meant that they were unable to adequately study local conditions and anticipate any hitches that might occur.

Dietrich, who knew that Operation *Watch on the Rhine* was a terrible waste of resources, with little chance of success, tried to rally his men:

> Soldiers of the Sixth Panzer Amy! The great moment of decision is upon us. The Führer has placed us at the vital point. It is for us to reach the enemy front and push beyond the Meuse. Surprise is half the battle. In spite of the terror bombings, the Home Front has provided us with tanks, ammunition and weapons. They are watching us. We will not let them down.[44]

On the ground Hitler's rejuvenated armies were energized. 'The morale of the troops taking part was astonishingly high at the start of the offensive,' said von Rundstedt. 'They really believed victory was possible – unlike the higher commanders, who knew the facts.'[45]

3

The Holy Grail

While Hitler's generals appreciated the need to counter-attack on the Western Front, few of them understood his obsession with retaking Antwerp. Model felt an attack at Aachen would produce perfectly satisfactory results and be less of a risk with their reinvigorated armies. Nonetheless, there was a sound strategic logic behind Hitler's plans. He firmly believed that if he denied Antwerp to the Allies once more, then their war effort would falter. Ever since D-Day the Allies had been reliant on trucks shifting vast quantities of supplies from the liberated French ports and across open beaches to the front. Before they could take the major Normandy port of Cherbourg, Hitler's garrison had comprehensively wrecked the harbour and it took the Allies until the end of September to clear all the debris. Access to the dry-docks was also destroyed.

Determined to slow the Allied advance, Hitler declared all the French Channel ports were to be held as fortresses once surrounded. In the event of them being taken, the dock facilities were to be systematically smashed and the harbours mined. Although the Allies had liberated the ports of St Malo and Brest in Brittany in the summer of 1944, they had given up trying to take Lorient and St Nazaire where the German garrisons defiantly held out. The garrison in Brest made sure that the harbour facilities were so compressively destroyed that the Allies were unable to use it as a major transit point. Furthermore, the Breton ports were really too far west to help Allied forces pushing eastward.

In the south of France, following their landings on the Riviera in mid-August 1944, the Allies had liberated Marseilles and Toulon in the space of just two weeks. Although the German garrisons had done all they could to wreck the docks, both ports were accepting Allied shipping by late September. However, Marseilles and Toulon were again too far away to have any real bearing on the fighting in north-west Europe. Fortunately for Hitler, the Allies' controversial Riviera campaign had significantly weakened their push on the Rhine, as it dissipated their forces and the Allied armies were left competing for increasingly scarce resources. Antwerp became the holy grail for the Allies, as it seemed to offer the answer to all their supply problems. They were only able to land just over 35,000 tons of supplies a day using the liberated Channel ports. It was simply not enough. Crucially, Antwerp's docks were capable of handling up to three times this amount.

Transporting supplies across Europe was a logistical nightmare for the Allies and a major undertaking. Just before D-Day, Allied air forces destroyed much of the French railway network to prevent German troop movements. This took time to repair, and at the end of August 1944 the Red Ball Express truck supply service came into being to keep the advancing Allied armies replenished.[1] At its height it employed around 6,000 trucks delivering 12,500 tons of supplies a day with road routes running from Cherbourg and Arromanches. The Red Ball Express had to continue until such time as Antwerp became available to the Allies and enough railways had been brought back into service.

In response to the British rolling into Antwerp in early September 1944, Hitler issued the following order:

> Because of the breakout of enemy tank forces towards Antwerp, it has become very important for the further progress of the war to hold the fortresses of Boulogne and Dunkirk, the Calais defence area, Walcheren Island, the bridgehead at Antwerp, and the Albert Canal positions as far as Maastricht.[2]

He had some 120,000 troops tied down in the various fortresses. Foolishly, instead of bypassing the Channel ports and concentrating on taking Antwerp and securing the Scheldt estuary leading to the docks, the Allies weakened their advance by diverting forces to take the Channel ports.

The German defence of Le Havre lasted until mid-September and the port was not reopened until the end of the first week of October. The garrison of fortress Boulogne lasted until late September, and they damaged the harbour to such an extent that it could not be reopened until mid-October. Calais fell in early October, but the wrecked port was denied to the Allies until November and then it could only handle personnel. Dunkirk remained firmly in Hitler's possession, which the Allies contented themselves with besieging. In the case of Antwerp, the docks fell intact into Allied hands thanks to the quick actions of the Belgian resistance.

However, Hitler was very pleased that despite the Allies sweeping into Antwerp so swiftly his forces managed to deny them the use of the docks for almost three months. He was in part helped by Field Marshal Montgomery, who failed to secure the shores of the Scheldt. Instead, Montgomery, intent on turning the Rhine at Arnhem in mid-September, had concentrated his efforts to the east of Antwerp. Hitler was very lucky that Montgomery foolishly gave little thought to the consequences of allowing the bulk of the German 15th Army to escape across the Scheldt. During September Montgomery only had two armoured divisions employed clearing the seaward approaches to Antwerp. They were instructed not to commit to offensive operations from 9 September onwards, as all resources were committed to Montgomery's 30th Corps about to drive on Arnhem.

In the meantime, the Germans dug in along the Scheldt's southern shores, creating the fortified Breskens pocket. They also dominated the northern shores by holding Walcheren and South Beveland. This meant that it was impossible for the Allies to get their supply ships along the Scheldt and into Antwerp without being shelled or hitting mines. It also enabled Hitler to continue launching his V-1 flying bombs and V-2 rockets with impunity from the Netherlands. He was able to quickly cobble together the 1st Parachute Army, which, along with elements of 15th Army, helped thwart Montgomery's ill-fated thrust on Arnhem.

Clearing the Scheldt after the German victory at Arnhem became an urgent priority for the Allies. Major General Kurt Eberding's 64th Infantry Division successfully held out in Breskens against the Canadian 1st Army until late October. Likewise, it took the Canadians until the end of October to fight their way north-west of Antwerp along the South Beveland Isthmus and through South Beveland. Field

Marshal von Rundstedt knew his hold on the Scheldt was slipping. He noted, 'In the area of the Scheldt Estuary a permanent recapture of the land connection with Walcheren can no longer be expected. CinC West therefore consents to the flooding of the area.'³ The defenders of South Beveland found their flank turned when two British brigades landed on the southern coast. On the island of North Beveland the small and dispirited German garrison decided to surrender rather than fight.

This left about 7,000 men trapped on Walcheren. To hamper the German defence, the Allies bombed the dykes, flooding much of the interior. Hitler wanted Walcheren held to the last but the quality of the garrison was poor, consisting of a collection of army, Luftwaffe and naval personnel. These forces had been thoroughly exhausted resisting the determined Canadian advance through the canals and flood waters of South Beveland. Many units were also weakened by sickness caused by the appalling conditions. Major General Wilhelm Daser, the senior army commander on Walcheren, was 60 years old and suffered from heart trouble. Daser's only hope was that the island's numerous gun batteries and concrete bunkers would slow the Allies down.

British forces launched amphibious assaults against Westkapelle and Vlissingen on the western and southern coasts of Walcheren on 1 November. Coordination between the German navy responsible for the coastal batteries and the German army was not good. Essentially the navy was responsible for the western defences and the army those to the east. The soaked and weary defenders proved no match for British commandos. Captain Frank Aschmann, the naval commander for the southern Netherlands, fled his headquarters in Vlissingen once the landings commenced. His deputy, Captain Otto Würdemann, was left behind to be captured. In the bitter street fighting for Vlissingen much of the sea front and docks were badly damaged. Resistance by Daser's weak 70th Infantry Division lasted only a week. A despondent Daser, finding his forces also under attack from South Beveland, surrendered in Middelburg on 6 November. Organized resistance on the northern part of the island ended two days later.⁴ The Allies were now free to reach Antwerp from the sea.

While Hitler was angry that fortress Walcheren had not held out as long as he had hoped, it would take Allied minesweepers until the end of November to clear the approaches to Antwerp. Hitler was granted 85 days from the fall of Antwerp to the point where the Allies could start using the port to bring in supplies. This meant that he gained a vital breathing space over the winter. It bought him vital time in which to gather his armies for his attack through the Ardennes with a view to recapturing Antwerp. The port had become Hitler's holy grail. The big question was, could his armies reach it with the resources available and in light of the inhospitable terrain they would face? It was a big gamble, but it was one Hitler was prepared to take, even if the very future of Germany rested on it.

4

How Many Rivers?

One of Field Marshal Model's biggest challenges was to get his armour over at least eight rivers in a timely manner before even reaching the Meuse. From north to south these included the Ourthe, Amblève, Salm, Our, Clerf, Wiltz, Sûre and Sauer. The problem was that the bulk of the army's assault and pontoon bridging was on the Eastern Front. During the course of the fighting there the Red Army, in the face of Hitler's invasion, had blown up all the major bridges. German engineers quickly replaced these with temporary crossings, which were then replaced by more permanent structures. However, Russian partisans kept attacking the latter, forcing the continued use of military bridging equipment across vast distances. After the Red Army's sweeping victories in the summer of 1944, much of this had been lost.

Inevitably the Americans would destroy some, if not all, of the river and railway bridges in the Ardennes in an effort to slow the German advance. Even if the bridges were captured intact, in some cases they would not withstand the weight of the panzers. One such road bridge was that over the Amblève at Petit-Spai. Intelligence showed that the road bridge across the Amblève at Stavelot was old and narrow. Just to the south-west at Trois-Ponts were two bridges, one road and one railway, over the Amblève and two road bridges across the Salm. This made the town a particularly dangerous choke point. All the Americans had to do was cut the Amblève bridges and that would impede access to the Salm crossings. An American report subsequently noted that the latter river 'was a perfect barrier against enemy armour'.[1] The railway not only passed over the Amblève at Trois-Ponts but also the Stavelot road on the near bank. If the latter was brought down it would block access to the La Gleize road. North-west of Trois-Ponts was another crossing over the Amblève at Cheneux. The approaches to this road bridge were horribly exposed. To the north-east of Stavelot there was a bridge over the River Warche at Malmedy.

At Crombach the Americans could slow the German advance on St Vith to the north-east by blowing the road bridge over the railway. Any German armour using the line or the open surrounding farmland would be exposed to American artillery and fighter-bombers. Key crossings over the Ourthe were at Hotton and La Roche. Likewise, the town of Bastogne sat astride the river Wiltz and the railway. There were also numerous railway cuttings to be bridged, such as the one near Losheim. Delays at any of these locations would derail Model's schedule and give the Americans time to build up their defences and summon reinforcements.

It seemed there was little the German Inspectorate of Engineers could do to help. Model's staff, on checking, found that Army Group B's engineers had just 14 B-type and eight J-type military bridges. These would be needed to get over the Ourthe and Meuse as they presented the largest barriers. Emergency bridges across the other waterways would have to be built using timber. General von Manteuffel noted 'plenty of lumber for the construction of bridges was made available to avoid the use of equipment of the bridge building columns at the Our and Clerf.'[2] German Schlauchboote (rubber dinghies), normally used as assault boats, at a pinch could be deployed by the Bautruppen (construction personnel) and engineers to build pontoon bridges. The problem with all this was that bringing the bridging equipment forward quickly and building the bridges potentially while under enemy fire would not be easy. If the weather cleared Model did not hold up much hope of the Luftwaffe keeping enemy fighter-bombers off his engineers or pioneers.

It was now that Model had cause to regret the army abandoning its armoured bridge-layers and assault bridges mounted on the chassis of the Panzer IV. Numbers of these had been built in 1940 to help overcome fixed enemy defences. When it became apparent that enemy fortifications could be easily bypassed and attacked from the rear, requirements for armoured bridge-layers were scaled back and then abandoned.[3] These would have been ideal for the Ardennes offensive as they could have kept up with the panzer divisions. Instead, Model, Dietrich and von Manteuffel would have to rely on vehicle-carried bridging. The ubiquitous Sd Kfz 251 armoured half-track used to transport panzergrenadiers had a variant produced for the pioneers. It had racks on the sides of the hull, which could carry a small assault bridge, but the latter was not designed to take the weight of a tank.

At army level von Manteuffel was assigned two battalions of engineers[4] and each of his divisions had a supporting battalion of engineers, though these were not all necessarily bridge builders. The combat engineer platoons assigned to the infantry regiments were unflatteringly known as 'maids for all work'[5] because they were expected to be jacks-of-all-trades. In contrast the divisional engineer battalions, considered fully fledged combat engineers, were often expected to fight as infantry.[6] Dietrich's allocation of engineers was not so generous. At army level he was reliant on slave labourers from a Todt brigade, but most of his divisions also had engineer battalions. Brandenberger only had a single battalion at army level, but he was not faced by so many river crossings. His troops would only have to get over the Our and Sauer. He was promised a brigade of engineers, but only received elements of this.[7] 'On 12 Dec 44, the engineer brigade finally arrived,' noted Brandenberger with some irritation. 'It consisted of two battalions, which had been trained only in obstacle construction and had no training in military bridge construction.'[8]

Model's commanders essentially had four types of bridging column available. These consisted of the bridge column with a 25-yard span which could take up to 16 tons; the engineer column of 55-yard span which could take up to 70 tons or four large ferries with the same capacity; and motor transport columns with a 60-yard span that could take any vehicle up to and including the Panzer IV, but not the Panther or Tiger. Many of the bridge columns' vehicles were commandeered to carry lumber for emergency bridge building, which meant unloading their bridging equipment. Brandenberger was promised six bridge columns equipped with 100 rubber pontoons. Once again he suffered problems receiving these. 'The arrival of the ... bridge columns was delayed by the difficult transportation situation on the west side of the Rhine,' observed Brandenberger.[9] He resorted to press-ganging the vehicles of his Volks artillery corps in an effort to bring them forward.

However, most of his bridging equipment had still not been brought up by 16 December. Generally, the bridging units were assigned as corps-level resources, although 2nd Panzer and Panzer Lehr Division each had one motor transport column.

To complicate matters infantry foot bridges would also be needed. This was especially the case over the Our. Fortunately for Model, German troops still held the western bank of the southern portion of the river. In consequence, foot and pontoon bridges could be completed beforehand ready for the drive towards the Clerf and on to Bastogne. On the northern section of the river von Manteuffel's 66th Corps would have to force a crossing from the eastern bank before striking towards St Vith. 'By order of the Corps the Div[isional] bridge commanders,' noted von Manteuffel, 'were assigned to direct the crossing of the Our after completion of the emergency bridges.'[10] In the meantime the 26th Engineer Battalion, belonging to Colonel Heinz Kokott's 26th Volksgrenadier Division that had units on the west bank, was instructed to construct foot bridges. The division was also ordered to move its artillery and horse-drawn wagons across using pontoon bridges. 'In addition,' said von Manteuffel, 'engineer units stood ready to enable the bridge commanders to repair any damage to bridges within their areas.'[11]

SS-Major General Priess recalled the rather optimistic orders received by his 1st SS Panzer Corps, which stated, 'Bridges in the sector Maas [Meuse] will be taken in undamaged condition by ruthless and rapid penetration. This will be accomplished by specially organized forward detachments.'[12] However, the situation for these 'forward detachments' was far from ideal. Peiper, on reviewing his 1st SS battle group, was unhappy to discover that his engineer company, under SS-Captain Rumpf, only had two platoons of men transported by armoured half-tracks; the rest had to ride in unprotected lorries or use bicycles. This was not an ideal situation if they were to support contested river crossings. Furthermore, Rumpf had no bridging equipment for Peiper's tanks. Likewise, the 1st SS Panzer Division's engineer battalion only had two platoons equipped with armoured half-tracks. The battalion's 3rd Company, commanded by SS-Lieutenant Sievers, which included the half-tracks, was assigned to support Peiper's battle group. Sievers' men, though, were only equipped with infantry assault bridges. The 2nd Company was allocated to Knittel's battle group. Skorzeny's ad hoc panzer brigade was allocated Bridge Building Column 2150 with a 60-ton capacity, which was supported by a company of combat engineers. The chance of it keeping up with the brigade seemed fairly slim. Likewise, the prospect of 1st SS Panzer's bridging column and the remaining engineer company being able to move along the terrible roads and through the rest of the division in a hurry was highly unlikely.

Peiper was understandably concerned that the crossings at Stavelot and Trois-Ponts might prove a problem. At both locations the bridges were overlooked by buildings, which could provide potential strongpoints for the Americans. In the case of Trois-Ponts, the northernmost road bridge over the Salm, which led to Werbomont, was overlooked by a four-storey building. However, intelligence available to Peiper and Skorzeny indicated that the bridges in their sector of operations were weakly defended. Skorzeny recalled, 'Malmedy had apparently been lightly held by the enemy.'[13] It was eventually to prove 'well held' and with 'strong defences, which could not be overrun without artillery support'.[14]

Skorzeny's main concern was the strength of enemy defences guarding the Meuse bridges at Amay, Engis and Huy. After much cajoling the Luftwaffe reluctantly conducted a reconnaissance flight using a jet fighter to photograph them. 'I almost jumped for joy,' said Skorzeny, 'when I observed that there were no signs of any special preparations for defence of the river crossings.'[15] However, he had to reach them first. If the Americans removed all the road signs, finding any of the bridges would be a problem. Maps were in short supply and those available were at the most 1:50,000 scale and produced in black and white.[16] Trying to read these at night would be almost impossible. If Peiper and Skorzeny were not quick, then the bridge builders would almost certainly find themselves in demand to repair blown bridges. Nonetheless, Skorzeny concluded rather rashly, 'No unpleasant surprises need be anticipated.'[17]

PART TWO
Scraping the Barrel

5

People's Grenadiers

Hitler's significant losses during 1943 and 1944 in Tunisia, Russia and France meant that he was facing a rapidly growing manpower crisis. Since the start of the war he had lost one and a half million dead and a similar number missing. Around double this figure was wounded. A particular blow was the loss of so many junior leaders and veterans whose experience was almost impossible to replace. Nonetheless, plans were formulated to replace these lost units with either new or reconstituted formations during the autumn of 1944; these were to be known as Volksgrenadiers or People's Grenadiers. This was to be achieved by extending conscription to encompass those between the ages of 16 and 50. The name was chosen for propaganda purposes in the hope that it would appeal to German patriotism.

Ironically the Volksgrenadiers were almost the death of Hitler. Colonel Claus von Stauffenberg had flown to the 'Wolf's Lair' at Rastenburg in East Prussia on 20 July 1944 to brief the Führer on progress with these new units. He had another motive as his briefcase also contained a bomb. It failed to kill Hitler, as had every previous attempt, and sparked a purge of all the conspirators including von Stauffenberg. A shaken Hitler realized that Germany was now fighting for its very existence and that he did not enjoy the undivided loyalty of the German people. Propaganda Minister Goebbels announced on 24 August 1944 a total mobilization that would muster the last of the country's manpower reserves. The year before, during a public rally held in Berlin following defeat at Stalingrad, Goebbels had called for 'Total War' but Hitler had not given him the sweeping powers he wanted to implement it. 'It takes a bomb under his backside to make Hitler see reason,' grumbled Goebbels.[1] He now found himself appointed Reich Plenipotentiary for the Total War Effort.

On paper at least, by September 1944 Hitler still had over ten million men under arms, seven and a half million of whom were serving in the army and the Waffen-SS. The problem was that Hitler, in refusing to give up any ground to the Allies, insisted on keeping these forces stretched over half of Europe. His men were left holding hopelessly exposed positions in the Baltic States, the Balkans and Scandinavia, when they would have been better deployed to defend Germany. He had clung to the Netherlands in order to launch his V-weapons against England; likewise he had clung onto Croatia and Hungary as their bauxite was needed for his new jet fighters. The Baltic coast, he argued, was needed for its training grounds and Norway as an operating base for his new U-boats.

During August, September and October 1944 some 500,000 men were rounded up for the army. In addition, men serving with the Luftwaffe and navy were also diverted to the army. Hitler ordered that 250,000 men be transferred from the factories to the army. Albert Speer, the Minister of Armaments and War Production, was horrified. If this happened, how was he supposed to re-equip Germany's armies? 'Such ill-considered intervention would only mean major disruption in the factories,' lamented Speer.[2] At the end of August, he objected to Goebbels' first transfer monthly quota, but soon found himself a victim of Nazi power politics. Hitler sided with Goebbels and Himmler, because the call-up was overseen by the regional governors or Gauleiters. They answered to none other than Martin Bormann, the Führer's private secretary.

Speer wrote to Hitler, complaining that 'Goebbels and Bormann had frankly expressed their view that my Ministry and my organization for industrial self-responsibility were "a collection of reactionary captains of industry", if not outright "anti [Nazi] party".'[3] When Speer handed his letter to the Führer, Hitler immediately passed it on to Bormann to deal with. Later Speer was summoned to see both Bormann and Goebbels. He was told in no uncertain terms that from now on he would answer to Goebbels. 'Bormann told me off in his usual loutish fashion,' recalled Speer, 'while Goebbels listened menacingly, making cynical interjections.'[4]

Speer was also unhappy that no provision was made to replace his conscripted skilled factory workers with women. Pre-war plans existed to mobilize females into the factories but Hitler refused to enact them. He preferred that women remain in the home and that domestic servants remained in service. 'Weapons are needed more desperately than soldiers,' argued Speer.[5] Hitler would not listen as he had an emergency on his hands. He needed to rebuild his armies as quickly as possible and he felt that production would not be affected until the spring of 1945. Instead, some foreign labourers were issued with special ration cards in the vain hope this might improve productivity. German women who were born between 1919 and 1928 were instructed to register for war duties, which often involved being in the auxiliaries. In another sign of Hitler's mounting desperation, school holidays were made indefinite for children over 12 so they could work or be recruited into flak units defending German cities. The Luftwaffe's anti-aircraft batteries ended up with over a million male and female Flakhelfer or Flak-helpers, tying up yet more precious manpower.

Troops and workers were also needed to garrison and rebuild the neglected Siegfried Line in order to hold the Allies at bay while Hitler refitted his armies. He resolved this problem by making rear echelon units operational. Static fortress battalions, training regiments and officer cadet schools were ordered to the Siegfried Line. Depot units were also called on to do their bit. Western Germany's Military Districts (Wehrkreise) were told their depot staffs were to form divisional headquarters. These were to arm engineers, signallers, ordnance specialists, military police, Luftwaffe and navy personnel and members of the Todt Organization. They were also to immediately summon men on leave and convalescing in hospital. These were formed into scratch battalions, regiments and divisions and sent to man the fixed defences of the Siegfried Line. In this way Hitler and Himmler succeeded in gathering 135,000 troops and workers to man and work on Germany's western defences. While this sounded like an impressive force, it lacked the mobility and firepower to tackle the Allies' armoured and mechanized divisions. Once the Allies had broken through there was not much these units could do to help contain the enemy.

Himmler, always keen on empire building, found the manpower of his Waffen-SS greatly expanded. Following the failed bomb plot, Hitler was not prepared to trust the German Army and therefore decreed that the newly raised Volksgrenadier divisions be placed under the control of the Waffen-SS. This move was supported by Bormann who hated the German Army, seeing it as an enemy of the Nazi Party. Although they would be the operational responsibility of the army, Himmler would be in charge of their administration and discipline. This stroked his ego, for as well as being Reichsführer, Minister of the Interior, and Chief of Police, he was now CinC Home Army. Hitler rather optimistically hoped that thanks to Himmler's fervent Nazi political leadership these poorly trained, under-equipped and under-strength formations would somehow be transformed into elite units. It was clearly a case of wishful thinking. To facilitate this the Ersatzheer or Replacement Army was also placed under Himmler's control.

Himmler faced an enormous challenge. On the Eastern Front Hitler's losses had been catastrophic thanks to Stalin's Operation *Bagration*, which had liberated western Russia and taken the Red Army into the Baltic states, East Prussia and Poland. According to German sources Hitler's Army Group Centre suffered 27 divisions badly mauled, 19 of which had to be disbanded; another seven were amalgamated to form just two divisions.

Hitler's losses at the hands of *Bagration* were far worse than those incurred at Stalingrad, Tunis or Falaise. During June–July 1944 alone Hitler's armed forces suffered in excess of 670,000 casualties on the Eastern Front, half of whom belonged to Army Group Centre.[6] It lost 31 corps and divisional commanders from a total of 47.[7] However, through the summer of 1944 the Red Army claimed to have driven back 124 Axis divisions of which 54 were destroyed. The German Army lost 75 infantry divisions on all fronts during 1944, which did not include motorized, mountain or panzer divisions. When Hitler saw the figures, he simply refused to comprehend what was happening; Germany was haemorrhaging manpower.

Replacement officers were left under no illusion as to what they faced. In Russia on average a battalion commander could expect to last up to four months before being killed or wounded. For a company commander the situation was far worse; if they were lucky they would last three months. When Himmler met some Volksgrenadier officers in late July 1944 he made no effort to sugar-coat the situation. Instead he called for self-sacrifice. 'I believe that each of you in the hour of difficulty and danger,' he said, 'will realize what a short second that is in the life of the earth … And during this short second the only thing that matters is that he … now does his duty…'[8] It is hard to see how this speech encouraged the men, who were being told in no uncertain terms to die for their country.

The intention was to refit 35 divisions that had been severely battered on the Eastern and Western fronts and create 15 new ones. The Volksgrenadier divisions were to be formed as a series of waves. The first six, dubbed category 30 and raised in August 1944, consisted of two entirely new divisions and four reconstituted infantry divisions from the east. The eight category 31 units initially had names and then were numbered. The 25 category 32 divisions included recruits of German extraction born outside the Reich. Some included Czech and Polish conscripts who spoke no German. Other divisions were converted from security and reserve units. One was formed around an officer training school regiment, which consisted of lieutenants who had gained battlefield commissions while fighting in Russia.

Speer could not understand the logic of re-forming destroyed units and creating new ones behind the lines. He felt they should concentrate on saving existing formations. During his visits to the Western Front it became clear that divisional commanders desperately wanted Speer's supplies shipped straight to them. He noted that Hitler and Himmler felt 'that it was better to hastily set up new units, the so-called people's grenadier divisions. As they put it, the beaten divisions might just as well be allowed to "bleed to death" completely.'[9]

Amongst those units reconstituted from the Western Front was the 352nd Infantry Division, which had ferociously defended Omaha beach during the Allied D-Day landings. By the end of July 1944, it had been so badly mauled by the Americans that it was no longer combat capable. It tried to refit to the south-east of Alençon, but the remnants were once again driven back by the American advance. On 21 September 1944 the survivors were combined with the 581st Volksgrenadier Division to create the 352nd Volksgrenadiers under Colonel Erich Schmidt. This unit was really a new formation and was built largely from Luftwaffe and navy personnel. Crucially, it was short of experienced officers and the level of training was poor. Likewise, General Hans-Kurt Höcker's 17th Luftwaffe Field Division, which had escaped from Le Havre, formed the basis of the 167th Volksgrenadier Division. Around 300 survivors from the 18th Luftwaffe Field Division, who had also escaped from France, helped form the cadre of the 18th Volksgrenadier Division. This unit was placed under the command of Colonel Günther Hoffmann-Schönborn.[10]

These Volksgrenadier units were formed along the lines of the Infantry Division 1944 organization. Whereas the previous infantry divisions had 17,000 men, this was reduced to 12,000 with the 1944 reorganization; the Volksgrenadier divisions were even weaker at 8,000–10,000 men. Often, though, they were put into the line as weak as 6,000. The fusilier battalion was reduced to a single company and one battalion was mounted on bicycles. Furthermore, the anti-tank companies were not issued with anti-tank guns, but instead had to make do with man-portable weapons such as the Panzerfaust and Panzerschreck. The Volksgrenadier divisions also had a much weaker allocation of supporting artillery. Each division had three infantry regiments, each with two battalions consisting of three grenadier companies apiece. These were generously armed with machine-pistols, plus a support company with medium machine guns and medium mortars.

Although the infantry-gun company only had four guns it was bolstered by eight heavy mortars. Divisional artillery support was reduced to about 60 per cent of the earlier infantry divisions with 32 field guns. In many cases, the equipment issued to these divisions was old or had been captured. While on leave gunner Klaus Ritter volunteered to join the 18th Volksgrenadiers rather than be sent back to the Eastern Front. He found the 105mm gun he was assigned to was towed by a captured tracked Russian tractor.[11]

Hopes of treating the Volksgrenadiers as a strategic reserve were soon dashed when they had to be sent to bolster the crumbling Western and Eastern fronts. Five divisions were sent to Lorraine to help the German 1st Army fend off American and French forces. Notably the 553rd Volksgrenadiers were deployed to help hold Nancy in the face of American attack. Similarly, the 559th Volksgrenadiers were committed to an unsuccessful counter-attack against the Americans near Château-Salins. Several divisions were also sent to the Netherlands and another one was lost defending Aachen. On the Eastern Front Army Group A was reinforced by half a dozen Volksgrenadier divisions. Two of these were positioned to contain the Red Army's bridgehead over the Vistula at Magnuszew. The unfortunate 6th Volksgrenadiers would end up obliterated at Magnuszew by devastating Russian firepower.

Himmler, in accordance with Hitler's wishes, viewed the Volksgrenadiers as 'political soldiers' who needed 'political officers'.[12] To that end the Army Personnel Office was instructed to appoint 'National Socialist Control Officers' to these divisions.[13] Himmler told them, 'Put the best, the most energetic and the most brutal officers of the division in charge.'[14] When General Guderian, Chief of the General Staff, heard that the officers of those units sent to the Eastern Front were reporting directly to Bormann, he was furious at this blatant disregard for the military chain of command. 'I decided that things were going too far,' said Guderian, 'and I put a stop to interference of this sort. I also saw to it that the guilty men were punished.'[15] This initiative was not new. In an effort to mimic the political indoctrination of the SS, the German armed forces had moved to introduce 'Nationalist Socialist Leadership Officers' at the end of 1943.[16] 'They will put up anyone that answers back against a wall,' said Himmler, explaining the role of these Nazi enforcers.[17]

This Nazification of the Volksgrenadiers was far from a success. Men began to desert at the first opportunity. Colonel Hoffmann-Schönborn was incensed when half a dozen of his men crossed over to the Americans. 'Rest assured the division will see that they never see home and loved ones again,' raged the colonel. 'Their families will have to atone for their treason. The destiny of a people has never depended upon traitors and bastards.'[18] His division was not the only one affected. Himmler made his views on the matter perfectly clear: 'Upon examination of the circumstances they will be summarily shot.'[19] Hoffmann-Schönborn resorted to anti-Semitic vitriol, warning his division, 'Deceitful Jewish mudslingers taunt you with their pamphlets and try to entice you into becoming bastards also.'[20]

The Volksgrenadiers did not have a distinctive uniform or insignia and were simply issued with the army's late-war-pattern military clothing and equipment. The former consisted of the new 'Field Uniform 44', which ironically was essentially a copy of the British battledress. To try to give them some sense of *esprit de corps* a badge, thought to consist of a monogram with the letters VGD, was planned on 8 October 1944. However, it was never put into production.

Just ten days later Hitler declared a *levée en masse*, calling up every able-bodied male between the ages of 16 and 60 to create the Volkssturm or People's Storm, a German version of the British Home Guard. It was also placed under the control of Himmler. Following Guderian's objection over the use of Nazi commissars with the Volksgrenadiers to politicize them, he noted, 'Needless to say the row that ensued, and the simultaneous mismanagement of the plans for the Volkssturm, did nothing to improve the general atmosphere at Supreme Headquarters.'[21] Hitler felt he had been forced into the 'total deployment of all Germans' thanks to 'the failure of our European Allies'.[22] Under pressure from the Red Army, the Bulgarians, Finns and Romanians had abandoned his cause. The Hungarians and Slovaks had only just been kept in the fight by occupying their capitals.

The Volkssturm were wholly unsuited for front-line combat. Unlike the Volksgrenadiers, the Volkssturmmann did not have a uniform as such. They wore civilian clothing and whatever military, para-military and party uniforms were available. Likewise, they used whatever equipment and weapons they could lay their hands on, much of which was ancient. The Allies, however, were confused by the terms Volksgrenadier and Volkssturm. The result was that they assumed these forces were one and the same thing – essentially a glorified Dad's Army. As a result, they significantly underestimated the firepower of the Volksgrenadiers.

On 13 November 1944, the self-seeking Goebbels moved to take full credit for the creation of the Volksgrenadiers, which further confused the Allies. 'Three months ago I received from the Führer the task, I may surely say the proudest task of my life,' he declared bombastically, 'to form more than one hundred new divisions within three months. Today I can declare before the world that they are formed...'[23] Such grandstanding simply highlighted his rivalry with Himmler as he sought to gain yet more favour from the Führer.

All this did nothing to help Field Marshal von Rundstedt. By mid-October von Rundstedt was holding a 625-mile front with 41 infantry divisions, which included the Volksgrenadiers, 30 motorized divisions and six weak panzer divisions. Manpower losses were such that the infantry only really equated to 27 infantry divisions. They were in contact with Allied forces, comprising 42 infantry and 13 armoured divisions, plus 11 tank brigades, which had almost the same tank strength as the armoured divisions. On 2 December, just a fortnight before the Ardennes offensive, it was reported that von Rundstedt was short of 3,500 officers and 115,000 men. The proficiency of those reinforcements he had received was poor. Three days later Hitler took the decision to make a further million men available to the German armed forces. Those being inducted into the Replacement Army rose from 1,960,000 in 1943 to 2,556,000 in 1944. Nonetheless, it was simply untrue when Goebbels claimed, 'we have regained the old fighting strength'.[24]

Goebbels was not opposed to supporting Himmler's self-aggrandizement. In mid-October Goebbels recommended to Hitler that Himmler be made Minister of War. This post was abolished in 1938, but by 1944 Himmler was effectively functioning in such a role. Although Hitler tolerated Himmler expanding his power base as a way of offsetting the influence of the army, he declined to grant Himmler the title. Himmler was not too vexed as he knew that he had successfully manoeuvred himself into becoming the second most powerful man in Nazi Germany. Nor did Himmler seem too worried when Goebbels began to encroach on his fiefdom. On 10 December Goebbels was appointed plenipotentiary to assess the manpower situation in the German armed forces. This was clearly an infringement of Himmler's authority but it caused no friction between the two men. Goebbels' task was to make recommendations for postings and transfers. By this stage of the war, with Germany scraping the bottom of its proverbial manpower barrel, any recommendations that Goebbels made would be little more than window dressing.

This cooperation between the two men was quite surprising, but times were desperate. Himmler had not always tolerated Goebbels, whom he considered a degenerate. 'Men of Dr Goebbels' type have always been alien to me,' Himmler remarked in 1939, 'though I have refrained from passing judgement.'[25] He was referring to Goebbels' profligate lifestyle and his reputation for being a sexual predator. Nonetheless, their combined recruiting drive would produce 50 Volksgrenadier divisions as well as 14 divisions for the Waffen-SS, which almost doubled its strength. Amongst the latter, which were also formed by the end of 1944, only two divisions were actually German, seven were recruited in south-east Europe, three in the Low Countries and two in Italy.

Another military reorganization took place on 10 December 1944 when the M1944 configuration of the army infantry divisions, which included six of the stronger Volksgrenadier divisions, was replaced by the M1945. This was designed to save manpower and was similar to that of the category 32 Volksgrenadier pattern, except that it had a full fusilier battalion on bicycles and the Panzerjäger battalion had assault guns as well as anti-tank guns. The field artillery was also stronger with 54 guns. Authorized divisional manpower stood at just over 11,000.

The army's panzer divisions were also weakened. Under the 1943 organization each was supposed to have a single tank regiment, with two battalions each of four companies, each with an authorized strength of 22 tanks. One battalion was supposed to be equipped with the Panzer IV and the other with the Panther. This gave a panzer division a total strength of about 170 tanks. In reality, unlike the Waffen-SS divisions and the army's elite Grossdeutschland Division, they rarely had half this number. Furthermore, the August 1944 divisional organization reduced the tank companies to 17 tanks.

However, Hitler clearly felt that Himmler's Volksgrenadiers would help form the backbone of his Ardennes offensive. The intention was to have ten Volksgrenadier divisions ready by 20 November 1944 and double the number available by 10 December. This would have given a force of some 200,000 men, but proved to be wishful thinking. By the time of the attack on 16 December just ten divisions were available to support the offensive and that included one held in reserve. This meant that only about a third of Hitler's strike force consisted of Volksgrenadier divisions.

The quality of these troops was variable with recruits consisting of occupation forces, Eastern Front and Normandy veterans, plus surplus Luftwaffe and naval personnel. Several were formed around the remains of the ill-fated Luftwaffe field divisions. On the whole these units were poorly trained. Two of the strongest were the 26th and 352nd Volksgrenadiers, which could field 17,000 and 13,000 men respectively. The former had been rebuilt under the old organization of three infantry battalions per regiment. Once the offensive opened another five Volksgrenadier divisions would be committed to the battle. Of these the 212th constituted the German 7th Army's best division, having been fleshed out with recruits from Bavaria. About half a dozen of the Volksgrenadier divisions were formed around the remnants of Eastern Front survivors who were grateful they were not sent back to fight the Red Army.

To try to concentrate artillery support, nine Volks artillery corps were formed, each with up to 100 guns. Seven Volkswerfer or rocket brigades were also created, each with over 100 launchers. Each consisted of two werfer regiments. These artillery corps and rocket brigades were combined with flak units to create army corps-level support assets. In the case of the 1st SS Panzer Corps it was allocated two Volkswerfer brigades and two Volks artillery corps. Sepp Dietrich was not pleased when he discovered that the artillery corps only had sufficient ammunition for two battalions and that a lack of fuel meant they could not move all their guns.[26]

6

Exhausted Panzers

From Mortain, via Falaise, to the ancient Norman capital of Rouen on the banks of the Seine, the Germans left a trail of charred and smashed equipment. Roads and river crossings were choked with the remnants of what had once been the most powerful and successful army in Europe. Men, beasts and machines became mashed into one obscene mess that blighted the Normandy countryside for months afterwards. General Fritz Bayerlein, commander of the once powerful Panzer Lehr Division, had watched as it was pulverized into oblivion by superior Allied firepower and devastating air power. Allied bombs, rockets and artillery had paved a way for the Allied breakout. Lacking Luftwaffe support, Panzer Lehr's strength had meant nothing. The terrible experiences of Bayerlein and his men had not been exceptional or uncommon.

To Hitler's generals it was hard to see how they could recover from their crushing defeats on the Western and Eastern fronts in the summer of 1944. It seemed as if there was nothing left to stop the Allies rolling into Berlin. Catastrophically, the 11 panzer divisions committed to the battle for Normandy had just 86 panzers remaining from a force of 1,800 by 1 September 1944. These losses included the six panzer divisions and a single panzergrenadier division which had been redeployed from the south of France to Normandy. Likewise, the independent panzer units deployed to Normandy were reduced from 458 panzers to just 44 by the same date. The panzer divisions lost 62,000 killed, wounded and captured from a total strength of

160,000 men. It appeared as if Hitler's armoured fist in the West had been completely spent.

Field Marshal von Rundstedt reported to Field Marshal Keitel at the end of the first week of September 1944 that his Army Group B had just 100 remaining tanks. He warned that 'The numerical superiority of enemy tanks compared to ours is indisputable. ... Enemy air force dominates the battle area and the lines of communication ...'[1] He then added, 'In agreement with Field Marshal Model, I recognize (near Aachen) the acute danger to the Westwall ...'[2] Von Rundstedt estimated that it would take six weeks to prepare their defences and in that time the Allies would have to be held at bay somehow.

Hitler's armies were simply running out of tanks. The German Army recorded that in July 1944 it had lost 1,969 tanks and assault guns on all fronts that month. However, within two weeks of Stalin's Operation *Bagration* commencing on 22 June 1944, the Red Army claimed 2,000 panzers and assault guns on the Eastern Front alone. By the end of July this figure had risen to 2,735. Albert Speer's weapons factories had only produced 1,256 replacements and most of those had been sent to the Eastern Front. The following month total losses were listed as 1,221 followed by 2,241 in September. However, half the latter are thought to have been lost in August but had not been counted at the time. Increasingly Speer's factories concentrated on building assault guns, rather than tanks. During June, July and August 2,438 Tiger, Panther and Panzer Mk IV tanks were produced; over the next three months this fell to 1,764 and not all of those could be delivered. Allied air attacks on the German railway network constantly paralysed the movement of ammunition and weapons.

Common sense dictated that now was the time to surrender, but Hitler was determined to fight on. This stance was not as pointless as it first appeared. When Hitler saw the figures from Normandy he was heartened to see that around 98,000 personnel from the panzer divisions had escaped Allied encirclement at Falaise. Himmler was particularly delighted because almost 58,500 of them belonged to his Waffen-SS units. This meant that Hitler's panzer divisions could be rebuilt if Albert Speer's weapons factories produced enough replacement tanks. Speer rose to the challenge and during August 1944 his workers built 1,613 tanks and assault guns.

The shrinking tank production was supposedly compensated for by assault guns, though these were essentially defensive weapons as they lacked a turret and the hull-mounted gun had very limited traverse. This meant that they could only fight effectively head-on and were vulnerable once enemy armour got past them. However, they were easier and quicker to produce. The assault gun had originally been intended to support the infantry divisions, but by this stage of the war they were used to arm the panzer divisions as well.

Many of the factories were located in Czechoslovakia and had avoided the attention of Allied bombers. More assault guns were built in the last three months of 1944 than in 1943. In August 1944 Speer's factories churned out 766 assault guns and this number had increased to 1,199 in November. Although Hitler was unable to replace more than half the panzers he had lost in France, he was able to bolster their firepower with these assault guns. During November the Western Front received 1,349 new or repaired panzers and assault guns. The following month it would receive 950.

Also, to compensate for the lack of tanks and anti-tank weapons Hitler's designers came up with a disposable man-portable single-shot launcher. Speer recalled, 'Another primitive weapon was the Panzerfaust (tank destroyer), a small rocket shot from the hand, which was to substitute for the anti-tank guns we did not have.'[3] These were produced in enormous quantities as Speer noted, 'Modelled on the American bazooka, 997,000 were produced in November 1944, 1,253,000 in December, and 1,200,000 in January 1945.'[4] On this occasion Speer's eye for detail failed him, as it was the larger reloadable Panzerschreck that went into service in 1943 which was based on the bazooka. This, however, was produced in much smaller quantities than the Panzerfaust and required two men to operate it.

Hitler ordered that his Normandy survivors be withdrawn to Germany, behind the protection of the Siegfried Line, where they could be rearmed and refitted. Some of them, however, would have to remain behind to help stabilize the shattered Western Front. Notably, his elite Waffen-SS units were moved out of harm's way so they could be brought back up to strength. The 1st SS, 2nd SS and 12th SS Panzer Divisions withdrew to the Eifel region in Germany. During November the 1st SS were re-equipped in Westphalia, while the 12th SS were re-kitted in Bremen. The 1st SS and 2nd SS were then put into reserve near Aachen.

The battered 9th SS and 10th SS were initially sent to a place called Arnhem in the Netherlands to refit. That was until the unwelcome arrival of the British 1st Airborne Division. During September the 12th SS was deployed to the Aachen area and the 17th SS Panzergrenadier Division withdrew to Metz. Of these units the tough 1st SS, 2nd SS, 9th SS and 12th SS were to be assigned to Dietrich's 6th Panzer Army.

In early September the 1st SS was ordered to withdraw to the area around Bitburg in Germany. Coming under 66th Corps and 7th Army the division benefitted from an influx of 3,500 replacements. Most of these, though, had only received the barest of training. After the 1st SS was assigned to the 6th Panzer Army it took part in rescue efforts in Cologne following Allied bombing. By December the division numbered about 22,000 men equipped with 84 tanks and 20 self-propelled guns. This made it one of the most powerful German armoured divisions. The 2nd SS crossed the Meuse on 7 September and halted at Rousen and St Vith, sheltering in the forests of the Schnee Eifel. Three days later it took up positions behind the German frontier and the Siegfried Line between Brandscheid and Liedenborn. The division found itself fighting alongside infantrymen from the Luftwaffe and the navy. It was not until mid-October that the 2nd SS was withdrawn to the Sauerland to refit.

After fighting at Arnhem, the much-depleted 9th SS Panzer Division was sent to Bad Salzuflen in Westphalia to reorganize. Various units were sent to Gütersloh, Hamm, Münster, Paderborn and Siegen. Manpower replacements were rounded up from reluctant ethnic Germans living in the border regions, including those from Hungary, Romania and Slovakia and even as far away as the Black Sea region of Russia. While the refit was underway the division conducted night-fighting training. The Luftwaffe's inability to protect the division's base areas meant that its units had to remain camouflaged during the day. In particular, vehicle movement was restricted to the hours of darkness. The 12th SS who had suffered about 8,000 casualties in Normandy by December had been brought back up to strength with around 22,000 men.

Thus, the two SS panzer corps of Dietrich's 6th Panzer Army were swiftly rebuilt. The two panzer divisions of Priess' 1st SS Panzer Corps totalled about 44,000 men with around 200 tanks and assault guns; notably the 1st SS Panzer Division was supplemented with Tiger tanks of 502nd SS Heavy Panzer Battalion, and the 12th SS, now under

SS-Brigadier Hugo Krass, was rebuilt, though it lacked experienced junior officers. The 2nd SS was reassigned to SS-Brigadier Heinz Lammerding, and the 9th SS reassigned to SS-Brigadier Sylvester Stadler. Bittrich's 2nd SS Panzer Corps was similarly rebuilt with better-than-average recruits, though the 9th SS lacked transport. According to Dietrich the shortage of fuel severely curtailed tank-driving training, with only enough for five hours per driver.

The German Army's panzer divisions were also quickly retrieved from the battlefield. The remnants of the 2nd and 116th Panzer were re-formed in Germany. The 9th was sent to Aachen for refit, but became involved in operations to hold up the American advance. The 21st Panzer fought in the Saar and Alsace and was then sent to Germany for refit. Its final destination would be the Eastern Front. The 2nd, 9th, 116th and Panzer Lehr were to come under von Manteuffel's gathering 5th Panzer Army.

All these divisions had suffered significant losses in Normandy. The 2nd Panzer sustained about 7,000 casualties, 9th Panzer some 3,500 while the 116th lost 4,348. Bayerlein's Panzer Lehr lost the most with 7,411 casualties. At the beginning of June 1944 it had almost 200 tanks, but when it was briefly deployed on the Saar front at the end of November it only had 72. 'I received sixty new tanks,' recalled Bayerlein when his division refitted at Paderborn, 'and I demanded more flak guns, in view of my experience with air attack.'[5] At the end of August, 2nd Panzer had only managed to cross the Seine with 1,200 men and just five panzers. Although the 9th Panzer was not trapped at Falaise and was able to muster 11,000 men it had barely any tanks left. Some 10,600 men and 21 panzers and assault guns of the 116th Panzer escaped the chaos of Normandy. As a result, the division was in constant combat, first in the Aachen area and then Arnhem and back to Aachen again.

The 116th Panzer Division did not enjoy a period of rest and recuperation. It was not ordered to replenish its strength until 23 November, and it was another three days before a battle group and the divisional artillery which had been detached were reunited with the division. Gathered south-west of München-Gladbach, the 116th was to put together another rapid reaction force for operations on the Roer. 'In response to our urgent request,' noted divisional adjutant Major Fritz Vogelsang, 'today we received 300 soldiers from the Luftwaffe.'[6]

They were followed by another 600 trained replacements for the panzergrenadier regiments, and by the beginning of December the division was anticipating the arrival of another 1,400 men. However, the steady influx of men was soon overwhelming the capabilities of the 116th's field replacement battalion responsible for training. This normally could handle 1,000 replacements, but it soon found it had to cope with 1,800 men until 600 were transferred elsewhere. By the beginning of December, although training was going well, the panzergrenadier regiments still lacked winter clothing and the panzer regiment was short of radio command tanks. By 10 December, 116th Panzer could muster 45 Panther tanks, 26 Panzer IVs and 13 assault guns. Crucially the division was short of 533 trucks and half-tracks, which curtailed the mobility of its panzergrenadiers.

Fearing his replacements would be little more than cannon fodder, General Siegfried von Waldenburg, commanding the 116th, did his utmost to minimize losses. He issued orders stating, 'It is more than ever the duty of every commander to use all means to avoid unnecessary casualties.'[7] Von Waldenburg wisely wanted the reinforcements 'split up among experienced personnel'.[8] He also cautioned his officers to avoid frontal attacks and to place their main defences on forward-facing slopes. 'Infantry must not hug the tanks for protection,' warned von Waldenburg. 'Tanks attract the fire of all arms.'[9] It was also clear that venereal disease was a problem, as he instructed, 'In future I will have anyone who does not observe regulations on this subject charged with self-mutilation.'[10]

Although the autumn output of weapons was barely sufficient to cope with ongoing losses on all fronts, let alone the losses of that summer, Hitler insisted that the bulk of new production go not to units on the front line, but rather those divisions being re-equipped or newly formed in Germany. Considering the disaster of Falaise and the ongoing efforts of the Allies' bomber fleets, the regeneration of 5th Panzer Army now under General von Manteuffel is little short of a miracle. The 2nd and 9th Panzer Divisions were successfully reorganized after their heavy losses in Normandy and by December each division had over 100 tanks apiece. The 9th included Tigers of the attached 301st Heavy Panzer Battalion. Two of 5th Panzer Army's three panzer corps commanders were familiar faces. General von Lüttwitz found himself in charge of 47th Panzer Corps, which included his old command 2nd Panzer as well as 9th Panzer and Panzer Lehr. General Krüger, still commanding

58th Panzer Corps, had responsibility for the 116th Panzer. General Karl Decker's 29th Panzer Corps would be brought up to direct 1st SS and Panzer Lehr at the end of December.

Transporting replacement tanks from the factories to the battered panzer divisions was not easy. Rolf Munninger, serving on Model's headquarters staff, observed that Albert Speer was a regular visitor. Munninger recalled the Armaments Minister telling Model, 'There was a tank factory in the east, about 150 to 200 kilometres [90 to 125 miles] from the front, but there was no fuel to transport them overland, the railway no longer functioned because of the constant bombing.'[11] Speer had apologized, saying, 'I could give you the best tanks built, but there is no way I can get them to you.'[12] What Model and von Rundstedt received was far from sufficient.

'There were no adequate reinforcements, no supplies of ammunition, and although the number of armoured divisions was high,' said von Rundstedt, 'their strength in tanks was low – it was largely paper strength.'[13] According to von Manteuffel, the 5th and 6th Panzer Armies combined mustered about 800 tanks or the equivalent of about eight panzer divisions.[14] Furthermore, fuel supplies presented another major problem. Von Manteuffel told Hitler that they needed five times the standard scale of petrol supply; in the event they only got one and a half times.

The equipping of the panzer armies came at great cost to the German war effort elsewhere. When Hitler had briefed his generals on 12 December he had told them, 'Gentlemen, on other fronts I have accepted sacrifices beyond the call of necessity in order to create here the preconditions for another offensive.'[15] He did not just mean the Italian and Russian fronts. General Brandenberger, commanding the 7th Army, felt that the panzer armies received preferential treatment to the detriment of his command. 'Not a single division had its full complement of assault guns,' he complained, 'some of them had none at all, and others no more than three or four.'[16] To make matters worse, his army 'was at least three or four divisions too weak to accomplish its mission'.[17] General Guderian agreed with Brandenberger's pessimistic assessment, remarking, 'this army lacked the mobile strength necessary for carrying out its difficult assignment'.[18] Guderian, who only had responsibility for the Eastern Front, could do nothing to help.

Between Brandenberger and Army Group Upper Rhine to the south was the remains of Army Group G with General Otto Knobelsdorff's 1st Army which was in a similar condition. He had lost the 3rd and 15th Panzergrenadier Divisions in October after they had been redeployed north to the Aachen area.

By the end of the year Knobelsdorff had just 86,000 men supported by 100 tanks. During November he had to fend off General Patton's US 3rd Army, which launched a series of attacks between Metz and Nancy, pushing towards Saarbrücken. His only armoured reserve was the exhausted 11th Panzer Division that had just 69 tanks.

In mid-November Knobelsdorff withdrew, leaving the 10,000-strong Metz garrison to its fate. They survived until 13 December and in the meantime the French 1st Army liberated Strasbourg on the Rhine on 23 November. Bayerlein's Panzer Lehr was deployed to Sarre-Union to launch a counter-attack to cut off the French, but, on the night of 27/28 November, was recalled to take part in the Ardennes offensive. Further south the French also liberated Belfort and Mulhouse, reaching the Rhine at Huningue. This left General Friedrich Wiese's German 19th Army horribly exposed on the west bank in a large salient jutting westward from Colmar. He also had few tanks, perhaps 40 at most. This lack of armour south of the Ardennes meant that most of Hitler's armies trying to hold the Western Front had extremely limited capabilities when it came to conducting even local counter-attacks.

In the Ardennes, though, Hitler put great faith in his panzer armies. 'Numerous testimonies of prisoners,' reported the chief of staff of the 62nd Volksgrenadier Division on 14 December, 'contend that the American soldier fears most the German tanks ..., next to the well-directed artillery fire.'[19] Somewhat surprisingly this report went on to add, 'According to prisoner's opinion, the German tank force fights far better in the Aachen sector than in Normandy.'[20] It remained to be seen how well it would fight in the Ardennes. Hitler instructed von Manteuffel, 'The armoured divisions were not to strike until the breakthrough had been achieved by the infantry mass.'[21] This was the complete opposite to the glory days of 1939–41.

General von Manteuffel knew that the survival of the panzers was paramount if they were to achieve their objectives. To that end he issued a directive on tactics to the divisions under his command at the end of November. 'Anti-tank guns must be destroyed,' he instructed. 'If the tanks or assault guns cannot do the job, they must be cut off by a pincer movement ... aided by our light and heavy weapons and artillery.'[22] He concluded, perhaps a little too optimistically, 'This will, in most cases, force them to withdraw.'[23] Some Germans had little respect for the ability of American tankers. 'According to all our observations American tanks will lose their aggressiveness,' reported Lieutenant Kahler of the 18th Volksgrenadier Division, 'and turn around as soon as they are attacked by close combat methods or artillery.'[24] Likewise a member of the 183rd Volksgrenadier Division noted, 'They advance with greatest caution. ... Whenever one tank was shot in flames, the group of enemy tanks withdrew most of the time. ... At dusk the enemy tanks always stopped their attacks.'[25] It seemed there were at least some grounds for optimism.

7

Unleash the Tigers

For the Ardennes offensive Hitler hoped that quality as much as quantity would give his panzers the victory he so desperately needed. He and his commanders were placing great faith in the abilities of the newer models of panzer, in particular the Panther and the Tiger II, which were by far the most powerful tanks in the German armoury. Although, thanks to the supreme efforts of Albert Speer's factories, Hitler was able to arm two whole panzer armies, there still remained a critical shortage of tanks. This was especially the case with the Panzer IV, Panther and the Tiger.

Field Marshal Model was able to gather about 450 Panthers, but not all these were fully operational. 'In my opinion,' said General von Manteuffel, 'the German Panzer V, the "Panther", was the most satisfactory of all, and would have been close to ideal had it been possible to design a lower silhouette.'[1] An improved design with a smaller turret was being developed but it was not ready in time. A new modification to the Panther, introduced in October 1944, which was welcomed by the crews, was a fighting compartment heating system. This drew warm air from one of the engine fans. What was not so welcome was the steel-rimmed 'silent bloc' road wheels that on some vehicles replaced the wheels with rubber-rimmed tyres. These were similar to those used on the Tiger and made for a less comfortable ride. Although this 'silent bloc' variant was only a trial production run, some were deployed to the Ardennes with the 1st SS Panzer Division.

The much newer turretless Jagdpanther tank destroyer, based on the Panther's hull, was armed with an 88mm gun similar to that on the

Tiger. This made it deadlier than the Panther and Panzer IV armed with 75mm guns, but very few were available. It was planned to build 150 of these a month but disruption by Allied bombers put paid to that. The factory managed just eight in October 1944, rising to 35 the following month. The result was that fewer than 400 Jagdpanthers had been built by early 1945. The 559th Panzerjäger Battalion equipped with Jagdpanthers was assigned to the Panzer Lehr Division while the 560th went to the 12th SS Panzer Division. A number of other battalions were deployed as army-level assets with 5th and 6th Panzer and 7th Armies.

Hitler had much greater hopes for the mighty Tiger II, which had gone into combat for the first time in the summer of 1944, when output of the Tiger I ceased. The Tiger II has been described as 'one of the most massive and spectacular tanks ever built'.[2] It featured many of the proven design benefits of the Panther, including sloped armour, copied from the Soviet T-34 medium tank. However, despite its powerful and improved 88mm gun and thick armour, the Tiger II was woefully unsuitable for use in the heavily forested and hilly Ardennes. The close terrain and resulting limited visibility would neutralize its long-range stand-off tank-killing capabilities. Likewise, its weight would be a problem on the narrow country roads and bridges.

Hitler refused to learn from the tough lessons gained in Normandy, where three battalions equipped with the Tiger I, along with a single company of Tiger IIs, had been committed piecemeal against the Allies. Although these tanks reaped a deadly harvest, most famously at Villers-Bocage, there had been too few of them to have little more than a tactical impact. Furthermore, the close confines of the Normandy hedgerows neutralized the Tigers' long-range guns and enabled Allied tankers to sneak up on them. It had also proved impossible to retrieve the last remaining Tigers that in consequence had to be abandoned along the banks of the Seine. The survivors from the 101st and 102nd SS Heavy Panzer Battalions were re-formed and re-designated the 501st SS and 502nd SS, alongside the army's existing 503rd.

After being refitted, SS-Lieutenant Colonel Heinz von Westernhagen's 501st Battalion first saw action with the Tiger II on the Eastern Front in the summer of 1944. The Tiger II once again did not live up to expectations and the battalion suffered heavy losses. This was in part due to problems with the engine, the transmission and the quality of the armour. The latter had a nasty tendency to crack on the welds and shower the interior of the tank with deadly metal splinters. Furthermore, no one had heeded General Guderian's mantra, 'The engine of the tank is no less a weapon than its gun.'[3] The Tiger II had the same underpowered engine as the Tiger I and at 68 tons was 10 tons heavier. General von Manteuffel agreed: 'In a tank battle, if you stand still you are lost ... speed and cross-country performance are the essentials.'[4]

The 506th Battalion belonging to the army had employed the Tiger II for the first time that summer, helping to destroy British forces at Arnhem. The fact that the British had resisted for so long showed just how poorly the Tiger crews performed. In one instance British infantry armed with just anti-tank mines and PIATs (Projector Infantry Anti-Tank weapons) had successfully stalked and destroyed five Tigers in the dark. Nonetheless, Otto Skorzeny was a fan of the Tiger II. He had deployed four from the 503rd Heavy Panzer Battalion to help secure Budapest when it looked as if the Hungarian government might defect to the Allies. He used one of them to dramatically force his way into Buda Castle in October 1944 after the garrison hesitated about letting the Germans conduct their coup.

Production of the Tiger II, though, was painfully slow and as a result only about 150 Tigers of both types were available by the winter of 1944. Hitler brought this situation upon himself. In mid-1943 Guderian had pleaded with him to relocate their tank factories before they were targeted by the Allied bomber fleets. Hitler, fearing the disruption this might cause, refused on the grounds that the Allies were too busy bombing Germany's aircraft factories. All Guderian could do was strengthen the air defences protecting Germany's main tank plants at Kassel, Friedrichshafen and Schweinfurt.

The moment Hitler had seen the wooden mock-up of the Tiger II on 20 October 1943 he had fallen in love with it and demanded it go into production. He saw it as another example of superior Nazi technological prowess. Just two days later the Allies bombed Kassel, where the Tiger I was being built and the Tiger II was under development. The result was that production of the former was delayed and only a single prototype for the latter had been built by the end of 1943. Allied bombers had then started attacking Hitler's other tank facilities in the Berlin area in November 1943. Limited production of the Tiger II had only started in early 1944, even though it had first been ordered a year earlier.

Hitler hoped that the manufacturer Henschel would manage 100 Tiger IIs a month from August 1944, rising to 140 from November 1944 onwards. In theory this could have given him up to 450 Tiger IIs to supplement the Tiger Is still in service. This would have represented a truly terrifying force. However, continual setbacks meant that the best month was August, when 84 rolled off the production line. By the end of the year just 376 Tiger IIs had been built, with another 112 following in early 1945.

The result was that just two Tiger battalions were assigned to 6th Panzer Army, the 501st SS and the 506th. At best the 1st SS Panzer Division spearhead would be supported by about 20 to 30 Tiger IIs from von Westernhagen's battalion, which was simply not enough. The 5th Panzer Army was sent the 301st Heavy Panzer Battalion, which was attached to the 9th Panzer Division. The battalion had returned from the Eastern Front to be equipped with 30 Tiger Is and remote-control demolition vehicles. When the time came, these three battalions could only muster 76 operational Tigers between them.[5]

These lumbering monsters were designed as breakthrough tanks but their weight meant that they were unable to use most of the local roads and bridges. Furthermore, as in Normandy the good stand-off capabilities of the Tiger and the Panther's guns were completely obstructed by the dense forests of the Ardennes. This meant that American tanks and Bazooka teams would be able to creep up on them and destroy them at very close quarters. The latter weapon could penetrate the hull sides and the rear of both types of Tiger. Furthermore, thanks to Allied air superiority the Tigers were vulnerable to enemy fighter-bombers. Bombs and rockets could damage tracks and vision devices. They could also knock the turret off its bearings, thereby jamming it, or fracture the welded joints in the armour. It took a brave tank crew to ride out a sustained air attack with all the hatches battened down.

The Tiger II's massive turret provided an easy target for enemy gunners. Its size was dictated by the need to house the KwK 43 L/71 gun, an improved version of the 88mm gun used in the original Tiger. The Tiger II turret also featured a massive overhang at the rear. This was designed to carry 22 ready-to-use tank rounds in racks, which were within easy reach of the breech of the gun. These were divided into two batches either side of the breech recoil area.[6] This meant that the crew only required minimal movement when loading the main armament, which sped up the rate of fire. The turret also contained a breech-loading mortar that could fire smoke grenades or anti-personnel fragmentation grenades. The latter could kill American bazooka teams, assuming that the crew spotted them first.

When the time came von Westernhagen's three company commanders, SS-Captains Birnschein and Möbius and SS-Lieutenant Wessel, were ordered to rendezvous at Tondorf ready to support SS-Lieutenant Colonel Jochen Peiper's battle group. Peiper placed them in reserve so they could later make use of the open countryside before the Meuse. Even Peiper appreciated that inevitably the Tiger II's weight would make it a liability. When von Westernhagen saw the routes they were to use, he was relieved he was not to open the assault. Even navigating the narrow streets of Tondorf would be a challenge. Turrets would have to remain resolutely forward or they would take out the windows with their long gun barrels.

The Tigers' greatest value in the Ardennes would be for propaganda purposes. Their appearance on the battlefield would help convince the Americans that every panzer they encountered was a dreaded Tiger. Möbius, commanding 2nd Company, summoned SS-Second Lieutenant Georg Hantusch, who was in charge of his 2nd Platoon, and told him that he needed a tank to be accompanied by an SS-Kriegsberichter or war reporter. The latter was to take propaganda photos at different locations. These would be used to help chronicle Hitler's anticipated triumph in the Ardennes. The combat cameramen, photographers and reporters of the 'SS-Standarte Kurt Eggers' Kriegsberichter Regiment had a tough reputation and did not shy away from putting themselves in harm's way.[7] Hantusch selected SS-Sergeant Kurt Sowa and the crew of Tiger II '222' for this job. They were to be recorded at Tondorf, Deidenberg, Kaiserbaracke and Ligneuville. Sowa took great delight in telling his men that they and the rest of the company were going to be war heroes. His crew found this funny, as they were so wrapped up from head to toe against the cold that no one at home would recognize them.

After the heavy losses in Normandy and Russia the Panzer IV, which formed the mainstay of the German panzer divisions, was understandably in short supply. Thanks to the efforts of Allied bombers and ongoing battlefield losses, the panzer divisions found it difficult to equip both a battalion of Panzer IVs and a battalion of Panthers. Increasingly Hitler had decreed that the Panzer IV production would be dedicated to building assault gun and tank destroyer versions on the grounds they could be churned out quicker. General Guderian, while serving as Inspector General of Armoured Forces, had told Hitler, 'production of the Panzer IV must be increased during the year 1944–45, so far as this can be done without damaging the production of Panthers and Tigers'.[8] He went on to urge that 'the Panzer IV should continue to be built until such time as a high level of mass production was absolutely assured for the Panthers'.[9] The latter, though, was never achieved because of Hitler's forever-changing priorities.

The resulting shortages of Panzer IVs meant that by November 1944 tank companies had as few as ten of them. The panzer divisions assigned to the two panzer armies each had between 26 and 42 Panzer IVs. Therefore, the eight panzer divisions deployed to the Ardennes offensive could only muster 259 Panzer IVs. Some of the panzer divisions could only field a mixed tank battalion of Panzer IVs and Panthers, which meant the second tank battalion had to be replaced by tank destroyers or assault guns. In the case of the 1st SS, they had to supplement their mixed tank battalion, of around 15 Panzer IVs and 15 Panthers, with the battalion of Tiger IIs. Notably the 2nd Panzer and 2nd SS Panzer Divisions had to employ two companies of assault guns to supplement their tanks. In the case of the 9th and 116th Panzer Divisions, they had no Panzer IVs at all. Instead they had to make do with three companies of assault guns.

The newest version of the Panzer IV, known as the Ausf or model J, which had gone into production in June 1944, suffered from certain wartime economies. Crucially, to allow space for extra fuel the auxiliary engine which powered the electric turret traverse was dispensed with, to the dismay of the crews. Instead they had to make do with a hand traverse. Shortages of rubber also meant that the road wheels had steel rims, which made for a bumpier and noisier ride. In addition, the steel side skirts, intended to offer additional protection from some anti-tank weapons, were replaced by cheaper wire mesh. This was easily snagged when manoeuvring and torn off. The Panzer IV needed 200 litres to cover 60 miles by road, which was only 40 and 60 per cent of the Panther's and Tiger's consumption respectively. Compared with the Panzer IV they were complete gas guzzlers. The Tiger consumed 500 litres and the Panther 350 per 60 miles by road.

Only a single factory continued to produce the Panzer IV, as all the other manufacturers had been ordered to build assault gun and tank destroyer variants instead. All these, though, lacked turrets, as the main armament was mounted in the hull in order to offer a lower profile. They were, like the earlier Panzer III-based versions, really defensive rather than offensive weapons as they lacked the flexibility of regular tanks. The tank destroyer units of the panzer divisions should have been strengthened by the new Panzer IV/70, a tank destroyer that carried a 75mm gun that was as powerful as that in the Panther. However, fewer than 140 were available for the Ardennes. Each division was supposed to get 21, but in the case of the 1st SS they only ended up with ten, under the command of SS-Captain Otto Holst. The thick frontal armour and the long gun barrel came at a price and rendered the Panzer IV/70 nose heavy. This made it hard work to steer and caused excessive wear on the front road wheels.

If it were not for the shortcomings of the American-built Sherman tank, Hitler's armoured capabilities might have looked inadequate. Instead, geography and Allied air power aside, it looked as if they almost had a fighting chance. 'Movement, action and surprise cannot be too fast,' observed General Bayerlein of their tank forces.[10] The success of Hitler's Ardennes offensive hung on these very three factors. Hitler was determined to unleash his Tigers on the unsuspecting Americans. SS-Lieutenant Colonel von Westernhagen's Tigers were painted in what was dubbed the 'ambush scheme', which implied a defensive role rather than a breakthrough one.[11] This camouflage was designed to help the tank blend in with woods and make it difficult to detect at close range.[12] Hitler, however, wanted his Tigers leading the charge, not lurking in the undergrowth.

PART THREE

Where's the Luftwaffe?

8

Fighter not a Bomber

While Hitler was rebuilding his infantry and panzer divisions, he also needed Reichsmarschall Göring to rebuild his battered Luftwaffe. By mid-1944 it had lost the air war over the Western and Eastern fronts as well as Germany's cities. Many of its veteran pilots were dead and increasingly Göring's fighters were piloted by inexperienced youngsters. By the autumn the Luftwaffe was in a similarly poor condition to that of the German Army. It could only muster 4,500 aircraft and the bulk of these were on the Eastern Front. In the West the Luftwaffe had just 1,000 operational aircraft, whereas the British and the Americans had around ten times this. On the Eastern Front Stalin's resurrected Red Air Force had expanded to almost 13,500 aircraft. Against this force the Luftwaffe had 2,199 of which only 1,624 were operational. The remaining 1,301 were in northern Italy and the northern Balkans. When the Red Army launched its massive counteroffensive in the middle of that year it was backed by nearly 6,000 aircraft. By then Hitler should have had a jet fighter-bomber with which to attack the Allied armies; instead, political infighting had held back this advanced wonder weapon.

Remarkably, in 1944, despite the best efforts of the British and American bomber fleets, German aircraft production continued to rise. In 1942 Hitler's aircraft factories had churned out 15,700 aircraft and in 1943 25,871 plus a further 18,600 repaired. The goal for 1944 was 51,800, of which 25,285 would be fighters. Albert Speer was grateful that the Allies were inconsistent with their targeting strategy, which had spared his vital aviation engine factories. The problem the Luftwaffe had was not replacement aircraft but pilots. It was engaged in a war of attrition that it could not win. Furthermore, the Luftwaffe was suffering from growing fuel shortages.

While Hitler survived the assassin's bomb on 20 July 1944, Colonel-General Günther Korten, the Luftwaffe's chief of staff, did not. In his place Göring appointed Lieutenant General Werner Kreipe, even though Hitler favoured General Robert Ritter von Greim. When Kreipe reported to Hitler on 11 August he was lectured on the performance of the Luftwaffe and the constant delays with the jet aircraft programmes. Hitler also wanted fighter squadrons redeployed from Germany to France, yet Kreipe knew that they were needed to protect Germany's synthetic oil refineries or the armed forces would run out of fuel.

This situation was becoming increasingly desperate. Thanks to Allied bombing, production of aviation fuel for the Luftwaffe was rapidly declining. Germany had produced 156,000 tons in May 1944; the following month it dropped by two-thirds to 52,000 tons. The Allies kept up their relentless pressure and in July this had fallen to 35,000 tons and in August to 17,000. The Luftwaffe had just five weeks of fuel by September 1944 and Germany's arms industries had soaked up the last of the raw materials that could not be replaced.

This systematic and concerted destruction of the synthetic oil plants also meant that by September 1944 petrol stocks, which had stood at one million tons in April, had fallen to 327,000 tons. Similarly, the production of diesel oil fell from 100,000 tons to 39,000 tons over the same period. The production of gasoline for vehicles plummeted from 134,000 tons in March 1944 to just 39,000 tons in March 1945. Germany's foreign oil supplies were also cut off. By the middle of 1944 Germany was receiving just ten per cent of the 2.5 million tons of oil it had received the year before from Romania and Hungary. Imports drastically fell from 200,000 tons in February 1944 to just 11,000 tons by the summer. When the Red Army drove into Romania in late August the loss of its oilfields mattered little as, by this point, they were contributing nothing to Germany's industries and the armed forces.

In an effort to consolidate his weapons production Hitler placed the aircraft industries under the control of Albert Speer. Field Marshal Erhard Milch, Inspector General of the Luftwaffe, was also put under Speer's authority. This was partly as a punishment for Milch's opposition to Göring's leadership and his defiance over jet development. Amongst his many tasks Milch was overseeing the long-awaited Messerschmitt 262, which was the world's very first turbojet fighter. It had two wing-mounted jet engines and with a top speed of 540mph was considerably faster than any other Allied aircraft. It also packed a punch with four 30mm cannons and air-to-air rockets. General Adolf Galland, commander of the Luftwaffe's fighter forces, was desperate for this aircraft. Luckily for the Luftwaffe, the Me 262 was fuelled with low-grade petrol, of which there was plenty, and was not greatly affected by the mounting oil crisis.

Initially Hitler and Galland had high hopes that this aircraft would drive the Allies from the skies and the Führer authorized production in November 1943. Hitler then decided he wanted it to function solely as a fighter-bomber to counter the anticipated Allied invasion of France, which meant major structural redesign work had to be conducted. Göring and his commanders were horrified when Hitler announced, 'In this aircraft, which you tell me is a fighter, I see the Blitzbomber with which I will repulse the invasion in its initial and weakest phase.'[1] He was adamant on the matter, adding, 'The aircraft does not interest me in the least as a fighter.'[2]

Milch chose to ignore Hitler's orders. Limited jet fighter deliveries to the Luftwaffe commenced in April 1944. When Hitler found out he was furious. 'Who pays the slightest attention to orders I give?' he ranted. 'I gave an unqualified order, and left nobody in any doubt that the aircraft was to be equipped as a fighter-bomber.'[3] Milch, pressing his luck, retorted, 'Mein Führer, the smallest infant can see that this is a fighter, not a bomber aircraft.'[4] It was at this point that Hitler ordered Speer to take over.

Both Milch and Speer later vainly tried to persuade Hitler that the fighter-bomber variant was a waste of time, arguing that their new jet would be better used to tackle the American bombers pounding Germany's cities and factories. As a bomber the Me 262 could only carry insignificant quantities of bombs, which would have little more than a tactical value. Furthermore, using it as a ground attack aircraft would negate its fast speed. Milch, firmly out of favour, briefed the newly appointed Kreipe to broach the subject with Hitler. 'In a growing temper he made short work of me,' noted Kreipe of his meeting with the Führer. 'Now I was stabbing him in the back as well!'[5] Göring reacted by ordering Kreipe not to talk to Milch ever again.

For some reason Göring seemed quite confused as to when Hitler had actually ordered the change of role for the Me 262. This may have been to avoid the Führer's wrath. When later questioned he said it was after Hitler first saw the aircraft in 1943, though test flights had commenced the year before. Subsequently he claimed it was in May 1944, after deliveries commenced. Either way it caused a fatal delay. By mid-September 1944 Speer resolved to write to Hitler in a final effort to get him to change his mind. Kreipe warned Speer not to do so, cautioning, 'At the very mention of the Me 262, Hitler was likely to fly off the handle.'[6] Kreipe had been in office long enough to know he would be held responsible. 'I would only be making trouble for him,' acknowledged Speer, 'since Hitler would assume that the air force chief of staff had put me up to it.'[7] Nonetheless, Speer still wrote to Hitler who took no notice, and Speer, with more pressing matters, gave up on the subject. Kreipe was right for his days were now numbered.

The Luftwaffe suffered another setback when on 1 October 1944 Milch was seriously injured in a car crash during a visit to Arnhem with Speer and hospitalized. Two days later an experimental fighter unit was set up with 40 Me 262s under 23-year-old Major Walther 'Nowy' Nowotny, a highly decorated Eastern Front fighter ace. This force operated from Achmer and Hesepe. Discouragingly its initial commander Captain Thierfelder had died in a ball of flames during a trial sortie. Nowotny was just the man for the job. He had commanded a squadron of Fw 190s in Russia where he had scored 255 confirmed kills. On 23 September 1943 Hitler had personally awarded Nowotny the Oak Leaves and the Swords to his Knight's Cross, which were known by the crews as the 'Cauliflower' and the 'Knife and Fork'.[8] Nowotny became the first pilot in the world to score 250 kills on 14 October 1943. He was the epitome of a fighter ace: handsome, dashing and daring.

Nowotny's jet pilots did not get off to a good start, as it soon became apparent that the Me 262 was vulnerable thanks to its slow take-off and landing speeds. 'This was clear from the outset to all experts,' complained Messerschmitt engineer Ludwig Bölkow.[9] Yet Test Detachment Nowotny's airfields were within reach of the Allies. On their first mission, from a force of six aircraft two were caught by enemy fighters as they tried to take off and another two were destroyed as they came in to land. Between them they only managed to claim three or four American bombers; it was a poor trade-off. Continual attacks by American fighter-bombers on Nowotny's two airfields meant they had to be constantly protected by Fw 190 fighters and anti-aircraft artillery.

Nowotny, under pressure from his superiors for immediate results, neglected training and gave little thought to developing new fighter tactics. Bölkow held the Air Staff responsible for these failings, not Nowotny. For many of the pilots their first experience of this revolutionary aircraft was flying circuits round the airfield. By the end of the month the squadron, which was grounded for ten days due to bad weather, had flown just three combat sorties a day. Thanks to technical problems Nowotny had only three operational aircraft. Allied pilots soon learned they could dodge the jet fighter's fire by side slipping, throttling-back and lowering their flaps.

On 8 November Nowotny was ordered not to take to the sky, but reports of returning American bombers were just too tempting. Not long after, he reported his 258th victory of the war. He also had 22 unconfirmed kills. His headquarters at Achmer waited anxiously for Nowotny and the last of the serviceable 262s to return. Fatefully that day there was no air cover at the airfield. When the radio crackled into life it was not good news. 'One engine has failed,' said Nowotny. 'Will try a landing.'[10] On the ground amongst those waiting for him was General Galland. They watched as Nowotny came into view with a pack of American fighters in hot pursuit. There was no way he could land, so instead he began to climb in order to dive back down amongst his attackers. After he turned, his jet exploded, having been hit by the Americans or due to some mechanical failure. The death of Walther Nowotny was a terrible blow to Luftwaffe morale. Nor was it a good advertisement for the overdue Me 262.

After Nowotny's death his unit was disbanded, having claimed 26 enemy aircraft. Another fighter unit was formed under Colonel Johannes Steinhoff, but after all the controversy over its use as a fighter it was clearly not producing the results that Milch and Speer had long hoped for. It began to look as if Hitler had been right all along. The first fighter-bomber unit, the 51st Bomber Group, was also established at Achmer and by the autumn another eight units were converting to the aircraft. By the end of October, the 51st was managing up to eight sorties a day, notably without breakdowns. This was in part because Test Detachment Schenk had already ironed out many of the teething problems.

Some 265 Me 262s had been built by the end of October, though 30 of these were lost thanks to Allied air raids on the Messerschmitt factories. Production was expected to amount to 130 during November followed by another 200 in December. Despite such potential numbers, availability of aircraft to the front-line units was poor. The jet engines were very unreliable and had a life of just 25 hours. The American destruction of the refineries meant that the severe fuel shortages impacted on introduction of the aircraft. Those sent to the Obertraubling factory awaiting flight tests had to be shifted to dispersal areas using the low-tech method of horses and oxen. Any hopes Hitler may have had of using the Me 262 over the Ardennes were completely dashed. The irony was that Milch's obstinacy had cost Hitler exactly the type of fighter-bomber he needed to attack Allied airfields. It could have swooped in to bomb and strafe, causing mayhem before the Allies realized what was happening, and then sped to safety. If sufficient numbers of the fighter variant had been available, it could have flown top cover for the attacking force.

Nonetheless, Hitler, deprived of his 'Blitzbomber', intended to support his Volksgrenadiers with a 'People's Fighter' or Volksjäger, which would be a single-motored jet fighter.[11] After all the problems with the Me 262 he wanted a jet in the quickest time and at the smallest cost. Messerschmitt introduced limited numbers of the Me 163 Komet into service in May 1944. This diminutive interceptor was powered by a rocket motor using a highly volatile fuel. The Komet's 596mph top speed meant it rapidly overshot its intended target, while heavy landings often caused the engine to explode, instantly killing the pilot. Preparations for the operational deployment of both the Me 262 and Me 163 had been under the supervision of Colonel Gordon Gollob. Galland, though, had been unhappy with Gollob's performance and transferred him.

The real candidate for the Volksjäger was the Heinkel He 162 Salamander. This was to be piloted by the Hitler Youth. However, this turbojet fighter was far from ready for mass production as the requirement had only been issued in mid-September 1944. The first prototype, featuring the engine mounted above the fuselage, crashed on 10 December 1944, killing the test pilot. He had conducted a high-speed low-level pass for the benefit of the dignitaries gathered to watch the demonstration. During this manoeuvre they witnessed the leading edge of the starboard wing tear off with catastrophic results. Subsequent prototypes were also found to be structurally unsound and suffered aerodynamic problems. As a result, a limited production run did not start until the New Year and by then it was too late to introduce it into active service.

Hitler had one other single-seat jet-powered aircraft in development that could conceivably support his Ardennes offensive. This was the Arado Ar 234 Blitz, which was the very first turbojet-powered bomber and the only one to be operational during World War II. It had a very chequered history and although work had commenced in 1940 it was three years before the first prototypes were flown. Four reconnaissance variants were issued to Sonderkommando Götz, an experimental unit, based in Rheine in the summer of 1944. The bomber version became operational in October that year with the 76th Bomber Group based at Achmer and Rheine. By 1 December 1944 it had been issued with 51 Ar 234s. However, these were hampered by fuel shortages and an engine life of just 25 hours. The engine was also prone to cracking. It was soon discovered that the cold weather caused a dangerous condensation problem on the inside of the canopy. While the Ar 234 could release its bombs in a shallow dive, it was certainly not suitable for dive-bombing. A multi-role version capable of ground attack was under development but was not ready for deployment. It seemed the Luftwaffe would be unable to support *Watch on the Rhine* with any of its new jet aircraft.

The Big Blow

Hitler hoped that, when he counter-attacked in the Ardennes, anticipated bad weather would screen his troops from the marauding Allied air forces. Dependent on the weather, the Luftwaffe was instructed to do all it could to help. Göring, fully aware of Hitler's current poor opinion of the Luftwaffe, knew that he needed to orchestrate some grand gesture. This was relayed to Hitler who was sceptical. 'The Reichsmarschall has ordered that all these new [fighter] groups now standing by should be deployed in a single day,' Luftwaffe General Eckhard Christian told the Führer on 6 November 1944.[1] Hitler was dismissive, remarking, 'The hope of decimating the enemy with a mass deployment is not realistic.'[2]

Just six days later the Luftwaffe's chief of staff General Kreipe was sacked and replaced by General Karl Koller. The latter inherited a hopeless situation. He now found himself having to oversee a massed air attack in north-west Europe. Koller stood dumbfounded when Göring pompously declared to the air staff, 'To stay alive at any price has always been the philosophy of the coward.' Those in the room understood the implications. 'Besides,' added Göring, 'the life in this world is by no means so sublime that I am not willing to pass on with great wonderment and curiosity to find out what it is like in the next.'[3] Few were convinced that he really meant it.

General Galland wanted to husband his fighter forces in order to launch a 'Big Blow' against American daylight raids on Germany. The nightfighter force would then pursue any crippled aircraft making for neutral countries after dark. After Hitler had sacrificed their fighter reserves over France, Galland persuaded Göring that they should not waste the fighters in day-to-day dogfights. He was well aware that many of the new pilots were being used as cannon fodder. The majority of them had few flying hours in front-line fighters and no combat experience. 'It was not uncommon for replacement pilots to arrive in the frontline having never flown the Fw 190,' said fighter pilot Fritz Wiener, 'or having practiced take-offs and landings in formation.'[4]

Galland's strategy was extremely ambitious. He wanted to hit the Americans with 2,000 fighters at once in order to shoot down up to 500 bombers in one go. This, he argued, would at least force the stunned Americans to postpone their relentless attacks. Hitler was not convinced in light of the Luftwaffe's failure to date to effectively defend Germany. Nonetheless, Galland planned to conduct a series of exercises to perfect tactics. The main problem was that his agile fighters, which were capable of breaking through the enemy escort screen, did not have the firepower to bring down the enemy bombers. His heavier fighters, although mounting sufficient firepower, could not penetrate the escorts.

Therefore, through October Galland greatly reduced operations in order to conserve fuel for the training of fresh pilots and to develop new tactics for co-ordinated massed attacks. He scheduled a major exercise for 2 November 1944, but this quickly turned into the real thing when 680 American bombers protected by 750 fighters penetrated German air space heading for the synthetic oil refinery at Leuna. Galland had no choice but to defend it. He was forced to commit his fighters piecemeal, and although they claimed 50 enemy bombers this was at the cost of 120 aircraft.

Galland was thwarted in testing his 'Big Blow' or 'Great Strike', as only an eighth of his force was involved and he was unable to overwhelm the Americans. However, two groups of heavy fighters totalling 62 aircraft did get through the escorts and shot down 30 of the bombers. If anything, this showed that Galland's tactics had the potential to work. Instead, Hitler latched onto the performance of the Luftwaffe's escort fighters. 'I send 260 fighters into action and I shoot down 20 bombers,' said Hitler. 'If I employ 2,600 I will shoot down 200 ... In other words, there is no hope of decimating the enemy with a mass assault.'[5]

Instead, it was decided it would be better to help the army by attacking forward Allied airfields just as the ground offensive commenced. This, though, could only happen if Hitler did not get the bad weather he was hoping would mask his assault. If heavy cloud persisted, then the Luftwaffe would only be able to offer sporadic and piecemeal assistance. A larger-scale attack would have to wait until such time as the weather cleared. Responsibility for this rested on the Luftwaffe's new commander in western Europe, General Josef 'Beppo' Schmid.

In senior circles, some officers did not hold General Schmid in very high regard. Schmid had served as the Luftwaffe's decidedly lacklustre intelligence chief during the Battle of Britain. When pressed on whether RAF Fighter Command could survive, Schmid had no idea how many aircraft they had left. Nor had his cooperation with General Wolfgang Martini's signals and cypher service been any good. This had led to a fatal underestimation of Britain's radar. Schmid also woefully underestimated British fighter production.

Up until his latest posting Schmid had been in charge of the 1st Fighter Corps, which was responsible for the air defence of Germany. He had got that job after General Josef Kammhuber was sacked over the persistent failure of Germany's nightfighters. The British had been delighted by this change of command because it signalled that Bomber Command was winning. Schmid fared no better than his predecessor, as the British and Americans were successfully jamming his radars. The Allies were also conducting spoof raids using 'Window', which were metal strips that created a false radar reading. For some senior commanders it was hard to understand quite why Schmid had been promoted to Luftwaffe CinC West on 23 November 1944.

However, it fell to Major General Dietrich Peltz, commander of the 2nd Fighter Corps near Altkirchen, assisted by Colonel Gollob, to formulate a plan to strike 16 enemy tactical airfields in Belgium, north-eastern France and the Netherlands. Ironically many of these had previously belonged to the Luftwaffe. Target selection was easy because it was obvious that the Allies would be forced to concentrate their aircraft at those airfields with hard paved runways during the winter months. To the great annoyance of Galland, the Special Fighter Command for the Ardennes offensive was placed under Gollob in whom he had no faith.

Around 600 aircraft would be mustered to conduct what was dubbed Operation *Baseplate*. To try to ensure this force included at least a smattering of veterans, instructors were called back to operational duties from the Luftwaffe's flight schools. Key amongst their targets were the

British Typhoon fighter-bomber and Spitfire photo-reconnaissance planes based around Eindhoven. Spitfire squadrons were also to be hit at Evere and Ghent.

Peltz was a veteran of the invasion of Poland and the Battle of Britain. He intended that the attack formations would be guided by Ju 88 nightfighters acting as pathfinders. Marker rockets would be used to designate the German front line, and coloured smoke flares would indicate turning points for the pilots. Beforehand considerable photo-reconnaissance flights were conducted over the target areas. These were used to help produce 1:500,000 scale maps for the crews to follow. 'The Air Wing will receive air photos of the targets allotted to them,' instructed Peltz, 'and will use their briefings to take every pilot through the operation in detail.'[6] Speed would be of the essence, as Peltz hoped not only to knock out the Allied airfields, but also catch as many of their aircraft on the ground as possible.

Göring had a role for at least a few of his Me 262 jets, which were to act as policemen to ensure that no pilots shirked their duty.[7] The jet crews were to report anyone not pressing home their attacks or jettisoning their bombs prematurely. Each group found itself allocated an Me 262. This was a complete waste of a limited but valuable asset and the jet pilots would much rather have acted as fighters. Flight Lieutenant Diether Lukesch's Blitz jet bombers of the 76th Bomber Group were also put on alert. They were to attack American troop concentrations and the railyards at Liège and Mamur. For the attacks on the Allied air forces they were allocated Gilze-Rijen, one of the British airfields near Eindhoven. This latter task would fall to Wing Commander Arthur Stark and half a dozen jet bombers. Air defence would be provided by Lieutenant General Wolfgang Pickert's 3rd Flak Corps, which had fought in Normandy. One of his key units was Brigadier Deutsch's 16th Flak Division based in Arnhem.

Despite his meticulous planning Peltz was not confident *Baseplate* would succeed. He was only too familiar with the overwhelming strength of Allied air power and their ferocious air defences on the Western Front. During early 1944, on Hitler's orders Peltz had reluctantly conducted a renewed blitz against southern England's cities and ports. In the process he had lost over half of the 630 aircraft committed to the attacks. Nor did this sacrifice have much impact on British morale or the Allies' preparations for D-Day. Following the landings, it had taken days for the Luftwaffe to scrape together just 60 aircraft to attack the Allied bridgeheads. Over Normandy the weak Luftwaffe had been consistently shot from the skies. At the end of June, it had gathered 200 aircraft, which managed to fly over 600 sorties in a single day. To counter this the Allies managed almost double the sortie rate. When the Luftwaffe tried to cut the bridges over the Waal at Nijmegen in the Netherlands in late September 1944 it was once more thoroughly mauled.

Peltz was concerned that Göring wanted two successive attacks. By the time the second attack was launched the Allies would inevitably have mustered aircraft from behind their lines and would be ready to retaliate. This meant the attackers would be intercepted over the target and on the way home. The real problem the Luftwaffe had was that the American P-51 Mustang fighter was faster and more manoeuvrable than both its Me 109 and Fw 190 fighters. With the addition of two drop tanks the Mustang had a range of over 2,000 miles, which left the Luftwaffe nowhere to hide. When the Mustang began to make its presence felt over Germany escorting American bombers, Göring had reportedly remarked, 'We have lost the war!'[8] Furthermore, for *Baseplate* to aid the ground forces it needed to be conducted before the ground offensive started. Any gaps in the weather would allow enemy fighter-bombers to pound the advance. As far as Galland was concerned, his 'Big Blow' against the enemy bomber fleet was a much better option that would produce much better results. However, neither Galland nor Milch was in favour with Göring or Hitler any more.

'Stubble-hoppers'

The Luftwaffe's support for the Ardennes offensive would not only be in the air. Its airborne forces would also play a ground role in the forthcoming fighting. The only other source of manpower for troops was Göring's exhausted parachute divisions that had been fighting as infantry or 'stubble-hoppers' in Normandy. Although they had suffered heavy losses they were partially reconstituted as part of the forces hurriedly sent to fend off the Allied thrust towards Arnhem in September 1944. These had included various elements of the 2nd, 3rd, 5th and 6th Parachute Divisions, of which only the 3rd and 5th were available for the Ardennes operation. Göring had already drained reserves to create the so-called 1st Parachute Army committed to the fighting in the Netherlands. The 3rd and 5th Divisions were brought back up to strength with the last influx of recruits, but in both divisions the commanders and troops were very inexperienced. Nor were they jump qualified. The resurrection of 5th Parachute was not anticipated by Allied intelligence, which reported, 'This is surprising, for at one time it looked as though remnants were far more likely to be incorporated in 3rd Parachute Division.'[1] Regarding the latter it assessed that during the battle for Normandy 'it had been reduced to almost nothing'.[2]

'The 3rd Para Div had no battle experience,' grumbled General Krämer, Chief of Staff of 6th Panzer Army, 'and besides their Commander had very little understanding about infantry matters.'[3] By December the 5th Parachute Division, commanded by Colonel Ludwig Heilmann, numbered almost 16,000 men. When he complained that the division lacked transport, weapons and training, Field Marshal Model rebuked him, saying, 'The parachute troops will find their way forward. I am confident of their courage!'⁴ A third unit, the 8th Parachute Division, was in the process of being formed, but it was not ready in time and was little more than regimental strength.

Luftwaffe General Kurt Student, commanding the German army group holding the Netherlands and CinC of Germany's parachute forces, lamented how his airborne troops had been wasted:

> On D-Day we had 150,000 parachute troops, and six organized divisions. Of the total 50,000 were trained, and the rest were under training. We were not able to complete their training as they were constantly committed to ground fighting, and by the time they were needed for the Ardennes offensive, five months later, only a handful were available – because they had been used up as infantry instead of being kept for their proper role.⁵

Hitler, with just over a week to spare, decided on 8 December that it would be helpful if the Americans were prevented from moving reinforcements by dropping parachutists west of Monschau. Thanks to the poor quality of Göring's airborne forces, limited numbers of transport aircraft and the inexperience of their crews, it meant any supporting airborne operation would have to be extremely modest in scope. Tough airborne veteran Colonel Friedrich August von der Heydte, who was in charge of the parachute school at Bergen Op Zoom, received a call to report to Student's headquarters in the Netherlands.

Student was in good spirits, having helped to thwart Field Marshal Montgomery's attempt on Arnhem. He explained to von der Heydte that the Führer was planning a major counteroffensive and that it was to be supported by an airborne operation. 'The Führer has ordered a parachute attack in the framework of a powerful offensive,' said Student. 'You, my dear Heydte, are ordered to carry out this task.'⁶ The colonel was surprised in light of Hitler having banned such operations after the costly occupation of Crete in 1941. His mission apparently was to drop behind the Red Army surrounding the German bridgehead on the Vistula in Poland. Where were the men to come from? asked von der Heydte. Student warned him that security was of the utmost importance; therefore he was not to recruit any of the instructors from

Bergen Op Zoom or men from his old regiment. 'Volunteers' were to be drawn from the four parachute divisions under Student's command. 'In a few days' time,' said Student, 'I shall send you 1,200 experienced paras to the collecting point at Aalten.' The colonel nodded, excited at the prospect of going into battle by air once more. 'But,' added Student, 'you must have your men organized by 13 December. Von der Heydte, with effect from 5.30 on the morning of the fourteenth you must be ready for action!'[7] The colonel's enthusiasm sagged in the face of the ridiculous time frame. Besides, what was he supposed to achieve with just 1,200 men?

Although the parachute regiments were instructed to provide their best men for this special mission, von der Heydte appreciated he would inevitably end up with those that no one wanted. Despite what Student had said, he hoped to employ members of his old 6th Parachute Regiment, and the word was quietly put out. After Normandy and Arnhem the veterans all remembered his pep-talk. 'From the moment a man volunteers for the airborne troops and joins my regiment,' he had told them, 'he enters a new order of humanity. He is ruled by one law only, that of our unit. He must give up personal weakness and ambitions and realize that our battle is for the existence of the whole German nation.'[8] In France three-quarters of von der Heydte's men had become casualties and, after the regiment was rebuilt, they had been thrown in the path of the advancing Allies in the Netherlands. During the defence of Eindhoven, he had got into trouble for conducting an unauthorized withdrawal, which had compromised the German line but saved his men.

He was provided with just over 1,000 men as promised. However, as German paratroops were deployed as infantry very few had ever made a practice jump. His staff reported that only about 200 of them were jump veterans. He was slightly heartened when they told him that 150 were from the 6th Parachute Regiment. German equipment on the whole was very well designed, but the airborne troops' RZ[9] parachute was another matter. This tended to pose a real danger to the user as it was impossible to control and difficult to land with. To the uninitiated it was a potential death-trap. Parachutists had to be thoroughly trained how to jump and then land safely. Recruits had to be very fit and with excellent reflexes as timing was everything. Annoyingly, Luftwaffe aircrew had much better parachutes, which were much more user friendly. Von der Heydte, though, did not have time to be picky or train his men.

Over the next few days von der Heydte and his staff worked hard to form a battle group consisting of four companies, supported by a company of engineers, a section of heavy mortars and a signals section. His company commanders included Lieutenants Le Coutre and Wagner, Sergeant Major Peters and Staff Sergeant Geiss, who was standing in for Lieutenant Wiegand as he was ill. He reported to Student on 13 December and said that he was ready except for mission orders and the all-important parachutes. Student told him that the parachutes would be supplied. Regarding the operation, von der Heydte was the responsibility of the Luftwaffe's Air Fleet West, which was attached to Sepp Dietrich's 6th Panzer Army. The mission was to take place in the Ardennes and not Poland as had been first suggested to him. A daylight drop would alert the Allies, so Operation *Hawk* would have to be conducted in the dark, just a few hours before Hitler's ground offensive commenced. However, the local geography made this impossible.

The colonel and his men were to move from the Netherlands to the training camp at Sennelager to make their final preparations. However, when they arrived the officious commandant was not expecting them and refused to accommodate them or feed them. An irate von der Heydte called the Luftwaffe's Münster Air Region headquarters. When he spoke to the chief of staff there the confusion continued. The man had no idea what von der Heydte was blathering on about nor had any knowledge of his mission. When the latter mentioned the airfields he was to operate from, the chief of staff said one of them had not even been built yet. Von der Heydte was told Münster Air Region had received no orders and could therefore not help him. News of the presence of the publicity-seeking, limelight-hogging Otto Skorzeny at Sennelager was the final straw. Why, wondered von der Heydte, had provision been made for Skorzeny but not him?

The colonel and his men were stuck as no one would take responsibility for them. Thinking on his feet, von der Heydte resolved to call an old comrade from his days with the 15th Cavalry Regiment. The man, now a chemist who lived in Oerlinghausen, was at first bemused then delighted to hear from von der Heydte. At 0400 hours the tired column of parachutists rolled into the village and were billeted with local residents. On 14 December von der Heydte was visited by Luftwaffe Major Erdmann, whom he had last seen during the invasion of Crete. Erdmann explained he had been instructed to use his Junkers 52 transport aircraft so von der Heydte's men could conduct a practice jump.

Colonel von der Heydte responded by saying they were to jump straight into combat. Erdmann thought this madness. Besides, all his pilots were straight from training school, had never flown in the dark and had no experience of dropping parachutists. When von der Heydte enquired about the airlift capacity, he was informed the Luftwaffe could muster about 120 transports. This was essentially enough to lift a regiment. Both von der Heydte and Erdmann knew such a force would be too weak to achieve much or survive long if it was not quickly relieved. Long gone were the days when Hitler could airlift and drop entire divisions. Erdmann explained that the failed attempt to keep the German army trapped at Stalingrad supplied had cost almost 500 transport aircraft – an entire air corps had been wiped off the Luftwaffe's order of battle.

When von der Heydte reported the situation to Commander-in-Chief Air Fleet West's headquarters, he was told to consult with the commander of the 2nd Fighter Corps, Major General Dietrich Peltz. However, Peltz knew nothing of the air drop so von der Heydte and Erdmann drove to Field Marshal Model's headquarters at Münstereifel. They arrived early in the morning and were greeted by Model's chief of staff, General Krebs. He explained to the colonel and major that Hitler's great offensive was to commence in just 48 hours. Von der Heydte told him how poorly prepared they were at which point Krebs fetched Model.

The field marshal listened with an expression of resignation. He then asked von der Heydte if he thought his mission had a 10 per cent chance of succeeding. The colonel thought probably 10 to 20 per cent. 'Lucky fellow. I wish the whole offensive had the same kind of chance,' said Model. 'Then it is necessary to make the attempt, since the entire offensive is the last remaining chance we have of concluding the war favourably.' Von der Heyte and Erdmann nodded glumly. Model, who appreciated that this was an all-or-nothing gamble, added, 'If we don't make the most of that ten per cent chance, Germany will face certain defeat.'[10]

The despondent colonel and major climbed back into their staff car
and drove on to Sepp Dietrich's headquarters. Dietrich's chief of staff,
General Krämer, ushered them in and they were confronted by a clearly
drunk commander. This did nothing to reassure von der Heydte and
Erdmann. 'Your battle group will hold the north-west crossing of the
Schnee Eifel heights at the junction of Malmedy-Vervier, 15km [ten
miles] north of Malmedy,' explained Dietrich grumpily, 'and keep those
crossing points open for 6th Panzer Army's advance.'[11] Operation *Hawk*
was to involve a parachute drop a few miles to the north of Malmedy
in the Baraque Michel mountain region behind the US 9th and 2nd
Infantry Divisions. The paratroops were to secure the Baraque Michel
road junction and hold it ready for the 12th SS Panzer Division's swing
north-west towards Liège. A second drop would be conducted south of
Eupen and the Meuse.

Colonel von der Heydte pointed out to Dietrich that dropping his
inexperienced parachutists into the forests and onto the moors of the
Ardennes at night was a suicide mission. Dietrich calmly reassured him
that he would only have to wait a few hours before his panzers arrived.
In this case it was to be a unit of 70-ton Jagdtigers which were hardly
very mobile. 'I should have to have the whole division if I am to hold
this area until the arrival of the armour,' said von der Heydte. 'These
objectives are also too far off.'[12] It was clear, though, that he had little
choice in the matter.

When von der Heydte asked about the level of resistance he was
likely to meet Dietrich responded angrily, 'I am not a prophet!'[13] This
suggested that the 6th Panzer Army's intelligence was poor. In particular,
the colonel wanted to know about the two American infantry divisions
in the Baraque Michel area. How mobile were they and how quickly
could they react? 'You'll learn earlier than I what forces the Americans
will employ against you,' snapped Dietrich. 'Besides, behind their lines
there are only Jewish hoodlums – and bank managers.'[14] This hardly
seemed accurate intelligence.

A radio officer, SS-Lieutenant Etterich, from the 12th SS, would jump
with von der Heydte's men in order to coordinate artillery support and
intelligence. In the event of the radio being damaged during the drop
von der Heydte prudently requested carrier pigeons. Dietrich, with
a million and one things to think of, laughed at the absurdity of it.
'Pigeons! Don't be stupid,' he growled. 'Pigeons! I'm leading my whole

damn army without pigeons! You should be able to lead one battle group without a damn menagerie.'[15] The hapless colonel looked to Krämer for help. 'What do you think I am?' added Dietrich. 'Running a zoo?'[16] An affronted von der Heydte stomped off firmly of the view that the pugnacious Dietrich was little better than a 'cur dog'.[17] To make matters worse he would have to jump with his right arm in a splint, as he had injured it a few weeks earlier in an aircraft accident in Italy.

Back at Oerlinghausen von der Heydte found that his problems were still far from over. Both the Luftwaffe and the army were continuing to disown his unit, which meant no one would organize transport for his men to the airfields at Lippspringe and Paderborn. The colonel was baffled by the Luftwaffe's logic. It had transported them to Oerlinghausen, but was now arguing that, as they came under the 6th Panzer Army, it was up to the Waffen-SS or army to arrange moving them. This stinginess over fuel was a clear indication of just how much the Luftwaffe was feeling the pinch. It was also systematic of the Luftwaffe viewing its paratroops as lowly 'stubble-hoppers'.

It seemed to von der Heydte as if there would never be any good news. When the parachutes finally arrived he was aghast to discover they were captured Russian ones. On closer inspection this turned out to be a good thing as they were triangular in shape, which reduced oscillation.[18] They also had better harnesses. A new German triangular design had been developed but it had not entered service. These parachutes might just help save his jump virgins. Von der Heydte had no idea where they had come from. The Red Army had only ever conducted one large-scale parachute operation involving two brigades carried out south-east of Kiev. They were swiftly trapped and wiped out. Another piece of equipment turned up that was to be used as a decoy. This comprised 300 straw dummies each kitted out with a parachute. They were to be dropped during daylight to confuse the enemy; a trick picked up from the Allies on D-Day. Von der Heydte's only worry was that there were not enough of them and that Major Erdmann's aircrew would have to risk their lives to deliver them. Far from being hawks, it felt more like his men were going to be clay pigeons.

PART FOUR
Into Battle

11

Peiper Leads the Charge

After weeks of arguing over planning and other practicalities, time ran out and the big day for Operation *Watch on the Rhine* finally arrived. 'Soldiers of the 6th Panzer Army!' signalled Dietrich in his order of the day, 'The Führer has placed us at the vital point. It is for us to breach the enemy front and push beyond the Meuse.' He knew that it would be a desperate race against time and added, 'Surprise is half the battle.'[1] At 0530 hours on Saturday 16 December 1944 the order rang out along the German gun lines, 'All batteries ready to fire! Fire!'[2] The gunners pulled their lanyards and their weapons jolted with the recoil. The morning tranquillity was shattered by the roar of field guns, mortars and rocket launchers. Scalding hot metal exploded skyward and shot towards its destination. Crews then raced forward to expel the spent shell cases where necessary and reload. The gunners had not really been given the chance to target effectively because of the need for complete secrecy. The preliminary bombardment was to last about 45 minutes. Many of the recipients of this barrage, asleep in farmhouses and barns dotted across the landscape, were given a rude awakening. Half-frozen men swearing and cursing scrambled for their kit, helmets and weapons. Others threw themselves into their foxholes and felt the earth tremble beneath them as if there were an earthquake.

The men of Hitler's two panzer armies gripped their weapons and prayed silently that they would survive the day. Many, though, were buoyed by the sight of all the massed vehicles and equipment around them. One excited tanker with the 1st SS Panzer Division leant out of his turret and yelled cheekily to the man poking out of a neighbouring tank, 'Good-bye, Lieutenant, see you in America!'[3] Another soldier rather optimistically said to his comrades, 'Wait till we get to Paris and all those sweet little French cheetahs.'[4] There was almost an air of intoxication and for many soldiers it felt good to no longer be on the defensive. If nothing else, they could surely drive the enemy away from the Rhine and their homeland.

Sitting in the path of Hitler's armoured steamroller were six American divisions numbering about 75,000 men. These units through no real fault of their own were in somewhat of a muddle. To the north, facing Dietrich's right, were two infantry divisions, the 2nd and 99th, from Major General Leonard Gerow's 5th Corps. The latter division had only been in the line for about a month and was disrupted by the 2nd moving through its positions to advance towards the Roer Dams. Also the movement of the 2nd Infantry Division had created a weakening to the south extending for two miles in the region of the vital Losheim Gap. It was this gap that Dietrich had earmarked for his advance.

This area was defended by an element of the 2nd Infantry, the 14th Cavalry Group, but it was poorly deployed and stretched thinly to compensate for the absence of the rest of the division. Confusingly the 14th Cavalry Group was still under the command of General Troy Middleton's 8th Corps, which inevitably was to cause problems if the unit was called upon to support Gerow's troops. The most northern of Middleton's units was General Alan Jones' 106th Infantry Division. They had only just arrived at the front and had been directed into the German Schnee Eifel region to take the place of the 2nd Infantry. This area was German populated and consisted of a salient made up of steep valleys and small sleepy villages. The 106th was exposed and von Manteuffel's right flank were tasked with chopping off the salient.

To the south of Jones was Major General Norman 'Dutch' Cota's veteran 28th Infantry Division. It had been sent to the Ardennes to recover from the battering it had experienced in the Hürtgen Forest. Cota's men had to hold a 23-mile front facing the Our River over which von Manteuffel's armour was to pour. On Cota's right were elements of another inexperienced division, the 9th Armored, which was to later claim fame grabbing the bridge at Remagen over the Rhine. A single combat command was occupying six miles of front, while the other two commands were held back as Middleton's mobile reserve. They would have to fight off General Brandenberger's assault troops from his 7th Army. Also in the firing line was the veteran 4th Infantry Division, which was likewise recuperating after Hürtgen.

To protect the northern shoulder of his intended breakthrough, Dietrich deployed Major General Otto Hitzfeld's 67th Corps, with the 272nd and 326th Volksgrenadier Divisions either side of Monschau facing the US 5th Corps. He hoped that, as his offensive progressed, these two units would join the attack. In reality they were not capable of effective offensive operations; having been created using survivors who had escaped from France they lacked experience and, just as importantly, adequate training. They were supposed to be supported by a third Volksgrenadier division, the 246th belonging to 15th Army, but it was still on its way. This had been formed around the few survivors from an infantry division of the same number that had been trapped at Vitebsk on the Eastern Front during the summer. Once refitted the 246th Volksgrenadiers had been thrown into the fighting at Aachen and suffered heavy casualties.

On his northern front Dietrich had first to barge the US 99th Infantry Division out of the way in order to take the Elsenborn Ridge, before breaking through the Losheim Gap. On his right to the south of Monschau this task fell to the 277th Volksgrenadiers, 3rd Panzergrenadier, and 12th Volksgrenadier Divisions with the 3rd Parachute Division opposite Losheim. Beyond them was von Manteuffel's 5th Panzer Army running south to Dasburg and Brandenberger's 7th Army. Once Dietrich's breach had been made his panzer divisions could make their dash for the Meuse. These would be deployed in two echelons: leading the armoured charge would be Priess' 1st SS Corps with 12th SS Panzer on the right and 1st SS to the left; behind them would come Bittrich's 2nd SS Panzer Corps with 2nd SS Panzer on the right and 9th SS Panzer on the left. As well as Skorzeny's 150th Panzer Brigade commando force cutting a path for the 1st SS and 12th SS Panzer Divisions, there were Battle Group Peiper and Battle Group Kühlmann respectively, each formed from their division's panzer and panzergrenadier regiments. They were to lead the way up the roads to Trois-Ponts, Stavelot, Malmedy and Elsenborn and onto the Meuse south of Liège at Amay and Huy. Support was provided by half a dozen other battle groups.

Dietrich and Krämer had calculated it would take a day to cut through the American defences, another day to cross the Hautes Fagnes plateau and two further days to reach the Meuse. Although their breaching force sounded quite formidable this was far from the case. All the divisions were second-rate units. Both the Volksgrenadier divisions, commanded by Gerhard Engel and Wilhelm Viebig respectively, were fairly weak and lacked veterans. In the case of the 277th Volksgrenadiers they could only muster about 1,000 experienced troops. The 3rd Parachute Division under General Walther Wadehn had been rebuilt after Normandy using rear-echelon Luftwaffe ground personnel who had no desire to fight as infantry. Its officers and men were also largely inexperienced. Brigadier Walther Denkert's 3rd Panzergrenadiers, which would provide armoured support, were not available until 21 December. After serving in Italy, the division had suffered heavy losses during the fighting around Metz and later Aachen. It was now 20 per cent under-strength, lacked 40 per cent of its equipment, and its armour consisted of a single tank battalion.

After the opening bombardment the German infantry and sappers surged forward under the cover of fog into the American lines. While the Americans on the receiving end of things were able to ride out the storm, the shelling did cause some confusion and severed communications. Many units were cut off from their chain of command so had no real idea of what was going on or what was expected of them. This meant that the opening day was soon to become a series of confused small-unit actions that would nonetheless cost the Germans valuable time.

At Dietrich's headquarters General Krämer reported, 'The 12th Volksgrenadier Division … had made good progress. … The attack group, 3rd Para Division, had met at the beginning stiff resistance, but a motorized group of the 1 SS Panzer Division was advancing on the road Honsfeld-Möderscheid.' Dietrich was determined to stick to his timetable and the scheduled movements of his troops come hell or high water. 'In no case was the 12th SS Panzer Division to be engaged in fighting against the enemy,' said Krämer, 'who would eventually attack from the north.'[5]

However, Dietrich soon found that the men of the US 99th Infantry were not going to be the push-overs he had expected. The defenders at

Buchholz Station beat off their attackers; likewise at Rocherath and Krinkelt the Americans did not withdraw, while in the far north in the Monschau-Höfen area they also held out. Nevertheless, things did not all go the Americans' way. At the road junction of Lanzerath a platoon of infantry was overrun by the 3rd Parachute Division. At Manderfeld a squadron of the 14th Cavalry Group was forced to withdraw south while the rest of the unit was destroyed, thereby opening up the Losheim Gap.

Dietrich was relatively pleased with his infantry's initial progress, but it did not last long. The 3rd Parachute Division's success had been hard won and Dietrich was forced to commit the 12th SS Panzer Division much sooner than he really wanted. 'They didn't meet very strong opposition except at Losheim,' he noted, 'where there were many tank traps. Also, the Krinkelt-Wirtzfeld-Büllingen triangle was heavily defended ... The 12th SS ... bogged down right away.'[6] The snow on the roads and the lack of bridging to get over the Our resulted in a huge sprawling traffic jam. It was clear that Dietrich's headlong dash through American positions to the Meuse was rapidly grinding to a halt. By the evening Dietrich was dismayed that the green US 99th Infantry had not disintegrated. When Hitler was told of progress he was delighted, exclaiming to one of his generals, 'everything has changed in the West! Success – complete success – is now in our grasp!'[7]

Staff Sergeant Karl Laun was with the 84th Flak Battalion, assigned to provide Peiper anti-aircraft cover. This unit belonged to the Luftwaffe but normally supported the army. His battery commanded by Major Koch was gathered at Dahlem ready to join the advance. 'H-Hour (0500) still finds us lying fitfully in an air raid shelter. Something must have gone hay-wire,' said Laun. 'Finally at 1700 we see Battle Group Peiper approaching.'[8] He was immediately impressed by the 501st Heavy SS Panzer Battalion. 'The Tiger Royals present an imposing picture as they thunder past us, their exhaust pipes aglow.'[9] The battle group had driven through most of the night and when they had stopped to get some sleep were constantly woken by V-1 flying bombs noisily passing overhead. In the morning they approached Losheim and came under air attack. Laun's commanding officer, Major von Sacken, drove his Volkswagen over a mine, but apart from being thrown from the vehicle was luckily unharmed.

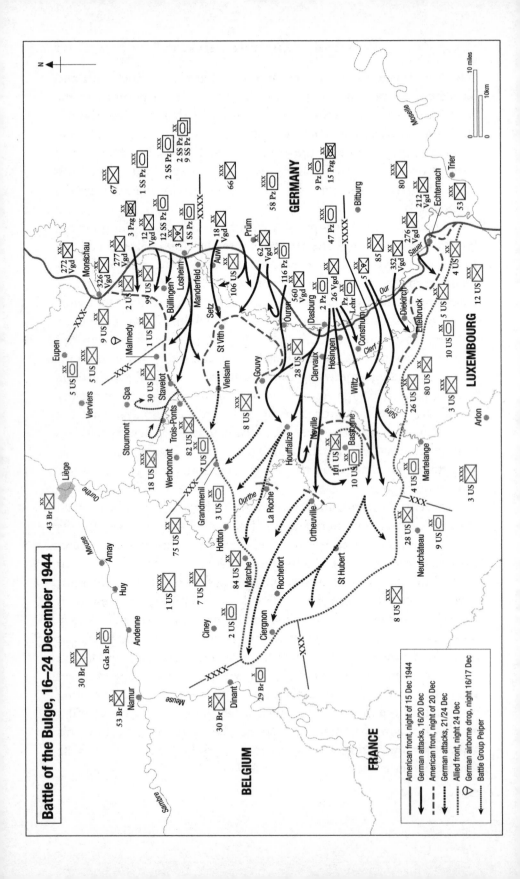

Battle of the Bulge, 16–24 December 1944

Legend:
- American front, night of 15 Dec 1944
- German attacks, 16/20 Dec
- American front, night of 20 Dec
- German attacks, 21/24 Dec
- Allied front, night 24 Dec
- German airborne drop, night 16/17 Dec
- Battle Group Peiper

Countries/Regions: GERMANY, BELGIUM, LUXEMBOURG, FRANCE

Rivers: Moselle, Sauer, Our, Sûre, Ourthe, Meuse, Sambre

Places: Trier, Bitburg, Echternach, Prüm, Diekirch, Ettelbruck, Monschau, Eupen, Verviers, Spa, Stoumont, Trois-Ponts, Stavelot, Malmedy, Billingen, Losheim, Manderfeld, Setz, St Vith, Vielsalm, Gouvy, Clervaux, Hösingen, Wiltz, Constbum, Clerf, Dasburg, Ouren, Auw, Werbomont, Grandmenil, Hotton, Marche, La Roche, Houffalize, Neville, Bastogne, Orfheuville, Ciergnon, Rochefort, St Hubert, Neufchâteau, Martelange, Arlon, Ciney, Dinant, Namur, Andenne, Huy, Amay, Liège

Units (labels): 272 Vgd, 326 Vgd, 277 Vgd, 3 Pzg, 12 Vgd, 12 SS Pz, 1 SS Pz, 99 US, 1 US, 2 US, 9 US, 5 US, 30 US, 67, 1 SS Pz, 2 SS Pz, 9 SS Pz, 2 SS Pz, 3 Pz, 9 Pz, 15 Pzg, 66, 58 Pz, 47 Pz, 5, 85, 352 Vgd, 276 Vgd, 212 Vgd, 80, 53, 4 US, 12 US, 10 US, 3 US, 80 US, 26 US, 28 US, 106 US, 62 Vgd, 560 Vgd, 116 Pz, 26 Vgd, 2 Pz, Lehr, Pz Lehr, 18 Vgd, 82 US, 7 US, 3 US, 75 US, 84 US, 2 US, 8 US, 101 US, 10 US, 28 US, 9 US, 43 Br, 30 Br, Gds Br, 53 Br, 30 Br, 29 Br, 1 US, 3 US, 8 US, 4 US, 9 US

Scale: 10 miles / 10km

On the second day of Hitler's offensive Dietrich's two most northern Volksgrenadier divisions moved to open the Monschau-Mützenich road. A battle group was sent past Höfen towards Kalterherberg. The 12th Volksgrenadiers were instructed to help the 12th SS secure the road across Weismes towards Malmedy. At the same time 3rd Parachute was to attack towards Manderfeld. By midday the 12th SS had got past Büllingen and the 9th SS was told to prepare for an attack to the left of 1st SS Panzer past Losheim, Amblève and Vielsalm. The 12th SS meantime became tied down in the Rocherath-Krinkelt-Büllingen triangle. Major General Hitzfeld's 66th Corps was instructed to bypass Monschau and swing south to clear the Americans from the Elsenborn Ridge; however, they quickly ran into mines and other enemy defences. Likewise, the 12th Volksgrenadiers were held up by American resistance in the hills to the south of Büllingen and did not break through until the afternoon. The town itself was not properly secured until the following day.

Dietrich and Krämer had intended for the 12th SS to make the main dash to the bridges over the Meuse. By midday on 17 December it was evident that its battle groups were still held up and that a change of plan was needed. It was vital that they overrun as much ground as possible to prevent the Americans solidifying their defences east of the Meuse. Likewise, they needed to grab as much territory as possible to allow their armour room to manoeuvre as they approached the better tank country near the river. Dietrich and Krämer agreed that the progress made by the 1st SS showed greater promise. Bittrich was told to pass control of the 9th SS to Priess so that it could operate on the left flank of the 1st SS.

That day Peiper's column was caught in an air strike and a flak tank was lost and several other vehicles damaged. However, his troops successfully attacked an American convoy near Baugnez, which surrendered after a brief firefight. Some of the 30 captured vehicles joined his column, their American drivers having 'volunteered' to drive to Ligneuville. Some American prisoners of war were subsequently shot in what became known as the infamous 'Malmedy Massacre'. Members of the 1st SS Panzer Division gunned down 362 American prisoners and 111 Belgian civilians in cold blood. The murders took place in a dozen locations, which included Honsfeld, Büllingen, Ligneuville, La Gleize and Stoumont.[10] These war crimes seem to have been committed for no reason other than the SS could not be bothered to escort their prisoners to the rear. It may also have been, in part, bloody revenge for the Allied bombing of Cologne.

American units trying to escape were shown no mercy either. Congested forest roads and country lanes provided the Germans with the opportunity for numerous turkey shoots. Vehicles jammed bumper to bumper and hub to hub were easy game. 'Today we overtook a fleeing column and finished it off,' reported Lieutenant Rockhammer. '... we pulled up along the road with sixty Panthers. ... a concentrated fire from sixty cannon and one hundred and twenty machine guns. It was a glorious bloodbath, vengeance for our destroyed homeland.'[11]

In the meantime, desperately short of fuel, Peiper, instead of pushing west, turned north to seize 50,000 gallons of American gasoline at Büllingen. Although his battle group had got to Stavelot via Büllingen and Möderscheid by the evening of 17 December, the rest of the division was still lagging miles behind. It was held up east of Büllingen by unwelcome traffic jams, while the 3rd Parachute Division was eight miles behind him. They were held up fighting at Waimes and Faymonville to the east of Malmedy. Likewise, the 12th SS Panzer was supposed to be on his right at Malmedy, but instead was bogged down by American resistance 14 miles to the east. The clock was steadily ticking.

From a hill east of the Amblève River Peiper could see Stavelot full of American trucks. Defending the place was a single squad from the US 291st Engineer Battalion. Deployed to the south side of the river bridge, equipped only with small arms, a bazooka and mines, this unit set up a roadblock. They knocked out Peiper's lead tank, forcing him to call a halt for the night. Although some American infantry reached the town during the darkness Peiper would breach their defences to the north the following day. His panzers would then be racing for the bridges at Trois-Ponts to the south-west, which would put him on the road to Werbomont.

At Trois-Ponts there were three road bridges to be taken: one over the Amblève and two over the Salm. The village was held by Major Robert Yates' Company C, 51st Engineers, who had arrived at midnight on 17 December. He had 140 men, with ten machine guns and eight bazookas. He ordered them to prepare the Amblève bridge for demolition and sent a squad to the railway bridge just to the north-east. They were reinforced by a 57mm anti-tank gun separated from a company of the US 526th Armored Infantry who had been driven from Stavelot.

'Before Stavelot the masses of SS concentrate,' observed Staff Sergeant Laun. 'Obviously there is trouble brewing in town.'[12] From 0630 to 0800 hours when it got light Peiper's artillery relentlessly shelled the town. Under the cover of this bombardment the 11th SS Panzergrenadier Company, under Heinz Tomhardt, from the 2nd SS Panzergrenadier Regiment, managed to reach the bridge and cross. In the process Tomhardt was wounded and a platoon commander killed. 'The bridge was taken,' said SS-Senior Sergeant Rudolf Rayer who was involved in the attack, 'but could not be held.'[13] Suffering heavy losses Peiper's troops had no choice but to withdraw. 'Enemy tanks continued to move and we expected a counterattack,' observed Rayer who found himself under fire from all directions.[14] He knew they needed the panzers to break the deadlock.

Panther tank commander Eugen Zimmermann with the 1st SS Panzer Battalion recalled, 'Colonel Peiper himself detailed off my tank to lead the attack through Stavelot ... The whole crew was given a very precise briefing.'[15] Peiper's panzers rolled down the hill and reached the bridge, which the Americans had still failed to destroy. On the way Zimmermann rammed an American tank destroyer out of his path. 'No sooner were we over the bridge than we were hit,' exclaimed Zimmermann.[16] Luckily, the anti-tank round did not penetrate their armour and he ordered his gunner to fire back but they missed. Instead, the Panther crushed the 57mm anti-tank gun that had shot at them and its crew fled. 'Great fire from all sides,' noted Zimmermann. 'Gradually it decreased and we were through.'[17]

The rest of the tanks crossed and pushed up the Chatelet road where they came under machine gun and anti-tank gun fire. Turning into a side street, the panzers bypassed the American anti-tank gun and reached the main street to Trois-Ponts. Behind them came their supporting panzergrenadiers. Laun's flak unit was also thrown into the attack. 'There is small arms fire, and mortar barrages aimed directly at us,' he said. 'I miraculously escape being hit by shrapnel.'[18] Once in town he witnessed the SS gun down three Belgian civilians allegedly because they did not know the password.

It took until 1000 hours for Peiper's men to secure central Stavelot. Some 45 minutes later 19 panzers coming up the road running north of the Amblève began firing on the Americans working on the river bridge at Trois-Ponts. However, at the railway bridge the column was brought to a halt by a concealed American anti-tank gun. It took the Germans 15 minutes to find it and destroy it along with the brave crew; this bought the American demolition teams enough time to destroy the Amblève bridge and the northern one over the Salm.

Cursing, Peiper was now forced north-east towards La Gleize and Stoumont. Some of his tanks headed for Werbomont, but the skies had cleared of low cloud and they were pounced on by four Thunderbolt fighter-bombers of the US 365th Fighter Group. They claimed two tanks and seven half-tracks. To make matters worse, ahead of him another squad from the US 291st Engineering Battalion had blown the bridge over the Lienne near Chevron. This stopped him reaching Werbomont and his thrust on the Meuse. Further north his men got over another bridge and swung south-west towards Werbomont only to run into an American ambush conducted by a unit from the US 30th Infantry Division. This was moving into position north-west of Peiper while the US 82nd Airborne were moving in from the west.

By the evening of 18 December Peiper knew that the only way for his battle group to head west was through the village of Stoumont. Earlier that day the 117th Infantry from the US 30th Division had reached Malmedy and Stavelot. The 1st Battalion recaptured Stavelot and cut the bridge over the Amblève. By the end of the day the 199th Infantry were at Stoumont, with the 3rd Battalion in the town, 2nd Battalion blocking the road westward and the 1st acting as reserve on the high ground to the north.

Dietrich was bogged down. Peiper's spearhead had been blocked at Trois-Ponts and Cheneux, and he would have a tough fight on his hands if he tried to take Stoumont. He was cut off from ammunition and fuel, and the 3rd Parachute Division was stuck holding the northern flank of the advance. Even worse, the 12th SS was some 20 miles behind him battling to get through the troublesome US 99th, 2nd and 1st Divisions on the Bütgenbach-Malmedy road. The 2nd SS and 9th SS Panzer Divisions, which constituted Dietrich's second wave, were still stuck back near the Siegfried Line thanks to the continuing traffic jams in front of them.

Early on 19 December Peiper threw his men at the American defences at Stoumont. His attack force included his mixed tank battalion with Panzer IVs and Panthers from the 1st SS Panzer Regiment and a few Tigers backed by a battalion of men from the 2nd SS Panzergrenadiers, an anti-aircraft gun unit, a battery of 105mm self-propelled guns and a company from the 3rd Parachute Division. Defending Stoumont was the US 3rd Battalion, 119th Infantry, supported by the guns of the 823rd Tank Destroyer Battalion. In the fierce close-quarter fighting that followed, two of the three American infantry companies were destroyed.

To the north the 1st Battalion had little choice but to withdraw covered by ten tanks of the US 743rd Tank Battalion via Targnon to Stoumont. When the panzers ventured beyond Targnon they were shelled by the 197th Field Artillery and forced back. Now running out of fuel and food Peiper gathered his battle group at Stoumont, La Gleize and Cheneux. He was running out of options. Staff Sergeant Laun at Stoumont noted, '200 Americans come out of the town. They gave up. But still I don't think we'll gain our objectives; the tanks are down to their last few gallons.'[19] The men were also very hungry. 'At last we find some grub,' adds Laun. 'They are "US field rations". Like animals we wolf down these delicacies.'[20] Their revelry was soon curtailed by enemy shell fire, which forced them to dig in only for them to be ordered to La Gleize.

At this stage more American reinforcements arrived to help the 199th in the shape of ten tanks under Captain James Berry from the 740th Tank Battalion. This was very much an ad hoc unit made up of mechanics and repaired tanks from the US 1st Army's workshops. The Americans now began to squeeze Peiper's forces. The US 82nd Airborne Division was pushing eastward from Werbomont; units were heading for La Gleize, Trois-Ponts and Hotton. Advancing from the north was the US 3rd Armored Division with Combat Command B moving to help the 117th Infantry at Stavelot and the 119th at Stoumont. The rest of the division moved west of the 82nd Airborne to block the Germans driving from Houffalize and Bastogne.

On 20 December the Americans struck back with 1st Battalion, 119th Infantry, and the tanks of the 740th advancing through Targnon. Company C with five Shermans under Lieutenant Powers bumped into a Panther which they knocked out at close range. A Tiger tank proved a tougher foe but this was successfully dealt with by a 90mm self-propelled anti-tank gun. Powers then destroyed a second Panther by bouncing an anti-tank round off the road and up into the underneath of the tank.

By darkness Company C was on the outskirts of Stoumont, having occupied the local Saint Edouard sanatorium. However, that night Peiper counter-attacked, driving the defenders out of 'Festung Sankt-Edouard' at midnight except for 11 men under Sergeant William Widener who clung on in a small annex building. Peiper's men captured 30 prisoners and accounted for five Shermans. When Task Force Jordan, from US 3rd Armored, tried to push south down the Spa road into Stoumont they were driven off by concealed Panthers. Nonetheless, Task Force Lovelady, also from 3rd Armored, cut the road between La Gleize and Trois-Ponts. They also intercepted and destroyed a supply column trying to get through to the beleaguered Peiper and his men.

For ease of command, on 20 December General Eisenhower reluctantly put Field Marshal Montgomery in temporary charge of all American troops north of the German breakthrough, which included the US 1st and 9th Armies. Understandably General Omar Bradley, commanding the US 12th Army Group (US 1st and 3rd Armies) was not happy with this arrangement, though it made sense. Monty meanwhile deployed 150 British tanks to the west of the Meuse as a blocking force. He then asked Bradley's Major General 'Lightning Joe' Collins, commander of the US 7th Corps, to put together a strategic reserve ready for a counter-attack.

While the US 504th Parachute Infantry, 82nd Airborne fought to drive the 2nd SS Panzergrenadiers from Cheneux, all three battalions of the 119th Infantry struck towards Stoumont again from the north, west and east and succeeded in retaking the sanatorium on 21 December. Peiper's men were shelled by anti-tank guns and tanks, but they had clung on to the smashed building until the very last. The roof had collapsed and the windows had been shot in during the previous round of fighting. Outside the crew of a flakpanzer tried to protect the entrance until they ran out of ammunition, while in the hallway a gun crew had fired every ten minutes for over an hour until they were silenced. In the cellar the wounded feared that the ceiling would fall in on them. Just 20 of the defenders managed to escape and headed for La Gleize.

The bad weather brought the fighting to a halt and Peiper withdrew the rest of his forces to La Gleize.

After losing Stoumont and Cheneux, Peiper was left holding just La Gleize, the hamlet of La Venne and a few neighbouring farms. The approaches to La Venne were defended by a single Panther and a Panzer IV. Despite his situation Peiper's morale does not seem to have faltered. In a cellar in La Gleize he struck up a conversation with an American prisoner, Major Hal McCown from the US 30th Infantry Division. 'He was completely confident of Germany's ability to whip the Allies,' recalled McCown.[21] 'We can't lose,' Peiper told him. 'Himmler's new reserve army has so many new divisions your G-2s [intelligence officers] will wonder where they came from.'[22] Peiper then added that 'a new submarine campaign was also opening up and they had been told that there had been considerable tonnage sunk in the English Channel'.[23] He also mentioned Hitler's V-1 and V-2 weapons and the Luftwaffe's new aircraft. McCown was worried about the fate of his men being held in La Gleize. He had heard rumours of massacres in Stavelot and Baugnez. When he pressed Peiper about observing the Geneva Convention, Peiper responded, 'I give you my word.'[24]

By now Battle Group Peiper had run out of ammunition and food and it was only a matter of time before it was completely overwhelmed. When Peiper relayed this to headquarters he was flabbergasted by the reply: 'If Battle Group Peiper does not punctually report its supply situation it cannot reckon on a running supply of fuel and ammunition. Six Tiger IIs are ready for action. Where do you want us to send them?'[25] These were stuck at Stavelot, and Peiper, knowing the tanks would never reach him, flippantly replied, 'Send via air lift to La Gleize. We must be allowed to breakout immediately.'[26]

He was refused authorization to push eastward to meet up with the 1st SS until Saturday 23 December. In desperation he signalled, 'Last chance for breakout tonight. Without wounded and vehicles. Please give permission!'[27] This was then finally granted for the early hours of the following day. Initially his request had been passed by Mohnke to Priess who then referred it to Dietrich who said no. Priess wanted to save what was left of Battle Group Peiper so delegated the decision back to Mohnke. The latter immediately agreed to let Peiper withdraw. It was clear to Peiper that his chain of command simply did not grasp the

severity of his situation when a message arrived stating, 'You may break
out but only if you bring all wounded and vehicles.'[28] This was the final
straw for Peiper, who lost his temper. Turning to his radio operator, he
raged, 'Blow the damn thing up. Permission or not, we're breaking out
of here on foot!'[29]

Peiper organized a small rearguard to hold off the Americans as
long as possible and to try to destroy as much abandoned equipment
as they could. The two remaining tanks were to hold La Venne and
an operational, though immobile, Tiger also remained to the east
of Petit-Spai. 'Out of the 2,000 men who so proudly advanced
through La Gleize on 19 December 1944,' said Staff Sergeant Laun,
'approximately 700 dejected souls remained.'[30] He strongly suspected
that Peiper would have fled on his own if he could have got away
with it. Peiper actually led 800 survivors through the woods along
the Amblève, north of Trois-Ponts and across the Salm River to
reach his division on Christmas Eve. Amongst them were Heinz von
Westernhagen and the survivors from his 501st SS Heavy Panzer
Battalion. They left behind half a dozen Tigers in the La Gleize area.
The men were warned not to try to surrender: 'If you fall behind you
will be shot!'[31] To speed up their escape they soon began to throw
away their weapons. First to be discarded were the heavy Panzerfausts,
which were followed by their machine guns, submachine guns and
rifles.

When they ran into a column of American infantry, Peiper's men
scattered into the forest forming small groups. Major McCown
recalled, 'suddenly tracer bullets flashed all around us and we could
hear the machine gun bullets cutting the trees very close over us'.[32] In
the confusion he managed to escape. One group of 200 men headed
for German lines south of Wanne, and some 770 survivors eventually
reached sanctuary at Wanne on Christmas Day. Staff Sergeant Laun
reached German lines at Ville du Bois near Vielsalm having gone via
Basse-Bodeux.

'The Tigers, Panthers, a large number of vehicles, self-propelled
guns, weapons, now become booty of the Americans,' noted Laun,
'providing they haven't been knocked out by Yank artillery already.'[33]
When the Americans entered La Gleize they found 300 German
wounded who had had to be left behind, 28 abandoned panzers,
25 self-propelled guns and 70 half-tracks. They also rescued 170

American prisoners of war, most of whom had been captured in Stoumont. German resistance in the area remarkably lasted for two more days; Battle Group Peiper, though, had ceased to exist. Upon reaching safety an exhausted Peiper slept for almost 24 hours. Only now did his optimism finally give out. While dozing off he thought to himself, 'I knew it was all over. We'd lost ... not only the Battle of the Ardennes, but also the war.'[34]

Krauts Speaking English

The three battle groups of Otto Skorzeny's 150th Panzer Brigade, assigned to the 1st SS and 12th SS Panzer and the 12th Volksgrenadier Divisions, were poised to leap ahead and make their dramatic dash for the Meuse on 16 December once the American defences were torn open. The battle groups were led by units dressed as American soldiers. These included 'special guides' who were kitted out in basic American uniform. To avoid accidental friendly fire, they were issued with a number of recognition signs that included a blue scarf tucked into the collar of the standard issue US Army field jacket, and the left chin strap was left loose on the M1 American helmet.

Before Skorzeny's brigade moved, his Einheit Stielau commandos rolled quietly forward and past the US Army's forward units to gather intelligence and cause confusion behind enemy lines. Wearing American uniforms, armed with American weapons and driving American jeeps, Skorzeny's raiders tried to look as nonchalant as possible by chewing gum and slouching in their seats. They were pretending to be members of the US 5th Armored Division. Some wore pink scarves with the second button of their field jackets left undone as recognition signs. On the near side of their jeeps' bonnets were stencilled the letters 'CD', 'XY' or 'Z', which would also tip off German troops that they were friendlies. If stopped by their own side they were to tap the side of their helmets twice. Skorzeny's reconnaissance patrols consisted of three or four men per vehicle, while the demolition teams consisted of up to six. Unbeknown to the commandos, US Army regulations stipulated that for safety reasons, principally because of mine casualties, only three men should ride in a jeep.

Some of the commandos had been sent to the American prisoner of war camps at Küstrin and Limburg to brush up on their English. Sergeant Heinz Rohde recalled somewhat worryingly, 'The performance of American films, especially war films, played a great role in our training.'[1] They were taught to use slang if challenged such as, 'Go, crap in yer hat, buddy!' and 'Go an' lay an egg'.[2] The plan was that they bluff their way past bemused checkpoints. Their final orders included the ridiculous advice from an instructor that, 'Just before they opened fire, they were recommended to change into German uniform!'[3] All the commandos knew they were running the risk that, if caught, they could be shot as spies.

In the early hours Sergeant Rohde and his three comrades headed in the general direction of Lanzerath to the west of Losheim. Some five miles to the south of the village they drove through the dense forest praying that they did not meet anyone. 'While the jeep bounced up and down like a young, frisky deer,' observed Rohde, 'the jeep team carried out a crazy striptease, getting rid of the [German] para-overalls to reveal the US uniforms beneath.'[4] They put on their American helmets as they passed a burning truck. In front of them they spotted an American gun crew struggling to manoeuvre their anti-tank gun. When a sergeant asked them for help they sped by, saying they were under orders not to stop. They cleared the trees and reached a country road only to bump into an American soldier. 'An Ami, as tall as a tree, was standing there,' said Rohde, 'and there was no missing the white stripes of the military policeman around his military helmet!'[5] He obligingly waved them onto a side road just as German artillery shells began to drop onto the route they had been going to take.

Rohde and the others sped westward; their objective was the crossing over the Meuse at Huy. They could not believe their good luck. Miraculously they drove unhindered for almost six hours before reaching their destination. Hiding up in some woods, they signalled Skorzeny's headquarters at Losheim using their radio. Afterwards they drove down to the river and hid the jeep in a bush. Three of them quietly approached the Huy bridge on foot. Concealed along the river bank, they watched American vehicles rumbling over the river. Reassuringly they could see no anti-aircraft or anti-tank guns. 'There were a number of typical American tents on the east bank,' observed Rohde, 'from which soldiers came and went all the time. Obviously they belonged to a guard company responsible for the bridge.'[6] There was no sign of any heavy weapons. When an American searchlight began to sweep the river, the commandos slipped back to their vehicle. They made their report and were given permission to return to German lines. Their intelligence was good news for Skorzeny as his brigade should be able to overcome Huy's weak defences easily.[7]

Skorzeny later confirmed a team, presumably including Rohde, did reach the Meuse where they observed lax security on the bridges. They then withdrew, laying mines and felling trees on three roads. On that first day another of Skorzeny's commando teams also claimed to have successfully reached Huy. There they set themselves up at a road junction, and when American tanks appeared their team leader, who spoke fluent English, calmly sent them in the wrong direction. The commandos then retreated, removing road signs and cutting a newly laid telephone cable as they went. Passing back through American lines, they successfully reached Skorzeny still at Losheim. Skorzeny noted that German intelligence later confirmed 'that the American Command were searching for one of their own tank regiments!'[8]

A third commando team arrived at Poteau not far from St Vith, which was held by two companies of American infantry. An officer approached the team leader, who was dressed as an American sergeant, demanding to know what was going on at the front. The sergeant told him that 'Krauts' had broken through and surrounded the village. In response the alarmed officer ordered his men to withdraw. Another team stumbled upon an American ammunition dump, part of which they blew up after darkness fell.[9] The commandos also reached Malmedy, Ligneuville, Aywaille and Liège.

Lieutenant Commander von Beer, a former German naval officer, now dressed as an unlikely looking American lieutenant, led his men into Malmedy with ease. Von Beer later claimed he had found the town by accident after getting lost, adding, 'At sea nothing would have happened to me.'[10] A Belgian civilian stopped their jeep and asked, 'Are the Germans coming back?'[11] Von Beer said he did not know. Although there were few signs of American troops, he appreciated that it was unwise to linger in the town. 'We got away with it that time,' he later remarked, 'because we had more luck than sense.'[12] A second team reached Malmedy and on the road to Eupen turned all the signs around, which caused an almighty traffic jam.

Disguised as Americans, Sergeants Manfred Pernass, Günther Billing and Corporal Wilhelm Schmidt drove like the wind to reach Aywaille on the Amblève to the north-west of Stoumont. On the way they told everyone they met that they were fleeing from a major German breakthrough. When they reached the village their luck ran out as they did not know the password and were promptly arrested. Schmidt, who had been masquerading as Private First Class George Sensenbach, admitted that they had been tasked with 'infiltrating through the Americans and reporting the condition of the Meuse bridges and of the roads leading to those bridges'.[13] Their presence so far west immediately caused panic. When questioned further about their mission, Schmidt added to the Americans' alarm by claiming they and other German commando units were out to capture General Eisenhower and his staff. When his interrogators pressed him harder, Schmidt confessed their mission was, 'To kill ... General ... Eisenhower.'[14]

It is unclear if this was a deliberate deception plan devised by Skorzeny and the enthusiastic young lieutenant from the commando company or simply arose from the rumour mill at Grafenwöhr. Schmidt's intelligence was 'confirmed' by Second Lieutenant Günther Schultz who was captured, along with three other Germans, reconnoitring a bridge on the outskirts of Liège. He claimed that there was an 'Eisenhower Action' group under Lieutenant Schmidhuber whose mission was to kidnap or assassinate Eisenhower. He embellished his story by adding that about 80 men, including Brandenburger commandos, were to rendezvous in Paris. The location of this gathering was Skorzeny's suggested Café de la Paix or the Café de l'Epée. The tough Brandenburgers were known to have carried out special operations in Belgium, Russia and North Africa, so Schultz's story seemed very plausible.

News of the German commando threat quickly flashed around the
Allies' headquarters. General Bradley, who was based in Luxembourg,
recounted with some amusement:

> Three times I was ordered to prove my identity by cautious GIs.
> The first time by identifying Springfield as the capital of Illinois (my
> questioner held out for Chicago); the second time by locating the
> guard between the center and tackle on a line of scrimmage; the third
> time by naming the then current spouse of ... Betty Grable. Grable
> stopped me, but the sentry did not. Pleased at having stumped me,
> he nevertheless passed me on.[15]

Donald Wallace, with a unit from the US 99th Infantry Division
deployed near Buchholz Station, was alerted to the danger of fifth
columnists. He remembered:

> During the night we pulled back into the forest. Word came down
> that German paratroopers in GI uniforms were infiltrating the area,
> and I delivered the message that everyone was to remain perfectly still
> and that they should shoot anything that moved. A short time later
> I was told to deliver a change of password.[16]

The assumption that the commandos were paratroopers may have been
based on the discovery of dumped para-overalls or smocks.

General Patton, always one to be over-excitable at the best of times,
told Eisenhower on 17 December, 'Krauts ... speaking perfect English
... raising hell, cutting wires, turning road signs around, spooking
whole divisions, and shoving a bulge into our defenses.'[17] Although two
of Skorzeny's teams were quickly captured, seven others successfully
ran circles around the bewildered Americans. In a panic, American
military police arrested American soldiers found to be in possession of
any items of German clothing. Later, advancing German troops caught
wearing American clothing to keep out the cold were also treated as
fifth columnists.

General Eisenhower's personal movements were completely
hampered by fears that Skorzeny's commandos were now on their
way to Paris to kill him. He found himself effectively under house
arrest at Petit Trianon or 'Hotel Eisenhower' for three days. When he

was let out he was escorted by a whole company of trigger-happy US military police who were taking no chances. One night at the villa of Eisenhower's chief of staff a gun battle broke out. In the morning the body of the assassin was located – it turned out they had shot a stray cat. On another occasion four French officers were killed by an overzealous American sentry. Any American soldier found on the streets of Paris with German military souvenirs was likely to find himself in deep trouble.

Paranoia swept through the American lines and jittery US military police started stopping everything that moved. Passwords were changed constantly, which caused American and British troops unending problems. While the Americans were thrown into a state of utter confusion, Field Marshal Montgomery was invigorated by the challenge of Hitler's offensive. He sent out his liaison officers to report on what was happening on his southern flank. At Spa they found General Hodges' US 1st Army headquarters almost completely deserted, apart from two officers still in bed. Everyone else had retreated at short notice for fear of capture by the commandos. In their haste to escape they had left classified documents on the desks and top-secret maps pinned to the walls. Although Hodges was not under Monty's jurisdiction, the field marshal told his liaison officers to find Hodges immediately and order him to block the Meuse bridges even if it meant using farm carts.

Once the Germans reached the Hohes Venn plateau Skorzeny's battle groups were to pass round their parent divisions, but things did not run smoothly as they became horribly tangled up in the massive traffic jam at Losheim.

Near Merlscheid SS-Lieutenant Colonel Hardieck, commander of Battle Group X, was killed after the vehicle he was travelling in detonated a mine. SS-Captain Adrian von Fölkersam, Skorzeny's chief staff officer, was sent to take over. Skorzeny realized by the evening of the second day of the offensive the element of surprise had been completely lost and that his 150th Panzer Brigade would never manage to reach the Meuse bridges. Instead he suggested that it serve as a regular combat force. This made his 'special guides' and to a lesser extent his commandos redundant. Skorzeny, under the direction of SS-Colonel Mohnke, was ordered to help take Malmedy to open up the roads to reach Battle Group Peiper.

At this stage many of Skorzeny's men cast off their American uniforms, which was sensible after one Einheit Stielau team was shot near Poteau and another captured at Aywaille. However, the crews from the 6th Panzer Division manning Skorzeny's Panthers modified to look like M10s retained some American kit. Lieutenant Peter Mandt and his crew and Senior Staff Sergeant Bachmann and his crew continued to wear American jackets and trousers over their black panzer uniforms. In contrast the crews of Skorzeny's assault guns preferred to remain in their field-grey versions of the panzer uniform. Mandt did not hold out much hope of success. 'We knew we were going to lose the war anyway,' he said, 'and regarded battle as a kind of gigantic lottery, with the big prize – survival.'[18]

On 18 December at Poteau an American sergeant challenged the crew of a self-propelled gun apparently belonging to the US 14th Cavalry Group. They explained they were 'from E Company' belonging to an American cavalry regiment.[19] This was immediately recognized as bogus because the cavalry used the term 'troop' or 'squadron' not 'company'. This mistake cost them their lives. When the commandos attempted to escape they were killed. Although the Einheit Stielau had been trained to recognize American rank badges, this particular team had clearly not taken enough notice of the organization of the US Army.

Apart from inconveniencing Eisenhower, one of Skorzeny's greatest indirect successes was the arrest of Brigadier General Bruce Clarke by his own men. Clarke, in command of Combat Command B from the US 7th Armored Division, was stopped by US military police on the morning of 20 December. His crime was to fail a test on the Chicago Cubs. 'Only a Kraut would make a mistake like that,' concluded one of the MPs.[20] When Clarke protested his innocence a policeman responded, 'You're one of Skorzeny's men. We were told to watch out for a Kraut posing as a one-star general.'[21] Clarke, who was responsible for the defence of St Vith, was held for 30 minutes before common sense prevailed.[22]

All three of Skorzeny's battle groups joined 1st SS Panzer and were to be thrown into the attack on Malmedy on 21 December after concentrating at Engelsdorf. However, any chance of them achieving a level of tactical surprise was lost when one of his men was captured the day before and spilled the beans. Furthermore, Battle Group Z led by Lieutenant Wolf did not arrive in time. Skorzeny had no idea where it was and at best could consider it a reserve should it appear. To make matters worse Skorzeny's planned attack lacked artillery support to soften up the defenders or conduct counter-battery fire when the American artillery inevitably retaliated. 'Our "heaviest" weapons were medium mortars,' said Skorzeny.[23] Luftwaffe fighter cover was also completely out of the question. 'My ten surviving tanks – the rest were temporarily out of action as a result of damage – ' noted Skorzeny with resignation, 'would have to suffice.'[24]

Captain Scherff with Battle Group Y on the right flank was met by such heavy shelling that he quickly broke off his assault. This was not the covert operation he had planned and trained for. On the left Battle Group X, now under the command of SS-Captain von Fölkersam, attacked with two companies of infantry supported by five fake M10 tank destroyers. They pushed from Ligneuville, through Bellevaux and along the Route de Falize, striking west of Malmedy. The main force headed towards the Warche River bridge and Rollbahn C. Trip-wire flares illuminating the early morning gloom quickly alerted the American defenders and the bogus M10s ran into a minefield. Nonetheless, the US 823rd Tank Destroyer Battalion command post was quickly surrounded and attacked.

Skorzeny watched from the hill on the Route de Falize as one of his M10s supported by infantry in an assortment of American and German uniforms attacked towards Malmedy. It was soon driven off by an American anti-tank gun. The other nine tanks valiantly attempted to capture a bridge over the Warche in order to reach Stavelot, but the first tank was lost to a mine and began to burn. American infantry manning a roadblock were forced back, but when the Germans attempted to cross the bridge GIs armed with bazookas knocked out two more tanks. Two American tank destroyers then accounted for two further German tanks. It was clear that the 150th Panzer Brigade was taking a beating. 'I had a good view of six of our tanks,' recalled Skorzeny, 'engaged in a hopeless struggle with a superior force of the enemy, while trying to protect the left flank of the attack.'[25] American shells rained down into the valley with the American gunners concentrating their efforts on Engelsdorf and its approach roads.

Skorzeny, seeing how badly things were progressing, ordered his men to fall back, but none of his remaining armour made it. One fake M10 was disabled at Malmedy; another crashed into the café at La Falize with its redundant gun barrel poking into the kitchen. A third belonging to Senior Staff Sergeant Bachmann crossed the Ambléve Bridge at Malmedy but was brought to a halt by American bazooka fire on the northern bank. Bachmann and his crew jumped out but were killed trying to reach the bridge. Only Corporal Karl Meinhardt, their radio operator, survived. He got to a nearby house where he prudently removed his American uniform. Meinhardt remained hidden until he was captured several days later. Some of Skorzeny's assault guns bearing American markings were abandoned in the open fields at Géromont. At least one of them was left booby-trapped by its crew and had to be dealt with by men from the US 291st Combat Engineers.

Skorzeny's troops suffered terribly at the hands of American artillery using the proximity fuse for the first time set for air burst. Lieutenant Mandt and his crew had reached the outskirts of Malmedy when their tank was 'rocked as if by a steel fist'.[26] The blast killed two crew, and a dazed Mandt with two other survivors clambered from their stricken steed. They crawled to the Café Lodomez but Mandt lost the others. Skorzeny's attack wilted in the face of sustained American shelling and mines. A German half-track carrying troops still in American uniforms ran over a chain of mines and was blown into the air. The maimed occupants were thrown across the road. One of them who was terribly burned survived and lay screaming amongst his former comrades. A captured American M8 light armoured car suffered a similar fate after hitting a mine. When Skorzeny's men reached the railway embankment to the west of Malmedy they were cut down by a deluge of American shells. Clinging to the soft earth, some tried to set up their machine guns but shrapnel quickly put paid to their endeavours, soaking the ground in their blood.

Mandt, who was the only survivor from his tank crew, was caught in this shelling and felt guilty for sheltering in a cellar. He was ordered to take command of some infantry, but found them understandably reluctant to leave the nearby cellars, which were also full of wounded. Mandt reluctantly crept out and rallied some men to renew the attack. 'Suddenly I felt a blow on my head, as if from a hammer,' he recalled. 'I lost consciousness. When I came to again, after how long I don't know,

I found my head soaked in blood and that I was lying between two men to whom I had been speaking when I had been hit. They were both very dead!'[27] SS-Captain von Fölkersam was wounded in the backside and, barely able to walk, had to be helped from the battlefield by a medical officer. The Americans dropped 3,000 shells into the Malmedy area that day.

On the morning of 22 December Captain Scherff made another unsuccessful attack east of Malmedy, and American engineers brought down the railway bridges on the N32 and over the Route de Falize and the bridge over the Warche west of Malmedy. For the depleted 150th Panzer Brigade the battle was now almost over. They had lost over 200 men in a week of fierce fighting, with Skorzeny himself badly wounded in the face by shrapnel. After jumping out of an armoured car that was under fire, Skorzeny recalled, 'I put up my hand and discovered a bleeding piece of flesh hanging down over my right eye.'[28] He was patched up at a dressing station and refused to go to hospital, instead returning to his command post. Artillery support belatedly arrived on 24 December; however, the officer in charge cautioned, 'I must inform you, sir, that I have only sixteen rounds for the whole battalion, and for the moment there is no prospect of my getting any more.'[29] Skorzeny was flabbergasted; there was nothing he could do to retaliate against the constant American shelling.

Short of rations and winter clothing, Skorzeny's men spent a miserable Christmas trying to keep warm. His orderly found a tree and placed a solitary candle on it, but this did little to cheer them up. The survivors were withdrawn from the line three days later and returned to Grafenwöhr where they were disbanded – officially ending the brigade's feeble attempt to pass itself off as Americans and dash to the Meuse. A knocked-out, snow-covered captured Sherman, belonging to the 5th Parachute Division, photographed outside the Hotel des Ardennes, aptly summed up the failure of Hitler's Operation *Griffin*. Skorzeny's fake M10s had got him nowhere; 2nd Panzer in fact had got closer to the Meuse than the 150th Panzer Brigade.

The only part of Skorzeny's command that achieved any notable results were his Einheit Stielau commandos. Most of his four-man undercover teams got behind American lines, with several successfully reaching the Meuse. In total 44 commandos got through. The last raid was conducted on 19 December and after that they reverted to their own uniforms for fear of being shot. Lieutenant Collonia, who had operated behind enemy lines as First Lieutenant George P. Ward, was awarded the Knight's Cross for his actions.[30] Skorzeny, once one of Hitler's favourites, found himself sent to the crumbling Eastern Front to face the Red Army.

13

The Losheim Gap

While Bradley, Hodges and Montgomery were trying to get a grip on the situation, Patton's divisions also found themselves under attack by Hitler's panzers. To the south von Manteuffel's operations went much smoother than Dietrich's. For a start the going was much easier and the American divisions were weaker. 'My storm battalions infiltrated rapidly into the American front – like rain drops,' said von Manteuffel.[1] The only problem was that the Losheim Gap, which formed the historic invasion route into Belgium from the Schnee Eifel, was also the boundary between Dietrich and von Manteuffel's armies. This inevitably caused problems for both of them.

In von Manteuffel's centre, General Walther Krüger's 58th Panzer Corps, with two divisions, the 116th Panzer and 560th Volksgrenadier, was tasked with getting over the Our near Lutzkampen. It was then to secure Houffalize; with the Ourthe River on its right it would move to cross the Meuse between Namur and Andenne. This certainly seemed achievable. The 116th Panzer, known as the 'Greyhounds', had suffered during the battles in Normandy and the Hürtgen Forest. However, its ranks had been fleshed out with fairly good recruits and it had over 100 panzers and assault guns. Although Colonel Rudolf Langhauser's 560th Volksgrenadiers were formed using troops on occupation duties in Norway and were poorly trained, they were to perform well. Initially Langhauser only had two of his three Volksgrenadier regiments available. These were supported by a regiment of artillery plus an anti-tank battalion and engineer battalion.

South of Dasburg on Krüger's left was General Heinrich Freiherr von Lüttwitz's 47th Panzer Corps with four divisions: 2nd Panzer, 9th Panzer, Panzer Lehr and 26th Volksgrenadier. His command was to get across the Our River and seize Clervaux, followed by the road junction at Bastogne. Von Lüttwitz was to cross the Meuse south of Namur. The 2nd Panzer Division was to attack westward from Dasburg towards Marnach and Clerf. In the 26th Volksgrenadiers' line of advance were Hosingen, Bockholz and Munshausen. Facing Panzer Lehr were Weiler and Holzthum.

The 2nd Panzer, under Colonel Meinrad von Lauchert, had been reorganized after Normandy and still had many veterans in its ranks. The division had over 100 panzers and assault guns. Its panzer regiment was equipped with 85 Panther and Mark IV tanks. Major General Harald von Elverfeldt's 9th Panzer including attached Tiger tanks had a similar armoured strength. Although virtually annihilated in Normandy, Panzer Lehr, under General Bayerlein, was rebuilding when it was committed to a counter-attack against Patton's US 3rd Army in the Saar region. As there was no time to draft in replacements before the Ardennes, the division was strengthened with ad hoc anti-tank and assault gun battalions. The panzer regiment could only muster 57 Panthers and Mark IV tanks. Major General Heinz Kokott's 26th Volksgrenadier Division, although an ad hoc formation, had a strength of over 17,000 men, so was able to offer welcome infantry support.

Another notable unit under von Lüttwitz's command that was quite powerful was the armoured Führer Begleit Brigade under Colonel Otto Remer. This was formed around Hitler's headquarters guard and included a panzer battalion from the Grossdeutschland Panzer Division, which was on the Eastern Front. To give it more punch the brigade had been reinforced with assault guns as well as 88mm and 105mm guns, in the shape of an artillery regiment and an anti-tank battalion. It also had its own flak regiment to help keep enemy fighter-bombers at bay. Infantry units comprised a panzergrenadier regiment as well as an additional grenadier battalion.

At Dasburg 2nd Panzer faced problems getting its tanks over the river. When Lieutenant Rudolf Siebert arrived with his armoured car company, he discovered that the engineers had mixed up the bridging equipment, which was causing delays and vast traffic jams. He decided to go ahead of his men using an amphibious Schwimmwagen to get across. It took all night on 16–17 December for the 2nd and 116th Panzers to cross the Our River road bridge at Dasburg. To the south the armour had exactly the same problem. 'By 1600 hours the Gemund bridge was completed by the engineer battalion of the Panzer Lehr Division using B-bridge equipment,' noted von Manteuffel.[2]

On Krüger's right units of General Lucht's 66th Corps were to cut off the Schnee Eifel salient prior to the capture of St Vith. Lucht's job was also to protect the junction of the 5th Panzer Army and the 6th Panzer Army. His command consisted of the 18th and 62nd Volksgrenadier Divisions. Both were of questionable combat value. Colonel Hoffmann-Schönborn's 18th Division had been formed in the summer in Denmark using a Luftwaffe Field Division and men from the navy. However, it had some two months of experience conducting defensive operations in the Eifel.

General Friedrich Kittel's 62nd Volksgrenadiers only arrived in the Ardennes ten days before the offensive commenced. It included many Czech and Polish conscripts who spoke no German. The division was tasked with breaking through south of the Schnee Eifel and blocking the exits from St Vith to the south and west. Both divisions were backed by 40 assault guns, but they had no tanks and little mobile artillery. Lucht's only armour was the 244th Assault Gun Brigade. For fire support he was mainly reliant on inaccurate rocket launchers. Kittel was to attack from the Schnee Eifel towards Winterspelt, while Hoffmann-Schönborn's men pushed on Auw and then Schönberg on the Our. The Germans had good intelligence on the latter village as a member of the Belgian SS had come home on leave completely unhindered by the Americans.[3] The two Volksgrenadier divisions were to converge on the key road junction at St Vith to the west of Schönberg, which was 12 miles behind American lines. The Führer Begleit Brigade would then move forward to exploit the breakthrough. The southern flank at St Vith would be protected by the 116th Panzer while to the north would be the 1st and 9th SS.

General von Manteuffel's line of advance meant that the brunt of his attack fell on Cota's US 28th and Jones' 106th Infantry Divisions. The 106th was compromised from the start, especially once the 14th Cavalry Group had been forced to give ground. The division's three regiments, the 422nd, 423rd and 424th, were soon cut off from artillery support after the Germans had got behind them. The assault companies of the 18th Volksgrenadiers relied on surprise and the wide spacing of American defences in the Losheim Gap. They had reached Auw some two miles inside the American front by 0830 hours. The US 14th Cavalry Group holding this area withdrew to Manderfeld Ridge. The Volksgrenadiers continued to pressure them and by 1600 hours they had been forced back to Andler and Holsheim some seven miles to the west. This exposed the northern flank of the 422nd Infantry who were positioned east of Auw. They were given a temporary reprieve as the two German regiments swinging round their northern flank were occupied pursuing the 14th Cavalry Group.

The 62nd Volksgrenadiers set about the 424th Infantry at the southern end of the 106th Division's defences. Although the Americans counter-attacked, by the evening the Volksgrenadiers had penetrated Winterspelt four miles inside enemy lines. Then the 62nd renewed their attack, and despite being confronted by Sherman tanks of Combat Command B from the US 9th Armored Division, they forced the 424th Infantry west past Elcerath and over the Our. Although von Manteuffel's attacks were held at Winterspelt to the south and at Bleialf in the centre, to the north American defences were pierced in the Losheim Gap. Jones at his headquarters in St Vith did not realize that he lay in the path of the northern wing of Hoffmann-Schönborn's 18th Volksgrenadiers.

In the meantime, von Manteuffel's 47th and 58th Panzer Corps were attacking Cota's 28th Division. He had deployed his three regiments north-south: the 112th which was nearest Jones, the 110th and then the 109th which formed the boundary with the 9th Armored Division. The 112th managed to frustrate the 116th Panzer Division by stopping it from taking two bridges over the Our, while the 109th fought off three German infantry battalions. German progress was so slow that the 116th Panzer was instructed to swing south.

Things did not go so well for Colonel Hurley Fuller's 110th Regiment. This had been deployed along an exposed supply route, dubbed 'Skyline Drive', that ran parallel to the front, where his men were manning isolated outposts. The 47th Panzer Corps' infantry had soon infiltrated through the American lines, but before they could press on they had little option but to liquidate the American pockets of resistance in the villages of Holzthum, Marnach, Munshausen and Weiler. Nonetheless, just after nightfall von Lüttwitz got bridges across the Our at Gemund and Dasburg, opening the road to Clervaux and Bastogne.

In the south, Brandenberger's 7th Army moved to protect von Manteuffel's flank. His 85th Corps, commanded by General Baptist Kniess, threw the 5th Parachute Division towards Wiltz, and the 352nd Volksgrenadier Division towards Diekirch. On their left flank General Franz Beyer's 80th Corps sent the 276th Volksgrenadiers to strike west of Echternach supported by the 212th. To the west of Trier, General Edwin von Rothkirch's 53rd Corps, with the 9th Volksgrenadier and the 15th Panzergrenadier Divisions supported by the Führer Grenadier Brigade, was in the process of gathering as a reserve. None of these units, though, were up to strength.

General Heilmann's 5th Parachute Division was supported by the 11th Assault Gun Brigade so had some punch, although Heilmann and his regimental commanders lacked combat experience. Erich Schmidt's 352nd Volksgrenadier Division was another of those infantry units that had been reconstructed and was green. Likewise, the 276th Volksgrenadiers was made up of inexperienced and poorly trained recruits. In contrast the 212th Volksgrenadiers with veteran officers and non-commissioned officers was the 7th Army's premier formation.

The 5th Parachute and 352nd Volksgrenadiers attacked the US 109th Regiment simultaneously with the main offensive. Likewise, the 276th Volksgrenadiers hit positions of the US 60th Armored Infantry Battalion between Bollendorf and Wallendorf, while the 212th Volksgrenadiers tackled the US 12th Infantry belonging to the 4th Infantry Division. Both American regiments with the support of a combat command of the 9th Armored held up Brandenberger's attacks. Then, once American reinforcements arrived, they dug in between Ettelbruck and Echternach. This meant that, like the northern shoulder at Elsenborn, American defences on the southern shoulder held firm, buying the Allies valuable time. At the end of 16 December German gains were quite modest, although they had breached the Losheim Gap and Skyline Drive.

Frustratingly for Hitler the American line did not collapsed wholesale and behind the scenes Eisenhower ordered the redeployment of the 7th Armored Division in the US 9th Army's sector and the 10th Armored with Patton's US 3rd Army in the south to the Ardennes. Similarly, Major General Matthew B. Ridgway commanding the 18th Airborne Corps was instructed to send his tough, battle-hardened US 82nd and 101st Airborne Divisions to Bastogne. Clearly the German high command had miscalculated for they had assessed the Allies did not have any reserves available, and yet within 24 hours Eisenhower had four divisions on the way to the battlefield.

By 17 December the 422nd and 423rd Regiments were left stranded on the Schnee Eifel. Of the two regiments of artillery in the Auw area one withdrew to St Vith and the other, under attack and at risk of being overrun, destroyed its own guns and fled. The 14th Cavalry Group had withdrawn to north-west of St Vith. The German 294th Grenadier Regiment moved south from the area between Andler and Auw to take Schönberg; this cut the main road from St Vith to the Schnee Eifel. One of the 294th's sister regiments captured Bleialf and reached Schönberg. A third American artillery regiment near Schönberg joined the 423rd Infantry but was soon out of ammunition.

The two American regiments on the Schnee Eifel tried to withdraw but found themselves blocked by German units and were both forced to surrender. The Führer Begleit Brigade, moving forward to help the 18th Volksgrenadiers capture St Vith, caught the 422nd Infantry in the woods to the east of Schönberg. Their tanks, artillery and mortars began to pound the trapped Americans who had little choice but to capitulate.

Colonel Descheneaux, commander of the 422nd Infantry, when he saw the Germans looting cigarettes and watches, said, 'Let my men keep one pack apiece.' A young German lieutenant overseeing the prisoners replied, 'Everything will be correct, Colonel.'[4] Everywhere it seemed the Americans, unable to withstand German tanks and infantry, simply surrendered. General Lucht's men took 8,000 prisoners of war. In the space of several days two-thirds of the US 106th Division simply vanished. As the dejected columns of American prisoners began to plod eastward their guards warned, 'Do not flee. If you flee, you will be machine gunned.'[5]

When the Americans attempted to relieve their forces trapped at Marnach they ran into the 2nd Panzer Division. Now that the Germans were in Clerf they were able to shell Fuller's command post in the Claravallis Hotel. Despite American reinforcements, the town was lost and Fuller captured along with an intact bridge. This opened the road west and 2nd Panzer rumbled towards Bastogne and Noville, followed by 116th Panzer, which swung north-west and headed for Houffalize. Meanwhile Bayerlein's Panzer Lehr crossed the Our at Gemund ten miles to the south and his reconnaissance battalion headed for Wiltz on 17 December. The town hosted the command post of Cota's 28th Division, which was protected by a company of infantry supported by a few tanks and anti-aircraft guns.

Before reaching Wiltz, it fell to Battle Group Kaufmann, comprising Panzer Lehr's reconnaissance battalion and the 39th Fusilier Regiment from the 26th Volksgrenadiers, to take Holzthum and Consthum. It then reached the Clerf River. To the east of Weiler the 26th Volksgrenadiers linked up with elements of the 5th Parachute Division. The former, though, were unable to prevent 200 men of the 3rd Battalion, 110th Infantry from withdrawing from Weiler, Holzthum and Consthum and reaching Wiltz. Also, further north, the 26th Volksgrenadiers took Hosingen, capturing 320 Americans.

Panzer Lehr, 2nd Panzer and the 26th Volksgrenadiers all experienced heavy congestion on the roads between the Our and the Clerf, which greatly hampered the drive on Bastogne. 'Speed was urgently needed,' said von Manteuffel, 'the more so, as according to an intercepted radio message on 17 Dec the American 101 Parachute Div was alerted and ordered to attack Bastogne.'[6] The following morning Panzer Lehr crossed the Clerf near Drauffelt.

Bayerlein decided to bypass Wiltz via Eschweiler and Mageret, leaving it to be taken by the 26th Volksgrenadier and 5th Parachute Divisions. 'We did not start from Mageret towards Bastogne before 19 Dec,' said von Manteuffel, 'having previously mopped up Mageret by dawn.'[7] Heilmann's new recruits had good reason to take Wiltz: they were cold and hungry. They wanted shelter from the weather and wanted to lay their hands on American rations, which would include tinned food, chocolate and decent cigarettes. By midnight on 19 December the American garrison had been overwhelmed. Cota's 112th Infantry escaped to the north-west to join the southern defences of St Vith, while the 109th moved south to join the US 4th Infantry Division forming the southern shoulder of the German bulge. A few hundred men from the destroyed 110th Infantry reached Bastogne and joined the stubborn defence there.

14

Falcon Takes Flight

At 0400 hours on 16 December Colonel von der Heydte found himself kicking his heels at Lippspringe airfield still waiting for half his men. They were unable to join him due to ongoing transport problems. He was supposed to have taken off but as always there were setbacks. Apart from Major Erdmann, he was really unhappy with the level of support he was getting from the Luftwaffe and the army. Major General Peltz, in charge of the 2nd Fighter Corps, had been particularly unhelpful from the start. Von der Heydte had requested that the Luftwaffe conduct reconnaissance flights over American positions to try to ascertain the level of resistance he might encounter. This was immediately rejected on security grounds. Nothing must be done to tip the Americans off that they were about to be attacked. In response he had requested any aerial photographs that the Luftwaffe might have of his drop zones. This request likewise fell on fallow ground. The colonel was completely unaware that the Luftwaffe had been conducting reconnaissance flights along the Meuse employing their Arado 234 jets since late November.

Despite Erdmann's efforts to help with transport, the plans for this part of Operation *Falcon* were far from encouraging. In an effort to help Erdmann's very inexperienced pilots find their way to the drop zones in the dark they were to fly from Paderborn along a corridor illuminated by searchlights. Once they were approaching their objective, the aircraft would regroup and follow a second avenue of lights. Fifteen minutes before von der Heydte and his men were due to jump, Ju 88 bombers would drop incendiary bombs to illuminate the area. This was to be followed by other aircraft that would deliver 'Christmas tree' flare markers both before and after the drop.

To try to confuse the US 18th Airborne Corps the Luftwaffe would illuminate two other areas to the north and west of the real main drop zone. These would also receive the paratrooper dolls. The hope was that the Americans, faced with three paratroop landings, would waste time trying to work out what was going on. This would slow down American attempts to contain von der Heydte's battle group and give him time to gather his men. He was alarmed to learn that SS-Lieutenant Etterich, the forward observation officer from the 12th SS, his own signaller and his runner had never jumped before. Nor had they received any training on how to land; it would be a miracle if they did not break their necks in the darkness. He had a few jump veterans such as Sergeant Lingelbach, but his last combat jump had been in Norway in 1940. A smattering of the other lads were veterans of the Crete campaign, but even that had been so long ago few really knew what to expect.

On the day before the army was scheduled to take von der Heydte's battle group to the airfields at Lippspringe and Paderborn ready for departure, sure enough, at 1700 hours on 15 December, a column of trucks had arrived to pick them up from Oerlinghausen; the only problem was that the vehicles had empty fuel tanks. Five hours were wasted while petrol was obtained. A second snag was then encountered when it was discovered there were insufficient trucks to shift the whole battle group in one go. An exasperated von der Heydte would only be able to go with about 400 men, just a third of his total force. When he reported this to Model's headquarters his staff at first rejected his estimate and then promptly cancelled the operation.

Von der Heydte and Erdmann were relieved by this news as, so far, the entire mission had been a chaotic shambles. However, this order was then countermanded by Sepp Dietrich's chief of staff, General Krämer. He told them that the offensive was not making the gains that had been anticipated and that there were concerns that the Americans would redeploy troops from the Aachen area to counter-attack 6th Panzer Army's right flank. Operation *Hawk*'s role had changed; it was no longer to hold open the routes for 6th Panzer Army; instead, von der Heydte was to block these routes and stop the movement of American forces and supplies. 'Hold on as long as possible,' instructed Krämer down the telephone, 'two days as a minimum, and do as much damage as you can to the reinforcements.'[1] Von der Heydte stood open-mouthed. Dietrich had said he would only need to hold for a few hours; now it had extended to several days. There was more bad news. 'By the way,' added Krämer, 'your dropping zone has been moved slightly south-eastward to the Belle-Croix crossroads near the Baraque-Michel.'[2]

By now all the men were gathered at the airfields. They had been issued emergency rations for two days, which included bacon, sausage, hard bread, energy tablets and a drug called Pervitin to keep them awake. They were also equipped with Losantin powder, designed to protect the skin from mustard gas. The non-commissioned officers struggled to prevent the younger recruits from eating everything while they were killing time. The sergeants and corporals warned them that they would need these rations once they had reached the drop zone. The men were tired from all the waiting around and there was much grumbling in the ranks. In the morning they had been keyed up and good to go; now all they could do was sit about smoking. It was noted by some of the waiting paratroopers that the SS men, 'these so-called "tough boys" were scared to death before their first jump'.[3]

It was not until just before midnight on 16 December that Colonel von der Heydte's parachute operation finally commenced. He stood with his men as they sang the paratrooper anthem 'Red Shines the Sun' before climbing into their planes. They tried to sound optimistic but the words 'When Germany is in danger, there is only one thing to do: To fight, to conquer and believe we shall die,' did not do much to raise their spirits. Each aircraft could carry up to 18 paratroopers and once on board the mood did not improve. Von der Heydte had watched as the Luftwaffe ground crews loaded the all-important air-dropped containers, which would carry the battle group's heavy weapons, rations, ammunition, medical supplies and communications equipment. These were carried on racks in the cargo bay or under the wings. As space was at a premium most were carried externally, ready to be released once the paratroopers were on their way.

A local priest had been summoned to bless them and the crews, but this seemed to do little good. Lieutenant Le Coutre's company was informed the road junction they were to secure would be marked by two fires. However, due to transport problems getting to Paderborn the drop for the first two of his platoons was scheduled for between midnight and 0300 hours. To make matters worse his third platoon would not land until 0500 hours. Some 106 Junker 52 transport aircraft took off from airfields near Paderborn.

Much to von der Heydte's dismay the jinx of Operation *Hawk* continued. The Luftwaffe had miscalculated the flying time. Above the Schnee Eifel the inexperienced pilots had not factored in the strong headwinds. They were using time to determine when to signal 'go' for the paratroops. In reality many pilots were miles from the drop zone. Furthermore, von der Heydte had been advised his drop would take place with a wind force of 4m to 6m (13–20ft) per second; instead it was 12m to 15m (40–50ft) per second with snow showers. Just before he had left, a Luftwaffe meteorologist had rushed over to warn him he faced up to 60kph (40mph) winds.

When 'Standby to jump' was called, von der Heydte, who was in the lead aircraft, climbed to his feet. Suddenly the plane rocked and the night was lit by tracer fire. Glancing out of a window, he saw enemy anti-aircraft guns bracket a neighbouring plane then hit it. This stricken Ju 52 juddered, fell from the sky and hit the ground. Undeterred, von der Heydte leapt from the exit door and into the darkness. He prayed that his Russian parachute would not be the death of him. Suddenly his fall was reassuringly arrested as the chute deployed, giving him a slow forward push. He was not used to the triangular shape and with his right arm in a sling struggled to control his descent in the strong wind. He hit the ground heavily, banged his head and was briefly knocked unconscious. When he eventually got to his feet he found no sign of any of his men. He cursed his luck; the same thing had happened to him in Crete in May 1941. Gathering his kit, he headed for their rallying point at the Belle Croix road junction. Remarkably the colonel's pilot had got him to his designated landing ground.

The rest of the drop was not such a success. Most of his signals platoon came down near Monschau to the east of Eupen and Malmedy and were swiftly rounded up by the Americans. Just 35 aircraft delivered their paratroopers anywhere near the drop zone. On the approach the transports were caught by flak and the novice parachutists were scattered from the Rhine to the Hautes Fagnes. Some even ended up beyond Aachen in the US 9th Army's area. This included three men from Le Coutre's company who were later captured that day. Another group of 200 men came down near Bonn some 50 miles behind their own lines.

In total, three-quarters of von der Heydte's force were dropped inside German-controlled areas. Two Ju 52s were shot down over Asselborn in northern Luxembourg and crash-landed intact not far from each other. Anti-aircraft fire claimed the lives of 37 of von der Heydte's men. One section from Lieutenant Wagner's company got lost and was captured intact. Sergeant Gall had been tasked by Staff Sergeant Geiss to secure a specific highway but had no idea how to find it and was swiftly captured.

Sergeant Lingelbach suffered an even worse landing than his colonel. He dropped into snow-covered trees and his chute snagged on the branches. The impact broke his left arm and he was left dangling six feet from the ground. He managed to struggle free and headed west in search of his comrades. Just as it was beginning to get light he came across a parachute canopy and its badly injured owner. Paratrooper Wiertz had hit the ground with such force he had broken both legs. Wiertz could not move and knew that he was done for. He urged Lingelbach to leave him, adding, 'Only first do me a favour of putting a bullet through my head!'[4] Instead the sergeant, using a makeshift sledge, miraculously dragged the injured man until he found a German patrol. Lingelbach was subsequently captured when the field hospital he was in was overrun by the Americans.

The only part of von der Heydte's ill-fated airborne drop that was successful involved the decoys. Near the Elsenborn Ridge some 300 dummy paratroopers were dropped, causing some confusion behind American lines. Fearing it was a real air drop, American patrols were sent on a wild goose chase looking for German soldiers who never materialized. Just five miles from von der Heydte, in Eupen, around 3,000 men from the US 3rd Armored Division were placed on alert. This was General Gerow's 5th Corps headquarters. When a German parachute was found in nearby woods rumours began to spread. It was not long before Allied intelligence was accurately estimating that around 1,500 paratroops had landed with the intention of seizing the crossroads on the Eupen-Malmedy road.

During the early hours, isolated groups of von der Heydte's men were engaged by the Americans. One man stumbled upon an anti-aircraft gun and, although challenged, managed to kill an American staff sergeant before escaping. A group of four, following a brief firefight, were not so fortunate and suffered one dead with the rest captured, two of whom were badly wounded. Two other men were discovered setting up their

light machine gun near another American anti-aircraft position. One
was shot and the other taken prisoner.

Initially, a dazed von der Heydte was able to round up just 20
of his 1,200 men. By daybreak his little force had grown to 125,
which included his signaller, runner and SS-Lieutenant Etterich.
Miraculously all three had survived. His group only had the weapons
and ammunition they were carrying. Their heavier weapons and spare
ammunition had been dropped in the containers but all these were
missing. Search parties were sent out and they eventually located
just six that held some ammunition, a mortar and a radio set. The
latter, as von der Heydte had feared, was damaged and inoperable. It
was clear that the built-in shock absorber on the container had not
worked sufficiently well enough to safeguard the radio. The loss of the
containers was a disaster. Normally it required 14 containers to equip
a full-strength platoon of 43 men. The battle group was supposed to
have 500 Panzerfausts but they could only find eight. This meant they
would not be able to take on American tanks for very long. Nor could
they summon any artillery support from the 12th SS should they
need it. A quick survey of support weapons showed they had just 14
machine guns and two mortars.

Three hours later the colonel had managed to gather 150 men, but
it was evident they were not strong enough to hold the Baraque Michel
road junction against determined American counter-attacks, especially
if they involved armour. Colonel von der Heydte had little choice but to
hide out in the local woods. Frustratingly the battle group was unable
to communicate with Dietrich's headquarters and therefore was unable
to pass on any intelligence it gathered on American dispositions.

The colonel's first encounter with an American convoy was a comedy
of errors. Some of his men were either side of the crossroads when
trucks came grinding round a bend full of infantry. As the Americans
were not expecting to meet any Germans they happily waved at what
they thought were men stuck on miserable guard duty in the middle of
nowhere. The frozen paratroopers, having failed to conceal themselves,
simply waved back as the convoy went on its way. The paratroopers
later captured a number of despatch riders from Eupen, but there
was no way of passing on the orders they were carrying. Calling for
volunteers, von der Heydte sent runners to try to make the 30 miles
to the German front lines, but none of them succeeded. When these

men were caught it further convinced the Americans that there were German paratroopers everywhere.

On the night of 17 December, the Luftwaffe attempted to drop extra ammunition, food and a 36-man heavy weapons platoon. If these were successfully delivered it could have helped boost von der Heydte's strength. At 1900 hours three Ju 52s took off from Sennelager, Paderborn, with orders to drop their cargo near a pre-arranged signal light. The pilots could not find the marker or the drop zone so released the containers and headed for home. In desperation, in the afternoon of 19 December von der Heydte sent an eight-man patrol to locate the missing containers. They found a few but these held ammunition and Panzerfausts with their fuses unscrewed. There was no sign of the food. When the men were sent out again two were captured and the rest returned empty handed.

On day three his force expanded when it linked up with another parachute battle group under Lieutenant Kayser of about 150 men. Kayser saluted and the two men compared notes; unfortunately, the lieutenant's force was in no better condition than the colonel's. Sporadic ambushes were being conducted but nothing on the scale that von der Heydte had hoped for. Nonetheless, their very presence had sown alarm and despondency amongst the American forces in the region. Half a dozen Americans from a rear echelon unit were captured but von der Heydte did not want to waste men guarding them. At nightfall he released them along with several injured paratroopers with instructions to return to American lines. Two of his men had each broken an arm during the drop and he sent with them a note addressed to General Taylor, commander of the US 101st Airborne Division against whom he had fought in Normandy. It said, 'please treat my jump casualties as well as my regiment has treated casualties of your division'.[5] In reality his opponents were the men of the US 1st Infantry Division.

The following day more Americans were captured but they were also released. Von der Heydte and his force spent four days watching elements of three American divisions rumble south across the Hautes Fagnes along the very road they were supposed to have cut. These were the US 7th Armored and the 1st and 30th Infantry, but there was no way he could relay this very useful intelligence to headquarters. Lieutenant Kayser was all for attacking the convoys but von der Heydte would hear none of it. 'Attack ... with three hundred men,' he replied shaking his head, 'and no heavy weapons?'[6] He appreciated that if they provoked the Americans they would soon be dive-bombed and overrun. Worryingly they could not hear any fighting, except for the sounds of artillery fire coming from the direction of Elsenbron. The promised Jagdtigers never made it beyond the railhead in the northern reaches of the Eifel thanks to American bombing.

The men of Operation *Hawk* by this stage had eaten all their meagre rations and barely had any ammunition left. All they could do was sit about freezing to death. The Luftwaffe made another feeble attempt to help them. A Ju 88 bomber spotted some of the paratroopers and dropped a wooden food container known as an Essenbomb. Some of the hungry men raced to it, tearing open the lid. Their joy turned to disappointment when they found no food but rather cigarettes and bottles of cognac, which would do little to alleviate their rumbling stomachs. On the fourth day it was decided to move east towards Monschau in the hope of reaching the German advance. Von der Heydte was beginning to feel weak as he had not eaten since before the jump. His clumsy landing ensured that his bad arm was hurting like fury and he was concerned that he might have frostbite in his feet.

The following morning the battle group, frozen and soaking wet after wading through the chest-deep Helle River, bumped into American infantry supported by tanks. The Americans were holding the nearby high ground and the paratroopers quickly suffered several casualties. Taking stock, von der Heydte sent out patrols to see if there was a way round the enemy positions, but they found all routes blocked by American armour. The Americans were slowly closing in on them and it would only be a matter of time before they were trapped and annihilated. 'Faced with this situation and with the ever-decreasing fighting strength of my hungry shivering men,' observed von der Heydte, 'I decided at noon on 20 December to disband the task force.'[7] They withdrew once more deep into the woods where von der Heydte divided his battle group into small three-man detachments in the hope that some of them at least might get through.

Von der Heydte, leading one of the last groups to depart, which included his executive officer and his orderly, set off through the deep snow and biting wind. They soon met three of his men who wanted to join them, but von der Heydte waved them on, saying, 'Each man must try his own luck at getting through.'[8] Exhausted, the colonel and his two companions stopped at a farmhouse to rest. He instructed them to go on without him as he was only holding them up. Upon reaching Monschau he took shelter in a school teacher's house. If the German offensive had been going to schedule the town should have been in the hands of the 326th Volksgrenadier Division, but instead it was clearly still held by the Americans. Mr Bouschery the local teacher took pity on von der Heydte and guided him into his kitchen to warm up. The unfortunate colonel had pneumonia as well as frostbite.

By now von der Heydte knew that it was hopeless and that there was no chance of getting away, as he was, 'Completely exhausted mentally and physically.'[9] In Normandy he had dramatically given the Americans the slip, but he knew this time there would be no escape. He sent Mr Bouschery's fourteen-year-old son on the morning of 22 December to find the nearest Americans with his offer of surrender. Throughout his airborne career he had always impressed upon his men the ethos of, 'Never surrender ... victory or death ... This is the point of honour.'[10] Colonel von der Heydte was in no fit state to carry on the fight. Shortly after, he became a prisoner of war when Captain Goetcheus and First Lieutenant Langland arrived to collect him. The town was immediately put on lockdown for fear it was harbouring more paratroopers. In the event only about 100 of von der Heydte's men ever reached safety. Von der Heydte's captors noted, 'He is extremely shrewd, speaks fluent English – and as could be expected, he offered only fragmentary information.'[11]

Unbeknown to von der Heydte, Staff Sergeant Willi Renner and other members of the 6th Parachute Regiment were dug in near Obermarch on the Belgian-German border oblivious to Operation *Hawk*. Renner was wounded in the legs while inspecting his company's positions and crawled back to his comrades. 'One of them hauled me across a turnip field and did his knee in,' recalled Renner, 'but we carried on and finally reached the company command post where there was a doctor.'[12] Von der Heydte's old regiment was stuck fighting as 'Stubble-hoppers'. Those men from the 6th who had bravely volunteered to join him were now either dead or captured. It was a miserable end to an illustrious regiment.

Despite the poor performance of the Luftwaffe, as far as von der Heydte was concerned his failure was down to Sepp Dietrich. He angrily told his interrogators, 'Dietrich is still a table waiter not fit to lead a German army.'[13] He also held the Reichsführer responsible. 'Army Group commanders now take their orders only from Himmler,' claimed von der Heydte. 'Von Rundstedt is a very old and very sick man. He is Commander-in-Chief in name only.'[14]

Von der Heydte also told his interrogators that his operation had involved 1,200 men. However, all the other prisoners agreed that the battle group only numbered 800–900 men. This led American intelligence to conclude, 'It is very probable that Lieutenant-Colonel von der Heydte was lying deliberately in order to mislead us.'[15] They assessed on 23 December, 'It can be reasonably assumed that in the wide areas of the snow-covered pine woods of Malmedy a number of parachutists with broken legs and collar bones are dying a slow death from starvation, freezing and exhaustion. … What happened to all of the approximately 900 men who jumped, will probably never be known.'[16]

PART FIVE

Race Against Time

15

Victory at St Vith

The St Vith road junction west of the Schnee Eifel was the centre of communications in the northern Ardennes. On 16 December St Vith was some 12 miles behind American lines and was acting as the headquarters for General Jones' US 106th Infantry Division. The town was also host to disparate maintenance and supply units. Unfortunately for the defenders the main routes west for Dietrich's 6th Panzer Army ran just to the north of the town, while those for von Manteuffel's 5th Panzer Army lay to the south. The problem for the Germans striking westward was that they could not bypass the town, as its continued occupation by the Americans would impede the flow of supplies and reinforcements. 'The taking of St Vith was of the same importance to the advance of the right wing of my Army,' explained von Manteuffel, 'as it was for the attack of the left wing of the 6th Panzer Army.'[1]

Once the German 66th Corps was attacking round Jones' northern and southern flanks, and the 1st SS had cut through the Losheim Gap, it was self-evident that St Vith was in danger of being cut off. Jones found his two forward regiments were trapped in the Schnee Eifel and German units were in Setz just four miles to the east. Although the American defenders lacked tanks, they were quickly reinforced by combat commands from both the US 7th and 9th Armored Divisions. The 7th Armored had been first blooded in the fighting in September 1944 near Metz and again in October in the Netherlands. In contrast the 9th Armored had yet to see action. German armoured units involved in the fighting for this town included the 1st SS, 9th SS and the 116th Panzer Divisions.

In Bastogne, General Middleton with 8th Corps instructed Brigadier General Hoge's Combat Command B, from 9th Armored, to move on St Vith. General Gerow's 5th Corps also ordered Brigadier General Robert Hasbrouck's 7th Armored, held in reserve north of Aachen, to make for St Vith. His Combat Commands A and B were soon on their way. Combat Command B, from 9th Armored, found the going tough as the 14-mile route between Vieslam and St Vith was jammed with American forces all retreating west. It was not long before Combat Command B, 9th Armored, along with the 424th Infantry Regiment were fighting to hold back the 62nd Volksgrenadier Division near Steinebrück to the south-east, while the 89th Cavalry Squadron held Wallerode to the north-east. In the meantime, the US 168th Engineer Regiment dug in on the edge of the pine forest just two miles out from St Vith.

Brigadier General Bruce Clarke's Combat Command B, 7th Armored, also suffered at the hands of US rear echelon vehicles clogging up the roads heading westward. In the end divisional commander Hasbrouck had to resort to threatening to barge the vehicles out of the way with his tanks if they did not clear the way. The rest of his division narrowly missed Peiper's panzers fighting south of Stavelot. By nightfall on 17 December St Vith was protected by an American horseshoe-shaped defensive perimeter, which ran from Burg Reuland to the south and Recht to the north-west. The US 17th Tank Battalion was tasked to defend Recht, some five miles from St Vith. The village also acted as the headquarters of Combat Command R, 7th Armored. Remnants of the 14th Cavalry Group, who had been driven back by the German attack through the Losheim Gap, were also in the area.

Defence of the St Vith-Schönberg road sector running north-west to Hünningen was the responsibility of the 87th Cavalry Squadron, 168th Engineers and Combat Command B, 7th Armored. The line to the south of St Vith was protected by Combat Command B, 9th Armored, and the 424th Infantry, which was all that remained of the 106th Infantry Division. Alarmingly, though, the Germans were now pressing to the west of St Vith. At Beho, six miles to the south-west, Combat Command A, 7th Armored, was in action as were the guns of the 16th Armored Field Artillery who were shelling German units heading westward. Colonel Austin Nelson's 112th Infantry Regiment, 28th Division, managed to reach the 424th Infantry and took up position on their right flank near Burg Reuland.

Adolf Hitler, with Reichsmarschall Hermann Göring (left). (Getty Images)

Field Marshal Walther Model, in command of Army Group B, with Hitler. (Getty Images)

Field Marshal Gerd von Rundstedt, CinC West. (Getty Images)

General Hasso von Manteuffel, in charge of 5th Panzer Army. (Getty Images)

Albert Speer, with Josef 'Sepp' Dietrich (right). (Getty Images)

SS-General Dietrich was
appointed to command the
newly forming 6th Panzer
Army. (Getty Images)

SS-Lieutenant Colonel Otto Skorzeny, who created 150th Panzer Brigade. (Getty Images)

SS-Lieutenant Colonel Jochen Peiper was tasked with spearheading the German breakthrough in the Ardennes. (Getty Images)

Colonel Friedrich von der Heydte commanded the ill-fated airborne element of *Watch on the Rhine*. (Getty Images)

Hitler placed great faith in the massive Tiger II to help cut through the American defences in the Ardennes. (Getty Images)

Hitler also hoped his range of new wonder weapons, such as the Me 262 jet fighter-bomber, would help him secure victory. (Getty Images)

Fighter-bombers like the proven Fw 190 took part in Operation *Baseplate*. (Getty Images)

Hitler planned to bombard Antwerp's docks with his V-weapons, including the V-1 flying bomb. (Getty Images)

The V-2 rocket was also used to target Antwerp. (Getty Images)

'Stubble hoppers', or German paras
fighting as infantry, from
3rd Parachute Division. (Getty Images)

Bemused SS officers trying to find a way through the traffic chaos on the second day of the offensive. (Getty Images)

German paratroopers preparing for a drop. Operation *Falcon* proved disastrous. (Getty Images)

American prisoners of war shot in cold blood in the Malmedy area. (Getty Images)

A Panther knocked out in La Gleize, where Battle Group Peiper made its last stand.
(Getty Images)

A German assault gun lost during the fighting at St Vith. (Getty Images)

Allied bombers pounded St Vith into oblivion. (Getty Images)

Cold looking German prisoners captured in the Bastogne area. (Getty Images)

Death and destruction wrought on the streets of Antwerp by a V-2. (Getty Images)

Allied troops and Belgian civilians killed by an indiscriminate V-1 attack. (Getty Images)

Germans killed in the last-ditch attempts to take Bastogne. (Getty Images)

German troops being rounded up by men of the US 4th Armored. (Getty Images)

Frozen German soldiers in early January 1945. (Getty Images)

An abandoned Tiger II on the streets of Stavelot. (Getty Images)

German losses during the Battle of the Bulge included 50,000 captured. (Getty Images)

The makeshift grave of a 'stubble hopper' from 5th Parachute Division found in the woods near Warnach. (Getty Images)

The German attack, however, remained greatly hampered by all the chaos on the routes of advance. It was not until 1400 hours on 18 December that the American northern flank at St Vith was tested when the 2nd SS Panzergrenadiers, supported by assault guns, forced Combat Command R, 7th Armored back to Poteau, two miles to the west. This unit was from the 1st SS Panzer Division and should have been supporting Peiper and his 1st SS Panzer Regiment battle group. Shortly after, the Americans were driven from Poteau. The survivors joined a scratch force known as Task Force Navajo and braced themselves for a third attack. Instead, the German battle group moved northward to try to reach the stranded Peiper at La Gleize. Over the next few days their attempts to get over the Amblève and Salm were thwarted by units of the US 30th Infantry and 82nd Airborne Divisions.

In the meantime, the Germans attempted to cut their way behind St Vith just to the north-west at Hünningen. While the village was only weakly defended with anti-aircraft machine guns and two troops of cavalry, a counter-attack led by Major Leonard Engemann with two companies of Shermans from the 14th Tank Battalion plus a company from the 811th Tank Destroyer Battalion gave the Germans a bloody nose. To the east of St Vith the fire of 275th Armored Artillery helped the 23rd and 38th Armored Infantry Battalions fend off two German attacks. To the south-east the US 9th Armored and 424th Infantry were forced back by Colonel Kittel's 62nd Volksgrenadiers pushing up the road from the Siegfried Line. This placed the Germans within three miles of St Vith. Seven miles to the south-west at Gouvy the 116th Panzer Division was thrusting towards Houffalize, which lay north-east of Bastogne.

In the afternoon of 18 December Combat Command A, 7th Armored, fought to retake Poteau. By nightfall the 48th Armored Infantry and 40th Tanks were in possession. However, the situation at St Vith did not look good. German armour was at Trois-Ponts, ten miles to the north-west, and had got past Gouvy ten miles to the south-west. On the 19th the Germans probed the Americans' perimeter. Field Marshal Model and General von Manteuffel were fed up with the delay and descended on the 66th Corps commander, General Lucht, and Colonel Hoffmann-Schönborn, commander of the 18th Volksgrenadier Division, gathered at Wallerode Mill at midday on 19 December. Model was not happy that the junction between the 5th and 6th Panzer Armies was proving to be such a problem and was causing friction with the Waffen-SS. Lucht was told in no uncertain terms to take St Vith as soon as possible.[8]

'It has to be taken fast. It's a stumbling block to my whole offensive,' grumbled Model to his commanders.[2] 'I know,' agreed von Manteuffel, looking at General Lucht. 'Encircle the town,' he ordered. 'Put your heaviest weight on the north and south. And do it fast.'[3] Lucht nodded but knew the Americans were not going to give up the place without a fight. 'We've got to have St Vith within twenty-four hours,' demanded Model. 'Dietrich is making complaints all the way back to the Wolf's Lair. He says even his 1st SS Panzer Division is being tied up because of the road jam.'[4]

This was too much for Lucht, who knew whose fault the delay was. 'Dietrich!' he exclaimed angrily. 'His people have been using my roads since yesterday. How can I mount an attack with him fouling up my rear? Yesterday I had to go out and personally arrest some of his officers.'[5] Model and von Manteuffel looked furious; nonetheless Lucht ploughed on with his denunciation of the SS. 'This morning,' he said, 'my horse-drawn artillery couldn't get through because Dietrich's people were stealing my roads. And they still are!'[6] 'Kick them off so they stay off,' responded von Manteuffel angrily. 'Without artillery you'll never take St Vith.'[7]

In a fury Model left the mill, exclaiming, 'I'll take care of this.'[8] He stormed out into the road and began directing traffic as if he were a member of the military police. Drivers drove by mouths agape when they realized they were being supervised by a man wearing a field marshal's uniform. 'Model himself directs the traffic,' observed a surprised Lieutenant Behman whose vehicle had got held up. 'He's a little, undistinguished looking man with a monocle. ... The roads are littered with destroyed American vehicles, cars and tanks.'[9] Another source of congestion was the large numbers of American prisoners being marched to the rear.

It was agreed the 18th and 62nd Volksgrenadier Divisions were to be reinforced by Colonel Remer's Führer Begleit Brigade. This consisted of a battalion of panzers, a battalion of assault guns, three panzergrenadier battalions, an artillery battalion and eight flak batteries. It had punched through the Schnee Eifel, causing the surrender of the US 422nd and 423rd Infantry Regiments. Once again traffic jams hampered Model and von Manteuffel's plans. 'This brigade could have been assembled by 19 December in St Vith,' said von Manteuffel. 'The delay in time, which proved decisive, occurred after its departure from the road Schönberg-St Vith to a highly unfavourable area for mobile troops to the north of the road (Wallerode-Meyerode-Born-Emmels).'[10]

Lieutenant Martin Opitz with the 18th Volksgrenadiers recalled in his diary, 'The roads are crowded with advancing columns. Via Prüm we slowly reach Schönberg. Traffic is extremely heavy. Prisoners, and more prisoners.'[11] Hoffmann-Schönborn was only able to attack with his 295th Grenadier Regiment from Wallerode. American artillery fire beat this force off and Hoffmann-Schönborn was badly wounded in the process. To the south-east the 190th Grenadiers, from the 62nd Volksgrenadier Division, ran into the US 27th Armored Infantry at Elcherath and were mown down. Both divisions desperately needed help.

General von Manteuffel observed:

The lack of marching experience of the Führer Begleit Brigade made it impossible for the latter to overcome the difficulties of the roads ... its full fighting power could therefore not be committed. For example, no more than about twenty-five tanks or assault guns out of eighty armoured vehicles of the unit were ever in contact with the enemy.[12]

Late on 20 December Panther tanks from Colonel Remer's 102nd Panzer Battalion probed American defences near Hünningen northwest of St Vith, while Dietrich's 1st SS and 9th SS swung even further west to Recht and Poteau.

American tank destroyers of the 814th Tank Destroyer Battalion were waiting in ambush on a reverse slope for Remer. Just as his tanks crested the rise the Americans fired seven rounds, knocking out four Panthers, which forced Remer to hastily withdraw. The fact that the panzer battalion belonged to the Grossdeutschland Panzer Division caused the Americans some confusion, as it was known that this division was supposed to be on the Eastern Front. Remer, though, was more interested in reaching the Meuse than helping take St Vith. He had decided it was more important to take the crossing over the Salm River at Vielsalm. The following day his panzergrenadiers fought their way through the woods to the west of St Vith. The 105mm self-propelled guns of the US 275th Armored Field Artillery Battalion firing at point-blank range only just stopped them. The survivors then had to retreat through a cordon of American Sherman tanks. This meant that the assault on the town was left to the Volksgrenadiers.

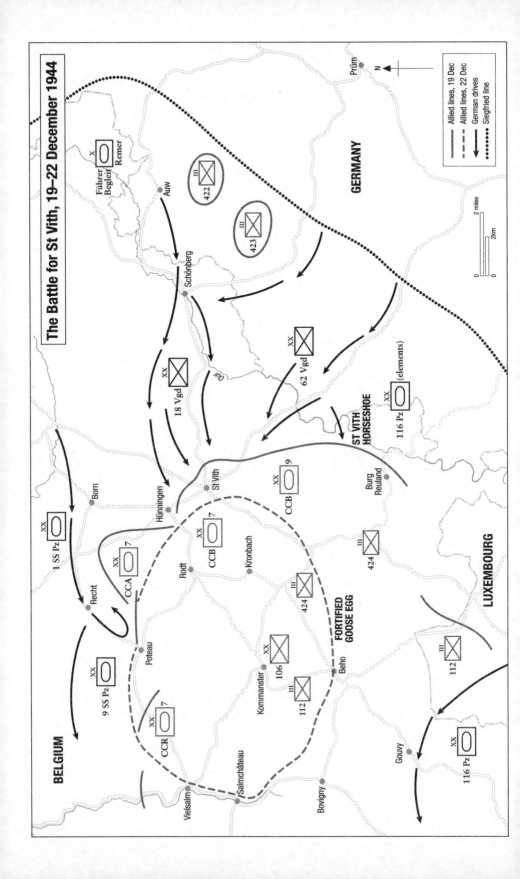

The Battle for St Vith, 19–22 December 1944

GERMANY

Prüm

N

Allied lines, 19 Dec
Allied lines, 22 Dec
German drives
Siegfried line

2 miles
2km

X Führer Begleit Remer

Auw

III 422

III 423

Schönberg

XX 18 Vgd

Our

XX 62 Vgd

XX 116 Pz (elements)

ST VITH HORSESHOE

Born

Hünningen

St Vith

XX 9

XX CCB 9

Burg Reuland

1 SS Pz XX

Recht

XX CCA 7

XX CCB 7

Rodt

Kronbach

III 424

9 SS Pz XX

Poteau

XX CCR 7

Kommanster

XX 106

III 112

Beho

FORTIFIED GOOSE EGG

III 424

III 112

LUXEMBOURG

BELGIUM

Vielsalm

Salmchâteau

Bovigny

Gouvy

XX 116 Pz

German patrols soon discovered that, although the Americans were dug in on the local hills and ridge lines, these defences were not continuous. Furthermore, the Germans were able to advance under the cover of the woods except for when they had to cross open fields. Followed by sustained shelling and rocketing of American positions, units of the two Volksgrenadier divisions began to slowly push in from the east. The defenders were particularly unnerved by the German Nebelwerfers which launched their rockets skyward, that then came crashing down on them. German mortars also joined in with the brutal bombardment.

'The attack on St Vith begins at 1515 after an assault by the engineers,' said Lieutenant Opitz. 'A new division – 62nd Volksgrenadier – passes through.'[13] He also observed, 'During the whole day no enemy airplane.'[14] They were shelled by artillery belonging to the US 7th Armored Division and the 275th Armored Field Artillery Battalion. On the southern flank the attackers came under fire from four tank destroyers supporting the 23rd Armored Infantry Battalion, which having expended all their high explosives resorted to using armour-piercing on the Volksgrenadiers. Seemingly undeterred, the Germans pressed home their attacks for over an hour and a half. They targeted American machine gun positions using stick grenades and Panzerfausts. Every time a new crew moved to take over, they too were killed. When the attackers infiltrated the positions of B Company, 48th Armored Infantry Battalion, they were able to capture and then drive off with 20 American half-tracks.

The arrival of six Tiger tanks from the 506th Heavy Panzer Battalion rapidly resulted in the destruction of five American tanks. The Tigers then turned their machine guns on the foxholes full of American infantry. The defenders had little choice but to give ground. The supporting Volksgrenadiers jumped on board the Tigers and by nightfall they were in town. With their forward companies completely overrun, the Americans had no choice but to set up a new defensive line in the shape of a goose egg to the west of St Vith formed around the villages of Kommanster and Kronbach. The American withdrawal carried out under the cover of a snowstorm was ironically helped by the poor roads which slowed the German pursuit. The chaos that the German advance experienced in the Losheim Gap and at Schönberg was repeated once more. When the German columns rolled into St Vith there was an almighty traffic snarl up. This was particularly the case on the southern approaches at the traffic circle near the former American headquarters in St Joseph's Kloster.

The three regiments of the 18th Volksgrenadiers and a regiment from the 62nd Volksgrenadiers surged into the town, eagerly looking to get out of the cold weather and loot anything the Americans had left behind. Officers and NCOs became exasperated as their men disappeared into the side streets on what was described as 'a kind of scavenger hunt'.[15] To add to the confusion units from 6th Panzer Army trying to avoid the jams in the Losheim Gap also arrived. Model, hoping to view St Vith, had to get out of his staff car and walk in on foot. It was hardly the triumphant entrance he had hoped for. 'Roads are still clogged, but traffic continues,' observed Lieutenant Behman. 'Vehicles are almost exclusively captured American equipment. It was a tremendous haul. St Vith has fallen.'[16]

Lieutenant Opitz noted, 'We move to St Vith and are billeted with a German family. The women sleep in a cellar and we have a room upstairs.'[17] He and his men soon moved into the cellar once the intensity of the Allied air attacks began to increase. 'Two bombs land close by,' he recorded, 'but nothing happens.'[18] The presence of the 18th Volksgrenadiers in St Vith seems to have been contrary to orders. 'St Vith was not to be occupied,' said Dietrich's chief of staff Fritz Krämer, 'because strong enemy air raids on this town were expected as soon as the weather changed. An engineer construction battalion was brought to St Vith, in order to secure the passage or the outflanking of this town.'[19]

Remer's men meanwhile were almost in Rodt to the north of Hünningen on the road to Poteau and Vielsalm. His brigade occupied the local high ground, which forced the Americans from Rodt. The presence of 9th SS Panzer at Porteau forced another retreat. By now the two Combat Command Bs from both the 7th and 9th Armored Divisions had lost half their Shermans and the surviving crews were exhausted. The combat command from 7th Armored had suffered almost 1,000 casualties. Likewise, the armored infantry battalions had endured heavy losses as had the 424th Infantry.

General Hasbrouck at Vielsalm signalled General Ridgway, his new corps commander, suggesting they redeploy their defences beyond the Salm. By dark on 23 December all his men had got over the Vielsalm bridge and were west of the river, which was held by the 82nd Airborne Division. In the meantime, the 62nd Volksgrenadiers swung south of St Vith and westward towards Salmchâteau to the south of Vielsalm, while the 9th SS moved west of Porteau and south towards Vielsalm. The battle for St Vith had cost the Americans about 5,000 men killed, wounded or captured. However, some 15,000 soldiers plus 100 tanks and most of their artillery had escaped the clutches of the Germans.

On Christmas Day, just as Krämer had predicted, 100 bombers from the US 9th Air Force pounded St Vith, flattening much of the town and causing huge clouds of dust and smoke to rise hundreds of feet into the air. 'I become from afar witness of the US bomber attack on St Vith,' recalled Staff Sergeant Laun. 'The forest forms a sound-proof wall against the rumbling detonation of the bombs, but thick smoke indicates that 6km [four miles] in front of me a town is dying by being disembowelled. ... How often have I witnessed such a modern Pompei.'[20]

Crucially the Americans had held up General Lucht's corps for a week and in doing so mauled the 18th and 62nd Volksgrenadier Divisions, as well as stopping the expansion of the gap formed by Peiper's lost battle group. 'There is no doubt,' complained von Manteuffel, 'that an attack properly carried out by the Führer Begleit Brigade on 18 and 19 December would have decided the issue of the battle at the left flank of the 6th Panzer Army.'[21] Once more valuable time had been lost.

Stalled at Bastogne

While the battle for St Vith was underway, further south fighting commenced for the other important road junction located at Bastogne. The Germans had to capture this quickly if they were to continue their surge westward. On 16 and 17 December they had successfully destroyed the US 28th Division's 110th Infantry Regiment and driven back its other two regiments to the north and south. General Middleton, the commander of the US 8th Corps in Bastogne, only had the Combat Command Reserve, US 9th Armored and two engineer regiments with which to hold up the panzers. It looked as if Bastogne would fall quickly. However, Middleton defiantly prepared to hold his ground.

By 18 December two American engineer battalions had taken up positions on the roads into Bastogne from the north-east, east and south-east. Early that day US Task Force Rose at Lallange came up against the 2nd Panzer Division's reconnaissance battalion. Shortly afterwards it was surrounded by Panzer IVs and Panthers of the 3rd Panzer Regiment and wiped out. That afternoon the Germans reached Allerborn, overwhelmed the defenders there and reached Longvilly. This, though, was defended by a scratch force supported by four tank destroyers and 105mm howitzers.

To try to help out Colonel Roberts with Combat Command B, US 10th Armored Division sent three armoured infantry groups designated Cherry, Desbry and O'Hara to the east of Bastogne. In the evening Team Cherry, comprising Shermans of Company A, 3rd Tank Battalion, some light tanks, Company C of the 20th Armored

Infantry plus a reconnaissance platoon of the 90th Cavalry, took up positions on the high ground just to the west of Longvilly. That night the Germans captured the village of Mageret to the west of Longvilly, cutting the main road into Bastogne. At 1140 hours the defenders of Longvilly began to withdraw through Team Cherry only to find the road blocked at Mageret, which the Germans had secured by 0200 hours. Team commander Lieutenant Colonel Cherry at his headquarters in Neffe Château to the west of Mageret was now unable to reach his men.

While the 2nd Panzer Division swung north of Bastogne a screen of anti-tank guns was left to protect its flank from the Americans still at Longvilly. To the left of 2nd Panzer, Bayerlein's Panzer Lehr had reached Niederwampach by 18 December. Here the poor roads and the horse-drawn transport of Kokott's 26th Volksgrenadiers held him up. Although Bayerlein's battle group, comprising 15 Panthers and a battalion of the 902nd Panzergrenadier Regiment, took Mageret, he was alarmed to learn that large numbers of Americans were still at Longvilly to the east of him. Bayerlein had no choice but to leave three panzers and some infantry as a blocking force behind him. Precious time was wasted. It was not until 0530 hours that he continued west towards Neffe. Outside the village one of his Panthers hit a mine and the road had to be cleared; in the meantime his panzergrenadiers attacked Colonel Cherry's command post. Bayerlein's tanks had got to Neffe station by 0700 hours, but they stayed there inexplicably for over an hour.

When the panzers finally rolled forward again it was at this stage they met Colonel Julian Ewell's US 501st Parachute Infantry Regiment, from the US 101st Airborne Division. He had been ordered to march east of Bastogne, locate the enemy and hold them. They successfully moved into Bizory, to the north of Neffe, with Mont to the south-west. The paratroops also got to Wardin to link up with Team O'Hara, but that day, in the afternoon of 19 December, seven Panzer IVs and elements of the 26th Volksgrenadiers drove them back to Mont.

Nonetheless, Bayerlein and Kokott were troubled by the gathering organized resistance at Bizory, Neffe and Mont as well as the continued American presence at Longvilly. Instead of pressing on, Bayerlein decided to destroy the American convoy on the road between Mageret and Longvilly. At the same time Team Cherry tried to break through the enemy, losing 175 men, 17 tanks and 17 half-tracks. Just a handful of men reached Bizory. At Neffe Château Colonel Cherry and his men held out until the evening, but with the building on fire he withdrew with the 501st Parachute Infantry towards Bastogne.

To the north the reconnaissance battalion of 2nd Panzer ran into men from Team Desobry at Bourcy at 0530 hours on 19 December. After a 20-minute firefight the Germans withdrew and the Americans redeployed westward to Noville five miles north-east of Bastogne. There, under Major William Desobry, was the 20th Armored Infantry Battalion (though his Companies A and C were with Cherry and O'Hara) supported by a number of other units that included 15 Shermans and a platoon of light tanks. Desobry had arrived at the village of Noville at 2300 hours on 18 December.

Looping north of Noville, 2nd Panzer cut the Houffalize road, knocking out two Shermans. At 0830 hours two Tiger tanks loomed out of the fog but were met by a hail of American fire from a Sherman, bazookas and a 57mm anti-tank gun. Both tanks were knocked out but the Germans then began firing from the west. When the fog cleared at 1030 hours the Americans saw 30 panzers in the open ground between Bourcy and Noville; another 14 could be seen to the south. Desobry, reinforced by a platoon of tank destroyers, managed to knock out nine German tanks and a shaken 2nd Panzer withdrew.

When Desobry requested permission to retreat to Foy he was reinforced by a battalion of paratroopers. Three companies of the latter counter-attacked towards the high ground to the east and north of Noville supported by Desobry's tanks. The Germans were waiting in anticipation of such a move. Only one American company reached their objective before being driven back to Noville. Reinforced by tank destroyers of the 2nd Platoon, Company C, US 705th Tank Destroyer Battalion, the defenders ensured they inflicted a heavy toll on the approaching enemy armour. Unfortunately, Desobry was severely wounded and the paratroop commander, Lieutenant Colonel James La Prade, was killed by an 88mm after shrapnel cut through their command post.

General von Lüttwitz and his 47th Panzer Corps were frustrated at every turn. While the 2nd Panzer Division was stalled by the American defence at Noville, the Panzer Lehr and 26th Volksgrenadiers had failed to get round or even penetrate Bastogne's defences. In order to press on westward only part of Panzer Lehr was to help the 26th Volksgrenadiers to take Bastogne.

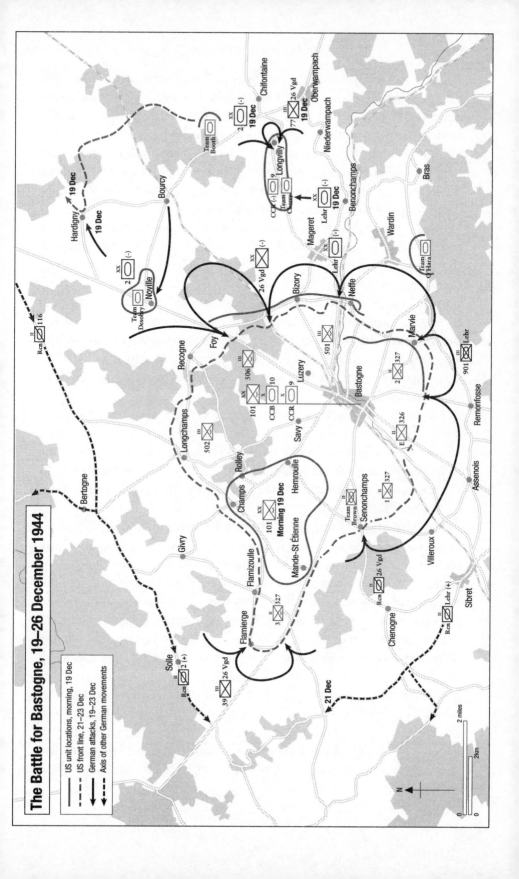

The Battle for Bastogne, 19–26 December 1944

— US unit locations, morning, 19 Dec
-·-·- US front line, 21–23 Dec
→ German attacks, 19–23 Dec
⇢ Axis of other German movements

Chifontaine
Oberwampach
Niederwampach
Benonchamps
Bras
Wardin
Magaret
Bourcy
Hardigny
19 Dec
19 Dec
Noville
Team Booth
Longvilly
Team Desobry
CCR (–)
Team O'Hara
Lehr (–)
Lehr
Foy
Recogne
Bizory
Neffe
Marvie
Longchamps
Luzery
Bastogne
Remonfosse
Assenois
Rolley
Savy
Champs
Hemroulle
Senonchamps
Team Brown
Villeroux
Givry
Flamizoulle
Mande-St Étienne
Morning 19 Dec
Sibret
Bertogne
Flamierge
Chenogne
Solle
21 Dec
19 Dec

2 (–)
26 Vgd
77
9
Team Cherry
CCR (–)
506
501
502
101 CCB 10 CCR 9
2 327
326 E
901 Lehr
327
327 1
3 327
26 Vgd
39 26 Vgd
2 (+) Rcn
Rcn 116
Rcn 26 Vgd
Rcn 1 Lehr (+)
101
2 (–)
26 Vgd (–)

0   2 miles
0   2 km

N

Early 20 December was again foggy and the Germans surprised the defenders of Noville. At 0730 hours two Panzer IVs rumbled south down the Houffalize road and into the village. The Americans, though, were swift to react and a Sherman supported by bazooka fire knocked out both tanks. What followed was a series of uncoordinated German tank and infantry attacks that were all beaten off. When the fog lifted the defenders were presented with the spectacle of 15 panzers and supporting infantry attacking from the south.

The American tank destroyers armed with 90mm guns knocked out four of the panzers, but a fifth, in the shape of a Tiger, got into the village. A Sherman tank crew dicing with death because their turret had jammed pumped three rounds into the Tiger. To their horror these just bounced off, but they were saved by what seemed to indicate inexperience on the part of the Tiger crew. The lumbering beast backed off and over a jeep, which fouled a track, causing the Tiger to swing round crashing into a half-track and over onto its side. The crew fled on foot and the Americans destroyed the Tiger with a grenade.

Major Robert Harwick, in charge at Noville, was now ordered to fight his way south to Foy. Just outside the village a traffic jam developed which was attacked by the Germans, and confusion reigned as everyone sought to negotiate road blocks created by knocked-out Shermans. In the meantime, the Germans were not only attacking Foy but also Mont, Neffe and Marvie; however, they were driven off.

The ongoing fighting was bitter and often confused. At Marvie, south-east of Bastogne, the defenders were attacked by four panzers and six half-tracks carrying infantry. Team O'Hara's Shermans engaged the enemy tanks, destroying two and driving a third back into the woods to the south-east. The fourth got into the village but was knocked out by a bazooka team. The half-tracks also got into the village and their troops fought men of the US 2nd Battalion, 327th Glider Infantry. The defenders lost five killed and 15 wounded; the Germans suffered 30 dead and 20 captured.

By this stage the US 9th and 10th Armored Divisions had lost 60 tanks, Combat Command R, 9th Armored, had ceased to exist and the 506th's 1st Battalion had lost half its men. The Germans, however, were now critically three days behind schedule and the Americans had successfully reinforced their defence of Bastogne. Many of the American stragglers, especially artillery units, were rounded up, turned about and committed to the town's defence.

On the evening of 20 December, a battalion of the 77th Grenadier Regiment, 26th Volksgrenadiers, attempted to reach Bastogne from the north-east. Although they tried to penetrate a gap between the US 501st and 506th Parachute Infantry, the Germans were cut off, losing 235 men killed or captured. The temperature now fell and it began to snow heavily. In the meantime, the 78th Grenadier Regiment pushed in from the east. Kokott's men also tried to break into Bastogne from the south.

'On the afternoon of 21 December, the reinforced 39th Fusilier Regiment fought its way up to Assenois,' reported Kokott, 'against stubbornly fighting enemy forces and penetrated the southern part of the village.'[1] On the fusiliers' right was the division's Engineer and Replacement Training Battalions, who made contact with the 901st Panzergrenadier Regiment belonging to Panzer Lehr that was positioned between Remoifosse and Marvie. To the left of the fusiliers the 26th Reconnaissance Battalion met stiff resistance at Senonchamps to the south-west of Bastogne. Attempts to reach the Mande-St Etienne road were also brought to a halt. To the east the 78th Grenadiers moved to replace units of Panzer Lehr holding the ground between Neffe and Marvie. The fighting that day cost Kokott up to 350 men killed, wounded or missing. Most of these losses were sustained by his reconnaissance and replacement training battalions.

'The elements of the division surrounding Bastogne in a wide arc,' noted Kokott, 'from Recogne to almost Mande St Etienne – could be supplied only with difficulty.'[2] The wide dispersion of the 26th Volksgrenadiers was not the only problem hampering support for his men; growing Allied air attacks meant supplies that were mostly horse-drawn could only be moved at night. The Doncols-Lutremange road along which most of his supplies had to be hauled was shared with Panzer Lehr and the 5th Parachute Division.

In the meantime, von Manteuffel was desperate to press on westward. 'I went forward myself with Panzer Lehr Division,' he said, 'led it round Bastogne, and pushed on St Hubert on the 21st. The 2nd Panzer Division pushed round the north side of Bastogne.'[3] Even further north of the town, Krüger's 58th Panzer Corps drove through Houffalize and

La Roche; this followed a brief shift to the right to clear resistance holding up the 66th Corps near St Vith.

That evening Kokott received orders that made his heart sink: 'With 2nd Panzer Division and Panzer Lehr Division being successfully on the advance to the west, the overall command for the encirclement front around Bastogne is being passed on to the commander of the 26th Volksgrenadier Division.'[4] He was also told that the 901st Panzergrenadiers would be subordinate to his command along with the 2nd Artillery Battalion of the 766th Volks Artillery Corps. In addition, the 5th Parachute Division was on its way to help out. Fritz Bayerlein was not impressed by the 26th Volksgrenadiers' and his own panzergrenadiers' efforts. 'In the evening of 21 December, 902nd Panzergrenadier resumed its attack on Bastogne from Neffe, but failed again,' he grumbled. 'The attacks of the two infantry regiments of the 26th Volksgrenadier west of Bastogne on the whole were also unsuccessful.'[5] The end result was that valuable time was still being lost and resources tied up.

However, German pressure on the town was starting to take its toll on the defenders. General Anthony McAuliffe, commander of the US 101st Airborne, was beginning to run out of artillery ammunition. By 22 December he was rationed to ten rounds per gun per day. His forward observers were instructed only to call on fire support if there was a serious threat. At this point General von Lüttwitz decided to take matters into his own hands without consulting von Manteuffel. At noon that day four Germans, consisting of an artillery major and a medical unit lieutenant and two enlisted men from Panzer Lehr carrying a white flag, arrived at the positions of Company F, US 327th Glider Infantry, bearing a written ultimatum. 'We are parliamentaries,' announced Lieutenant Hellmuth Henke in perfect English by way of introduction, 'and we want to talk to your officers.'[6] He then conferred with his superior Major Wagner in German, then added, 'We want to talk to your commanding general.'[7] The two German officers were escorted to Captain James F. Adams who contacted his regimental headquarters.

Von Lüttwitz's ultimatum said that there was 'only one possibility to save the encircled USA troops from total annihilation: that is the honourable surrender of the encircled town'.[8] It went on to say that the American garrison commander had two hours in which to make up his mind. If he failed to comply, German artillery would flatten the town and everyone in it. The ultimatum even claimed that von Lüttwitz had massed an entire artillery corps and six anti-aircraft battalions to carry out this task. It also went on to say that any civilian losses would be the garrison commander's fault. This threat was sent to McAuliffe at Heintz Barracks whose famous response was 'Aw, nuts!'[9] This was relayed back to the Germans by Colonel Joseph H. Harper, commander of the 327th, with the explanation that 'nuts' meant 'go to hell'.[10] Henke and the major were dumbfounded. 'I will tell you something else,' warned Harper defiantly, 'if you continue to attack, we will kill every goddamn German that tries to break into this city.'[11] Henke was clearly unmoved and responded, 'We will kill many Americans. This is war.'[12] Henke was then taken aback when Harper added, 'And good luck to you.'[13]

When von Manteuffel discovered what had transpired he was angry because they lacked the artillery to make good von Lüttwitz's threat. Instead, he called in the Luftwaffe to bomb Bastogne. General von Manteuffel was also annoyed at Bayerlein's slow progress. The previous day he had ridden a tank to the approaches of St Hubert far beyond Bastogne. From there it should have been possible to push on north-west to Rochefort and Celles before reaching Dinant on the Meuse. When he arrived at Bayerlein's command post he shouted, 'There's nothing out west. Get your damned people moving!'[14] The problem was that in many places the Americans were defiantly clinging to their positions, clogging up the German lines of communication.

That afternoon McAuliffe received welcome word from 8th Corps that the US 4th Armored Division was fighting its way north to relieve Bastogne. Inside his defensive perimeter the supply staffs scoured local farms, shops and warehouses to boost their meagre food rations. After the 101st Airborne Division's field hospital had been captured on 19 December, the 501st Parachute Infantry's aid station in Bastogne became the main hospital. Wounded were evacuated to the west until 21 December, when the Germans cut the road. Two days later the skies began to clear and German columns were pinpointed by the tracks they left in the snow. Some 250 sorties a day were flown by US fighter-bombers in support of the garrison. 'The Battered Bastards of Bastogne', as the 101st styled themselves, were grateful that they had not been forgotten by the flyboys.

Kokott, despairing of ever taking ruined Bastogne, renewed his pressure. There followed a bitter battle for Marvie, with the Americans almost being driven out. American fighter-bombers harried the retiring

Germans units, but also mistakenly bombed Marvie twice, much to the dismay of the American defenders. Kokott's control of the battle was now rapidly slipping because on his southern flank the German 5th Parachute Division was giving ground to the US 4th Armored. This necessitated him despatching units to help the paratroops.

Kokott was far from happy with the situation:

It is an uncomfortable feeling to have someone launching a drive to your rear. I feared 4th Armored. I knew it was a 'crack' division. I talked to General von Manteuffel on the telephone and told him I could not watch two fronts. He told me to forget 4th Armored, that it was quiet for the moment. The only solution was to attack Bastogne, and devote all my efforts to the attack from the north west.[15]

Kokott switched to attacking Bastogne from the west with Champs, Flamizoulle and Hemroulle as his objectives. At Champs the American 502nd Parachute Infantry fought hand-to-hand with the German 77th Grenadier Regiment. Some 18 German tanks rolled through the positions of the 3rd Battalion, 327th Glider Infantry, and divided into two, with one group heading for Hemroulle and the other north to Rolle. A single Panzer IV made it into Champs where it was pounded into flames by a 57mm anti-tank gun and bazookas. At Hemroulle a lone Panzer IV got into the village and was captured intact.

Team Cherry, part of Combat Command B, 10th Armored Division reserve, was moved out of Bastogne to reinforce the 502nd and 327th, but they and their supporting tank destroyers had already stabilized the situation. All of the German tanks and most of the two infantry battalions committed to the latest attacks had been destroyed, killed or captured. Without capturing Bastogne Hitler's Ardennes offensive was now completely stalled. American defiance there was effectively derailing *Watch on the Rhine*.

Clear Skies

Up until Saturday 23 December, thanks to the weather the bulk of the Luftwaffe and the Allied air forces had been largely grounded. Both sides had managed only minimal sortie rates. That day, though, the sun dramatically burned through the fog and ground mist to reveal a clear blue sky and a snow-shrouded landscape. Major General Peltz knew that this meant Allied fighter-bombers and bombers would soon set about the German ground forces and scrambled his fighters to intercept them. The Luftwaffe would manage 800 combat sorties, but this paled into insignificance against the 3,153 by the Allies. 'Contrary to the Wehrmacht weather forecasters' predictions,' said Colonel Otto Remer, commander of the Führer Begleit Brigade, 'the skies cleared after the first week and the Allied air forces took full advantage.'[1]

Major Fritz Vogelsang, adjutant of the 116th Panzer Division, reported, 'Right away, across the entire western horizon, the countless streaks of white vapour trails moved across the sky, an impressive but scary show. The air is filled with uninterrupted humming. The number of bombers, fighter-bombers, and fighters cannot be counted!'[2] For those Germans who had fought in Normandy, they knew exactly what to expect – relentless and terrifying air attack. At Florennes, Foy-Notre-Dame, Rochefort, Soy and Stavelot they soon came under sustained air strikes.

Around Bastogne the German flak gunners braced themselves for inevitable air attack. 'The first enemy fighter-bombers appeared towards 0900 hours,' noted General Kokott, commander of the

26th Volksgrenadiers, 'swooped down on communication roads and villages and set vehicles and farmyards on fire.'[3] One of the first units on the scene was the US 513th Fighter Squadron, whose P-47 Thunderbolts targeted tanks, troops and guns. They were greeted by the most intense flak they had ever experienced and lost several new pilots.

According to the US 9th Air Force's intelligence, there were about 700 German 20mm quad anti-aircraft guns in the Bastogne area. This seems an implausibly high number and is probably more a reflection of the density of German flak in the Ardennes. Nonetheless, the German Army, knowing that it could not rely on the Luftwaffe, was well equipped with towed and self-propelled anti-aircraft guns. Notably the panzer divisions were protected by the Wirbelwind, consisting of a 20mm quad mounted on the chassis of a Panzer IV, and the Möbelwagen with a single 37mm flak gun also on a Panzer IV. A newer version of the latter known as the Ostwind had also just entered service, but only in very limited numbers. The 1st SS Panzer Division had 16 Wirbelwind and Ostwind, but some of these were on loan from another unit.

Some self-propelled flak guns caught in the open had already been lost during earlier Allied fighter-bomber attacks. For example, several, including a 37mm gun mounted in a half-track and another one on a truck, were destroyed near Lodometz on 18 December. In several instances American troops captured a number of Wirbelwinds intact which had been abandoned due to a lack of fuel and ammunition.

Above Bastogne the air soon became full of Thunderbolts from the 365th Fighter Group. On the ground, as well as their anti-aircraft guns, the Germans shot back with rifles, submachine guns and even pistols. One American pilot recalled, 'the flak tracers were like garden hoses with projectiles arcing lazily through the air towards me'.[4] The main concern of the flak gunners was that they were using up ammunition at an incredible rate and it would be difficult to replace it. The Luftwaffe did what it could to intervene and the sky became full of swirling vapour trails. 'The German air force produced their maximum contribution during the Ardennes offensive,' reported Field Marshal Montgomery's chief of staff, Major General Francis de Guingand. 'In the first place they provided tactical support on a larger scale than had been achieved for many months.'[5]

Despite the efforts of the Luftwaffe, everywhere German troops found it hard to avoid air attack. Tracks left in the snow showed where vehicles were sheltering in barns or under the trees. Trying to hide in the forest often did no good. 'I cannot praise enough the brave young American fliers who went into the Battle of the Ardennes,' wrote American war correspondent John Hall. 'I watched them actually scraping the treetops to search for hiding enemy tank units.'[6]

SS-Second Lieutenant Fritz Langanke with the 2nd SS Panzer Division concealed his Panther in the shadows of a row of conifers. 'Every time the aircraft approached, we felt great anxiety in our panzers,' he recalled. 'The fighter-bombers, flying at a very low altitude, had to pass right overhead and we were never sure if we might be their target. Only when they were directly overhead would we start to breathe again.'[7] Luckily for Langanke the planes were preoccupied by a 37mm flak gun that was firing at them from the sanctuary of a quarry. 'Because of the lay of the terrain, the aircraft could only use a certain path of attack,' observed Langanke. 'The gun fired without hesitation, regardless of how many fighter-bombers showed up. An exemplary action!'[8] Both the anti-aircraft gun and Langanke's tank survived to fight another day.

When members of the 5th Parachute Division began withdrawing on 23 December through Hompré, which was the location of Kokott's command post, they immediately came under air attack. 'Enemy fighter-bombers swooped down on Hompré and pushed their thrusts of fire into the fluctuating and congested mass,' observed Kokott. 'All rifle carriers inside the village and anti-aircraft forces located close by were firing wildly at the planes.' They could do little to ward off their attackers and the effects were devastating. 'Houses caught fire, vehicles were burning,' said Kokott, 'wounded were lying in the streets.'[9] It was a scene of utter destruction.

A column of panzers and half-tracks belonging to the 2nd Panzer Division were caught in a sunken road just south of Celles. They were alerted to impending trouble when a light spotter plane buzzed overhead. Shortly after, RAF Typhoons appeared to deliver a hail storm of rockets. Unable to go forwards or backwards, the trapped column was soon a blazing wreck. On one occasion south-east of Celles, when a German column came under attack by Typhoons they tried to distract them by firing red smoke, indicating an Allied target, onto an American position. The pilots took no notice and continued their air strike. Throughout the bulge German troops had to endure a deluge of bombs, cannon fire and rockets.

Panzer Lehr was not spared either. 'My rear columns were taking severe losses from air attack,' reported General Bayerlein. 'A flak battery was caught on the march and badly cut up. And worse both my tank recovery vehicles were destroyed from the air. ... My tank repair shops were badly bombed.'[10] He had lost 30 panzers during his advance and was now unable to retrieve any of them.

The American 19th Tactical Air Command (TAC), supporting General Patton's US 3rd Army pushing up from the south, flew 493 sorties on 23 December. The Luftwaffe opposed many of these but only managed to shoot down 11 aircraft. They in turn lost 23 aircraft, with the Americans claiming another four probables. The net result was that Patton's fighter-bombers managed to drop 54 tons of high explosive, fragmentation bombs and napalm. They claimed 26 German tanks and armoured vehicles, 250 motor vehicles and 36 gun positions. Unknown to Model and the others, Patton attributed the clear weather to a prayer that he had requested from 3rd Army's chaplain Colonel James O'Neil. As far as Patton was concerned it was divine intervention.

The chaos inflicted on the German advance was far-reaching. 'On the roads our convoys or single motor transport could not move during the day,' said Field Marshal von Rundstedt. 'We could never count on when a certain division would arrive at its destination.'[11] Many German artillery batteries, fearful that they would give away their positions to the roaming fighter-bombers, stopped firing. Major General Karl Thoholte, Model's artillery commander, observed, 'As soon as the enemy air force appeared the effect of the artillery was reduced to fifty or sixty per cent.'[12]

Despite the warming sunshine on the ground, German soldiers were soon missing the bad weather. 'This morning, fighter-bombers and bombers turned La Roche,' noted Major Vogelsang, 'into a smoking pile of rubble. Our anti-aircraft guns were able to shoot down some of the attackers.' Looking up at the clear skies he then cursed, 'If only the weather would turn bad again!'[13] High above them German soldiers in the bulge could see the ominous vapour trails of enemy heavy bombers heading for their homeland.

The 18th Volksgrenadiers in St Vith was temporarily spared. Lieutenant Behmen with the division's artillery regiment recorded in his diary on the 23rd, 'We sight strong bomber formations flying towards Germany. Saw two of them shot down.'[14] The following day he was almost killed: 'Dive bombers attack and hit a house in front of me. Two more metres and it would have been me.'[15]

Hitler had wilfully chosen to ignore the fact that his supply routes supporting those troops thrown into the Ardennes offensive would inevitably become choke points. German communication centres and railheads in the Eifel were targeted. In particular, American bombers hit Bitburg, Nideggen and Prüm. American troops could actually hear trains operating from Prüm, and Bitburg had five roads feeding into it, making them both prime objectives. Although these locations were well defended by flak guns, they did little to deter the enemy from pressing home their attacks. Likewise, the bridges being used to bring German supplies across the Rhine were attacked.

During the day on 23 December, the defenders of Cologne once again found themselves fending off the RAF's Lancaster bombers. However, this was unusual as they normally came at night. The city was an easy target to navigate thanks to the Rhine and the distinctive twin towers of the cathedral. Alongside the latter was Cologne's main railway station and one of the rail bridges over the river. The Gremberg railway marshalling yards and the crossings over the Rhine at Cologne were a key link in Hitler's supply line. When the sirens began to wail and the flak gunners swung into action it soon became apparent the bombers were after the marshalling yards, which were full of supplies for von Rundstedt's forces. The city centre had already been devastated during the Allies' 'Big Week' raids in February 1944, which had claimed the lives of over 4,000 people. Two years before that Cologne had been a victim of a 'Thousand Bomber' raid. Remarkably there were only 500 fatalities on that occasion, though over 5,000 people were injured and 45,000 had been made homeless.

During this latest raid the Luftwaffenhelfer, consisting of 16-year-old school boys, ran to their anti-aircraft guns. After peering skyward, they were soon blazing away with some success. The cloud over Cologne had cleared unexpectedly, giving them a perfect view of their attackers. The Luftwaffe's fighters latched onto the lead Lancaster. Two of the bomber's four engines hit by flak caught on fire and there was fire and smoke in both the bomb bay and the nose. It seemed as if it must fail in delivering its target markers, but the pilot Bob Palmer bravely pressed on. He kept the aircraft on a straight and level course, successfully delivering its bombs before the plane spiralled to earth in flames. A fighter spotted a second burning bomber, which had been hit by flak just after making its bomb run, and raked the cockpit with cannon fire. The stricken bomber crashed into the ground and exploded. The Germans claimed five Lancasters and a Mosquito over the target area, but it was small recompense for the damage caused. The inhabitants of Cologne had no way of knowing that they were caught up in a battle being fought over a hundred miles away in Belgium and Luxembourg.

The following night the bombers returned to hit the rail yards in the industrial district of Cologne-Nippes. German nightfighters and the Luftwaffenhelfer resisted the raid for an hour. Nonetheless, the bombers got through, destroying an ammunition train, four traffic installations and closing a section of line between Cologne-Neuss. The whole of the Nippes marshalling yards' superstructure was destroyed. The damage was such that it would take a week to repair. It was a week that Field Marshals von Rundstedt and Model did not have.

The Nippes railway workshops had been first flattened in 1942 and yet the resilience of the German railways was such that the line was soon up and running again. At the time a disbelieving Göring had accused Josef Grohé, the Gauleiter of Cologne, of lying about the scale of the attack. By 1944 there was no hiding the level of destruction wrought on the once magnificent city along the banks of the Rhine. Miraculously the cathedral remained standing, but only just. The RAF would revisit the Gremberg marshalling yards in the first week of February 1945. Once again the flak was ferocious and once again the RAF deemed the raid a success.

During the course of the war Cologne received almost 29,000 tonnes of bombs and had almost 2,000 acres flattened. Australian war correspondent Chester Wilmot felt the RAF's attacks on the Rhineland were increasingly a waste of time. He wrote, 'in cities like Cologne and Essen there was nothing left to burn, and the blast-bombs, which caused great havoc when the buildings were intact, now did little more than convulse the rubble'.[16] Wilmot, though, failed to fully comprehend that the RAF was not just targeting Hitler's weapons factories. Certainly Field Marshal von Rundstedt and Gauleiter Grohé did not share Wilmot's prognosis.

When the 6th SS Mountain Division passed through the city by train its troops were horrified by the damage. Private Schmidtchen, who came from Cologne, had thrown open the door to his wagon and exclaimed, 'Oh my God! Look! See that? I didn't know it was as bad as that!'[17] His friend Johann Voss pushed his way to the door. 'I remembered towering rear walls of the business and housing districts on both sides of the thoroughfare, but there was total emptiness now,' observed Voss. 'The city of Cologne was gone. Even in the dark we could see that much.'[18]

Ahrweiler, Dahlem, Ehrang, Homburg, Jünkerath and Kaiserslautern were also bombed on 23 December by the Americans to impede von Rundstedt's lines of communication. These raids forced the Luftwaffe to put up large numbers of fighters to defend the towns, resulting in heavy losses on both sides. The Americans also attempted to attack Zülpich or Lommersum. The former was a railhead for Brandenberger's 7th Army. Instead they ended up accidently bombing Malmedy, killing 37 of their own men. These attacks, though, had the desired effect. 'The consequences were disastrous,' lamented von Rundstedt. 'It meant that we could not get supplies or troops forward. ... The deep penetration of heavy bombers east of the Rhine against our communications was painful for moving our troops, our supplies and our fuel.'[19] The Luftwaffe paid a heavy price that day, suffering 98 casualties, comprising 63 pilots killed and 35 wounded. Two days later the RAF and USAAF hit 13 Luftwaffe airfields with mixed results.

The reality was that the Luftwaffe had been losing the bomber war since 1943. Allied technical innovation and developing tactics meant that while the Luftwaffe's losses were steadily rising those of the British and American air forces were going down. For example, between 1 October and 31 December 1944 the RAF only lost 136 bombers out of 14,254 sorties flown. During the same period the US 8th Air Force managed a staggering 66,294 sorties against Germany and the occupied territories with the loss of 618 aircraft.

General Josef 'Beppo' Schmid, the Luftwaffe's Commander-in-Chief in the West, was furious that Germany's fighter forces were failing. 'I am astonished that in spite of pains, admonitions, and orders throughout the whole year,' he said, 'I have not succeeded in bringing the fighter divisions at least to a point of being able to distinguish in what strength and in what direction the enemy is approaching. In my view there is no excuse whatever for this failure.'[20] However, he had no one to blame but himself. Nonetheless, the loss of 27 Allied bombers on 31 December showed that the Luftwaffe should not be underestimated or written off.

The clear skies on 23 and 24 December enabled the Americans to drop 244 tons of supplies to the hard-pressed garrison at Bastogne. This arrived in the nick of time as the American artillery battalions defending the town were down to their last rounds. It had become a question of whether relief would arrive before the ammunition ran out. Model had no idea how close he had come to overwhelming Bastogne. Despite the deteriorating weather, further supplies were dropped and brought in by glider over the next two days.

General Kokott received a warning at midday on 23 December, which simply stated: 'Attention! Strong enemy formation flying in from west!'[21] When he first saw large aircraft escorted by fighters, he feared they were going to be carpet bombed. Anti-aircraft gunners in the Clochimont, Sibret and Salvacourt areas were relieved when the 'bombers' turned off as they approached Bastogne. They then watched as parachutes billowed out from behind American C-47 transport planes, spreading their cargoes over a wide area. 'In a short time,' recalled Kokott, 'the sky was covered with a multitude of cargo chutes, dangling slowly to the ground.'[22] The pilots flew low and steady past an old cemetery on the outskirts of Bastogne using a drop zone marked by airborne pathfinder teams.

To some Germans, including Kokott, it looked as if the planes were bringing in airborne reinforcements. At Hompré a flak battery, which had been blazing away at enemy fighter-bombers, was now ordered to 'about face' and prepare to repel enemy armour or enemy paratroopers. Kokott and the others could only curse the Luftwaffe for failing to stop these resupply flights. 'Not a single German aircraft could be seen in the skies!' he noted bitterly.[23] The Luftwaffe tried to intervene but were swiftly chased off.

The German units gathered around the town opened up on the resupply flights with 37mm and 20mm flak guns as well as machine guns and caused some losses. One C-47 pilot, after his aircraft was hit by 20mm anti-aircraft fire, successfully made a forced landing near Bastogne. The vital stores he was carrying were swiftly retrieved by the garrison. The Germans discovered those planes shot down between Chenogne and Hompré were carrying artillery ammunition and medical supplies. Some 19 aircraft were brought down and 50 badly damaged. However, the daily sight of these massed formations of transport aircraft was a sobering demonstration of America's military might. Furthermore, frozen German soldiers regularly found themselves under attack by the fighter-bombers escorting the transports. 'The results of this resupply and simultaneous reinforcement of the fighting strength by paratrooper units were felt by the German forces after only a few hours,' noted Karl Wortmann, commanding a flakpanzer with the 1st SS.[24]

The Luftwaffe retaliated by conducting a series of night attacks on Bastogne. On Christmas Eve, Ju 88 bombers flew over the town dropping flares to illuminate their intended targets. The bombers then tried to destroy the railroad overpass near the Heintz Barracks. The flak was minimal because the Americans had deployed their anti-aircraft guns in a ground support role on the perimeter. Bombs fell on an American hospital, killing 20 wounded trapped in the building. The Hotel Lebrun, the command post of the US 10th Armored Division, was also hit, inflicting casualties. At least one plane made two strafing runs and machine-gunned the streets. This raid was followed by a second similar attack. In total the Luftwaffe managed to drop about two tons of bombs and by morning the buildings around Bastogne's main square had been gutted by the explosives and resulting fires. The Luftwaffe returned once more on 29 December, delivering deadly 'Butterfly' bomblets. This was followed by an even bigger and thoroughly pointless raid the following night.

By the evening of 23 December von Manteuffel's tanks had stalled just four miles from Dinant. Although the Germans had control of two good east-west roads, thanks to the clearing weather they were under continual heavy attack by Allied aircraft. It was the very situation that Hitler's generals had feared from the beginning. Despite its best efforts the Luftwaffe could not cope, although it managed 600 sorties on Christmas Day. By that stage General Richard Metz, von Manteuffel's chief artillery officer, was warning that moving ammunition was increasingly a problem. Thanks to the clear weather and Allied fighter-bombers, 'the available transport area was from now on measurably smaller'.[25] The attacks on the trains was also causing him difficulties. 'In this connection,' he added, 'there also existed a tense transport situation to the Ardennes front.'[26]

The Luftwaffe continued to target Patton's troops in an effort to stop them reaching Bastogne. It launched 94 attacks on the US 3rd Army involving 143 aircraft on 24 December. American anti-aircraft gunners were waiting for them, shooting down 17 aircraft and damaging another six. The following day the Luftwaffe managed to send 103 planes against 3rd Army, but 22 were lost to American fighters and flak. In total the 19th TAC flew 1,157 sorties on Christmas Day and Boxing Day and in that time claimed 108 tanks and other armoured vehicles as well as 1,160 motor vehicles. They also hit three marshalling yards. The Luftwaffe lost 15 aircraft and 11 damaged. At the end of the month 19th TAC began systematically targeting German railways, destroying 78 trains, 861 railroad cars and nine marshalling yards. Although the German forces in the bulge were slowly being strangled the fighting was far from over. 'Things started to turn very bad for us in the Ardennes,' said Hans Behrens with the 9th Panzer Division. 'We suffered great losses. It was very, very cold. Food was becoming difficult, so was fuel.'[27]

PART SIX

Here Come the Americans

Almost to the Meuse

Hitler's assumption was that in the face of the panzers American units would flee or surrender. In some cases, this happened, but crucially not enough to tilt the battle. Hitler's generals could have done without the distractions caused by determined American resistance at St Vith and Bastogne. Their goal was always the Meuse and beyond, but instead they were bogged down by the frustrating battles for the key road junctions. They had grossly underestimated how long this would take and the constant need to keep feeding troops into localized battles.

While the fighting was still going on around Bastogne, Colonel Meinrad von Lauchert's 2nd Panzer Division was ordered to concentrate on the Meuse. His division, although it had suffered heavy losses in Normandy and been subsequently reorganized, still had many veterans in its ranks and was equipped with over 100 tanks and assault guns. On 23 December the vanguard battalion of the 304th Panzergrenadier Regiment overwhelmed the US 4th Cavalry Group at Harsin and by nightfall was at Hargimont.

On von Lauchert's right von Waldenburg's 116th Panzer Division found Houffalize undefended and its reconnaissance battalion reached Bertogne and Salle to the south-west, seeking a crossing over the Ourthe. American engineer and tank destroyer units thwarted them by blowing the bridges. This caused General Krüger, commander of 58th Panzer Corps, to instruct the 116th Panzer to get over the Ourthe at Houffalize and strike north-westward. This did the Americans a big favour as the original route was not well defended, whereas the panzers were now on a collision course with the US 3rd Armored and 82nd Airborne Divisions.

By noon on 20 December both the 116th Panzer and 560th Volksgrenadier Divisions were north of the Ourthe and heading for Samrée and Rochefort. Both towns were defended by supply units of the US 7th Armored Division who were swiftly driven out. In Samrée the 116th got their hands on 15,000 rations along with 25,000 gallons of petrol. This windfall was welcome and enabled von Waldenburg to refuel his vehicles. A counter-attack by Task Force Tucker, from 3rd Armored's Combat Command A, was driven off with the loss of half a dozen Shermans. Two Shermans and a tank destroyer were also lost in the Samrée area.

In the Germans' path lay Hotton on the Ourthe, which was defended by 200 men from the 3rd Armored and a platoon from the 51st Engineers. They were supported by just one 37mm anti-tank gun, two medium tanks, two light tanks and two 40mm anti-aircraft guns. American reinforcements from Soy to the east helped beat off the attack, though German armour got into Hotton, where the Americans knocked out three tanks including a Panther. Resistance at Hotton convinced Krüger that he could not get to the Meuse via this route. He decided to withdraw to Roche, cross the Ourthe and move on Marche to the west.

On his right Lammerding's 2nd SS Panzer Division was to strike for Manhay, which posed a threat to American defences stretched from Hotton eastward to Trois-Ponts. This 25-mile front was only thinly held by the 82nd Airborne and 3rd Armored Divisions. The key point was the junction between the two American divisions at the Baraque de Fraiture crossroads south of Manhay. On the morning of 21 December, the American defenders drove off a patrol from Rudolf Langhauser's 560th Volksgrenadiers; they also captured an officer from the 2nd SS who was scouting a route for the panzers. The division was just nine miles to the south waiting for fuel. Not long afterwards, men of the 4th SS Panzergrenadier Regiment supported by some tanks moved north of Baraque de Fraiture and cut the road to Manhay. In the process they captured four tank destroyers from the US 643rd Battalion, 3rd Armored, that were heading for the crossroads. On 23 December the Germans attacked Fraiture, just to the north-east, which was held by the US 325th Glider Infantry, and were driven off.

In the meantime, the Germans began shelling the crossroads. Then two panzer companies and two panzergrenadier battalions fell on the defenders. Although defence of the crossroads was reinforced by three Shermans, Captain Junior Woodruff with Company F, 2nd Battalion, 325th Gilder Infantry, asked to pull out at 1700 hours as their situation was precarious. Permission was denied and his men were overrun an hour later. Just 44 of Company F's 116 men reached Fraiture. One of the panzer companies under the command of SS-Lieutenant Horst Gresiak claimed 17 enemy tanks that day. By about 2200 hours the US 7th Armored Division was withdrawing north-west of Baraque de Fraiture to Malempré. During their retreat SS-Master Sergeant Frauscher, commanding two Panther tanks from the 2nd SS, slipped into an American armoured column unnoticed in the darkness. They then swung back out and opened fire, destroying nine trapped Shermans in the process.

The American position now looked quite critical as the 2nd SS were threatening Manhay and the 116th Panzer were moving on Marche and Hotton. To the south 2nd Panzer was pressing for the Meuse. By the evening of 22 December, von Lauchert's 2nd Reconnaissance Battalion was just four miles from the river, having reached Celles to the east of Dinant. They were tantalizingly close to their first major objective. In reality, though, the Germans were horribly overextended and had exposed their lines of communication. Fuel supplies were also a constant worry.

Certainly, elsewhere things were not going so well for the Germans. To the south-east of 2nd Panzer, Bayerlein's Panzer Lehr Division had taken until Christmas Eve to secure Rochefort. On the northern shoulder of the German bulge, SS-Colonel Hugo Kraas' 12th SS Panzer Division had failed to break through the US 5th Corps. This stopped the Germans from widening the breach created by the 1st SS. Only now were the 2nd SS and 9th SS Panzer Divisions able to get forward, but it was much too late.

'I telephoned Jodl,' said von Manteuffel, 'and asked him to tell the Führer that I was going to withdraw my advanced forces out of the nose of the salient we had made – to the line La Roche-Bastogne. But Hitler forbade this step back.'[1] It was a blow as von Manteuffel was increasingly fearful that an Allied counteroffensive on either side of the salient would cut off both panzer armies. 'So instead of withdrawing in time,' lamented von Manteuffel, 'we were driven back bit by bit under pressure of the Allied attacks, suffering needlessly heavy casualties.'[2]

The danger for the Americans, though, was far from past. The German threat to the Meuse remained, as did the threat in the north with the commitment of the 2nd SS and 9th SS Panzers supported by the 560th Volksgrenadiers. In the north, controversially, Field Marshal Montgomery had been given temporary command of the US 1st Army, 5th, 7th and 18th Corps. General Ridgway, commanding the latter, was not happy when Montgomery ordered the US 82nd Airborne to withdraw from their Vielsalm salient to a shorter line through Bras to Manhay. The Germans had their sights set on Manhay. Lammerding's 2nd SS was to take the town then turn west to Érezée via Grandménil to link up with Langhauser's 560th Volksgrenadiers.

On Christmas Eve, at 2200 hours, Panthers and Panzer IVs led by a captured Sherman from 2nd SS Panzer moved along the road to Manhay. 'Bright moonlight flooded the Ardennes landscape covered in deep snow,' recalled panzer ace SS-Technical Sergeant Ernst Barkmann commanding Panther 401. 'Above us a full moon in a clear starry night unveiled all the contours ahead. Everything was going according to plan.'[3] The highly decorated Barkmann was a veteran of the Eastern Front and Normandy, who along with his unit the 2nd SS Panzer Regiment had re-equipped with the Panther in early 1944. The experiences of Barkmann and his crew in the Ardennes were typical of the confused and chaotic nature of the fighting there. While experience was invaluable, luck also played its part.

The Americans hesitated because elements of the US 3rd and 7th Armored Divisions were holding the line Trois-Ponts-Manhay-Hotton so there were concerns about friendly fire. Panzergrenadiers armed with Panzerfausts swiftly destroyed four Shermans and severely damaged two others. Two Panthers received direct hits but the rest of the column sped through the broken American positions. At this point Barkmann got lost and drove alone onto Highway N15. In the darkness Barkmann, thinking his comrades were in front of him, pressed on. Some 50 yards ahead and to the right he saw a tank with its commander standing in the turret. Assuming it was from the 2nd SS, Barkmann drew up to the left-hand side of the tank. Instructing his driver to kill the engine, he removed his radio headset. At that point the other commander dropped into his tank and slammed the hatch shut. Then the driver's hatch popped open on the other tank and Barkmann noticed the instrument panel light was not the same as a Panther's (wine red rather than green).

Realizing it was an American-crewed Sherman, he instantly ordered his crew to fire. The gunner quickly traversed only to catch the L/70 gun barrel on the enemy's turret with a loud clang. The impact jammed Barkmann's turret. The quick-thinking driver started the engine and backed up a few yards and the gunner slammed a round into the rear of the Sherman. Rumbling past the burning enemy tank, Barkmann spotted two more Shermans coming from the forest on the right of the road. These were also dealt with in quick succession. 'When everything remained quiet,' said Barkmann, 'we slowly increased our speed. The trees thinned out. Then suddenly, in front of us was a large open area bordered by woods.'[4]

Rounding a large S-bend, Barkmann ran into nine partially dug-in American tanks. 'All aimed the muzzles of their barrels threateningly at our Panzer,' said Barkmann.[5] He knew that to stop would be suicide, so he ordered his driver to press through them and for some reason the enemy tanks did not engage. Instead the American crews bailed out. 'Only bluffing could have saved us,' added Barkmann.[6] His Panther reached Manhay only to be confronted by three Shermans coming from the direction he needed to take towards Grandménil and Érezée. Heading north-west, he rumbled past yet more enemy tanks that were parked with their crews dismounted. The Americans watched as a Panther roared by, then waking to the danger leapt into their tanks, but as they were nose to tail they could not target Barkmann. The Panther's crew hastily threw out a smoke bomb to cover their escape. Barkmann estimated they passed more than 80 enemy tanks, having stumbled into the assembly area for the US 7th Armored Division, as well as the US 82nd Airborne and 75th Infantry Divisions.

The chaos, though, did not end. An American jeep promptly ran headlong into Barkmann's Panther which crushed it, but in doing so crashed into a stationary Sherman. The Panther's drive sprocket became entangled in the Sherman's tracks and its engine stalled. The driver restarted the engine and backed up, successfully freeing the Panther. It rolled on past more American vehicles and equipment, but now with growing numbers of Shermans giving chase. Barkmann coolly traversed his turret and knocked out the lead tank; by doing this several times he closed off the road behind him. Barkmann and his men finally took shelter in the forest and calmly dismounted to take the morning air and marvel at their quite remarkable luck. At such close quarters Panther 401 should have been destroyed numerous times. 'I saw grinning faces,' Barkmann said of his crew. 'Everything had worked out well once again.'[7]

As they stood about they could hear Panthers firing from the direction of Manhay. Retracing his steps to re-join their company, Barkmann counted 20 American tanks that had surrendered. 'The road to Liège lay open in front of us,' said Barkmann triumphantly.[8] The bitter battle for Manhay cost the Americans, along with the lost tanks, 100 killed and wounded. Although the Germans were left in possession, they headed west instead of turning north into the rear areas of the US 1st Army. At Soy the 2nd SS were stopped by the US 75th Infantry Division. Ridgway instructed General Hasbrouck to retake Manhay, which he did on Boxing Day. At Marche and Hotton 116th Panzer was driven back, while at Celles the British Household Cavalry came up against 2nd Panzer.

Bayerlein had tried to help 2nd Panzer on Christmas Eve. Sergeant Otto Henning of the 130th Panzer Lehr Reconnaissance Battalion was just about to tuck into captured American rations in a requisitioned Belgian house when he was ordered out by Staff Sergeant Keichel. Henning and his men secured a local bridge and stood around enduring temperatures of about minus 10°C. Just after midnight they became aware of approaching troops. Keichel gave the order to open fire, but his soldiers hesitated just as the cry went up: 'Don't shoot. Don't Shoot.'[9] Henning went forward and discovered about 15 bedraggled members of 2nd Panzer. 'They were older than us,' he noted, 'and completely exhausted. Some of them just fell to the ground, shaking all over.'[10] These fortunate survivors were sent back to Panzer Lehr's lines.

On Christmas Day General Harmon's US 2nd Armored Division, striking south-west from Ciney, split 2nd Panzer in two in the Celles area. At Foy-Notre-Dame, just four miles from Dinant, elements of 2nd Armored and the British 3rd Royal Tank Regiment, 29th Armoured Brigade, attacked 2nd Panzer's reconnaissance battalion and some of its artillery units. They resisted until they were overrun, losing seven Panthers and 148 prisoners. Further south a panzergrenadier regiment, panzer battalion and the rest of the artillery under Major Cochenhausen were caught in the woods between Celles and Conjoux. They were pounded by Allied artillery and fighter-bombers then 2nd Armored's tanks moved in for the kill. Cochenhausen with some 600 men fled on foot south and reached Rochefort where the remains of 2nd Panzer had gathered.

'Our unit was supposed to reinforce the 2nd Panzer Division,' recalled Sergeant Henning, 'but the enemy's artillery fire was so intense we didn't dare move out of the forest.'[11] He and his comrades, fearful for their lives, were relieved when they were ordered to return to their own lines. 'All this happened on Christmas Day,' added Henning, 'and, of course, we knew that the Ardennes offensive had failed.'[12]

Captain Hingst at Noville, commanding the remains of the 1st Battalion, 3rd Panzer Regiment, 2nd Panzer, foolishly launched a counter-attack with his Panthers in an exposed skirmish line. Standard orders were to operate in echeloned depth with the support of eight-wheeled armoured cars. The latter meant the panzers could offer mutual support to each other, with the armoured cars guarding the flanks, whereas in a line they were clearly vulnerable. During a 45-minute engagement American Shermans claimed half a dozen of his Panthers. Hingst was immediately replaced by Captain Scheer, commander of the 2nd Battalion, and the survivors were combined to create Battle Group Scheer.

Colonel von Lauchert, desperately short of fuel, wanted to withdraw the lead elements of his division, but permission was refused. East of Rochefort at Hargimont he had led a battle group almost as far as Celles, but was confronted by massing British and American armour. His men came under artillery fire and air attack and pulled back towards Rochefort. Attempts by Panzer Lehr to reach Celles were halted by Allied fighter-bombers now prowling the clear skies like angry hornets. Abandoned in the open in the Celles area for want of petrol were numerous staff cars, lorries, half-tracks, armoured cars and artillery pieces belonging to 2nd Panzer. Hitler reluctantly agreed that day, 26 December, to the withdrawal of 5th Panzer Army's spearhead and demanded the immediate capture of Bastogne. Although the fighting was not over, Boxing Day marked the end of Hitler's Ardennes offensive.

Colonel Alfred Zerbel, one of von Lüttwitz's staff officers, recalled, 'An Army order at 1530 hours authorized the immediate withdrawal of the advanced detachment of the 2nd Panzer Division to the bridgehead of Rochefort. The order was transmitted immediately by radio.'[13] The following day Zerbel noted, 'At 0100 hours the division reached the bridgehead at Rochefort. A great deal of its materiel had to be left behind.'[14] This bridgehead was held by elements of Bayerlein's Panzer Lehr until relieved by members of 9th Panzer.

American Counter-attack

The Battle of the Bulge was exactly the type of rough-and-ready scrap that General Patton excelled at. He greatly enjoyed the excitement and sense of urgency created by Hitler's breakthrough. Thinking on his feet is what he did best. Just three days after Hitler's offensive opened, Eisenhower ordered Patton and his US 3rd Army, comprising the 3rd, 8th and 12th Corps, north to attack the left flank of the German assault. Patton, though, was ahead of the game; his 3rd Corps had already been ordered to move from Metz north of Luxembourg. Its 4th Armored Division under Major General Hugh Gaffey deployed to Longwy, while 12th Corps' 80th Infantry Division was sent to Luxembourg. Both these tough divisions had most recently seen combat during Patton's push to the Saar River and they were also veterans of Normandy. Gaffey's 4th Armored had seen heavy fighting in Lorraine and Major-General McBride's 80th Infantry had fought hard to get over the Moselle River.

Patton's 12th Corps under Major General Manton Eddy also included the 4th and 5th Infantry Divisions and the 10th Armored Division, minus Combat Command B which was in Bastogne, plus Combat Command A of 9th Armored and the 109th Infantry from the 28th Division. The plan was that Major General John Millikin's 3rd Corps would relieve Bastogne. Millikin was told by Patton to 'Attack in column of regiments and drive like hell.'[1] The only snag was that some of the routes north and the bridges had been destroyed by the Americans to stop the Germans turning south. Patton appreciated that without Bastogne the Germans were ultimately going nowhere.

General Barton's 4th Infantry were highly experienced. They were D-Day veterans, having landed on Utah beach. After fighting in Normandy they had helped liberate Paris, then penetrated the Siegfried Line on the Schnee Eifel and fought in the Hürtgen Forest. General Irwin's 5th Infantry had arrived in Normandy in July and had suffered heavy losses during the fighting for Metz. In contrast General Morris' 10th Armored were largely greenhorns. His division had not entered the line until late September in Lorraine in time to take part in the encirclement of Metz and the drive to the Saar.

In Patton's line of advance to Bastogne was Heilmann's 5th Parachute Division, which was tasked with holding Martelange, Warnach, Burnon and Chaumont. It consisted of the 13th, 14th and 15th Parachute Regiments with supporting anti-aircraft guns, artillery and engineers. At Martelange where the bridge had been cratered by a bomb, Heilmann hoped to stop the Americans getting over the river Sûre. If nothing else, it would force them east towards Arsdorf and Harlange. Kokott could not help because he had been told by von Manteuffel to concentrate his 26th Volksgrenadiers on attacking Bastogne. As a result, he ordered the commander of his 39th Fusilier Regiment, which was deployed in the Assenois, Salvacourt and Sibret areas, to 'continue facing Bastogne and not form a front to the south'.[2]

Patton's H-Hour was 0600 hours on 22 December. On his right flank the US 80th Infantry moved on Merzig and came into contact with the 352nd Volksgrenadiers, whom they cut through to reach Heiderscheid and Ettelbruck to the east of Arsdorf. The Volksgrenadiers were not in defensive positions but were on the march from Ettelbruck so were caught on the open road. The US 26th Infantry Division hit the head of their column, while 80th Division struck the centre and the rear.

This helped take pressure off 4th Armored's thrust towards Bastogne by holding up both the 352nd and 79th Volksgrenadier Divisions' move west. The latter had been released to conduct a counter-attack to regain control of the Ettelbruck-Bastogne highway but it soon found itself under air attack. On the left the US 26th Infantry took Grosbous from the Volksgrenadiers but was checked at Arsdorf and Rambrouch by the powerful Führer Grenadier Brigade, which consisted of a battalion of Panzer IVs and Panthers, a battalion of mechanized panzergrenadiers and a battalion of infantry. The 26th Infantry, commanded by General Willard Paul, had only just been pulled from the line to take in replacements after fighting near Verdun so was nowhere near combat ready. Fortunately for them the Führer Grenadier Brigade was committed piecemeal and its commander Colonel Hans-Joachim Kahler was critically wounded by American shelling that evening.

On the western flank Millikin's 3rd Corps was led by Combat Command A, 4th Armored, which pushed up the Arlon-Bastogne road, with Combat Command B to the west using the secondary roads. At Martelange Combat Command A were held up by a company from the 15th Parachute Regiment until 23 December when the village was secured and the bridge over the Sûre repaired. In contrast, Combat Command B reached Burnon by midday on 22 December, which was just seven miles south of Bastogne. Here, though, they were delayed by more demolition damage and elements of the 5th Parachute Division. The village was not secured until midnight and heavy resistance was encountered at Chaumont by a company from the 5th Parachute, which was also defended by Luftwaffe fighter aircraft. Some 22 Shermans of the 8th Tank Battalion and supporting infantry moved round the village and, despite a slight thaw that bogged down some of the tanks, captured Chaumont.

General Kokott was not complacent about this threat developing on his left flank and launched a counter-attack with units from the 11th Assault Gun Brigade and his 39th Fusilier Regiment. He was able to supplement his ten assault guns with five lumbering Ferdinand tank destroyers from the 653rd Heavy Panzerjäger Battalion.[3] They had been shipped from Italy and were supposed to have been sent to Alsace. Their parent unit was being re-equipped with the new Jagdtiger. As far as Kokott was concerned they were heaven sent. His force emerged from the woods to the north of Chaumont and drove down the hill into the village before the Americans could react. Very swiftly, 65 Americans were killed and 11 Shermans lost. By the end of the day Chaumont was once more in German hands.

That same day, 23 December, the US 35th Tank Battalion, 4th Armored, attacked the Germans occupying Warnach to the north of Martelange. The village, which hosted the headquarters of the 15th Parachute Regiment, was held by a parachute battalion and a battery of assault guns, which successfully drove off the first assaults. The following day the Americans struck from three sides and once in Warnach fought house to house. The defenders did not give up easily and counter-attacked, claiming four Shermans and 68 American lives before being driven out. Once the village was secured the Americans found 135 German dead and a similar number of prisoners. When Bigonville was taken on the 23rd by 4th Armored the village yielded 328 German prisoners from the 13th Parachute Regiment.

There was no hiding German losses had been heavy. 'At night one could see from Bastogne back to the West Wall,' observed Colonel Heilmann, 'a single torch light procession of burning vehicles.'[4] Despite the ferocity of the fighting the German paratroops still found time to bury their dead. In the woods near Warnach an American patrol came across a simple solitary grave, a cross made from branches against which was propped the dead man's Mauser rifle and his para helmet.

The stubborn German resistance was a blow to General McAuliffe in Bastogne who signalled 4th Armored, 'Sorry I did not get to shake hands today.' He then added rather pointedly, 'I was disappointed.'[5] General Millikin's armoured thrust had been weakened by the efforts of Heilmann's men, so he decided to recuperate ready for another go on Christmas Day. The men of the 4th Armored were impressed by the tough fighting capabilities of the 5th Parachute Division. One tanker observed, 'I want to describe these bastards because some observers have underrated them. They were to be sure, inexperienced ..., but the fact is they didn't act inexperienced. They were slick, savage, ... almost sullen in their bloody determination.'[6] Although McAuliffe was understandably disappointed, he was optimistic 4th Armored would punch its way through.

Tintange was lost by the Germans after a costly struggle along with Hollange and Chaumont. On the left Remonville was pounded by four US artillery battalions. When the German defenders from the 3rd Battalion, 14th Parachute Regiment, who had been keeping their heads down attempted to reach their firing positions, they were mown down by American tanks using their machine guns and supporting

American riflemen. When the fighting stopped the Americans had captured 327 prisoners.

The Germans stubbornly resisted the US 3rd Corps at both Heiderscheid and Kehman on 24 December. Also they continued to build up their forces in the US 8th Corps area around St Hubert. However, once they had withdrawn to the north bank of the Sauer, they offered only limited resistance against the US 12th and 20th Corps. A regiment from the US 26th Infantry Division advanced to Eschdorf and Arsdorf, while another made its way eight miles north-west of Diekirch. A third regiment had reached Tintange.

General von Manteuffel knew that time was against him. He simply did not have the forces to take Bastogne and reach the Meuse at the same time. To add to his difficulties, the attack by Brandenberger's 7th Army had not come far enough forward to protect his southern flank. It would only be a matter of time before the Americans counter-attacked from the south in significant strength once they had cut a corridor to Bastogne. His northern flank was also exposed because Dietrich's 6th Panzer Army had only got as far as the line Monschau-Stavelot. To the west, after eight days of fighting it was obvious that the Allies would have significantly strengthened their defences along the Meuse. This meant it would be unlikely that the Germans would now be able to force a crossing.

On Christmas Eve a despondent von Manteuffel telephoned Hitler's headquarters where he spoke to General Jodl. 'Let me know this evening what the Führer wants,' he said. 'The question is whether I shall use all my strength to overcome Bastogne, or continue masking it with small forces and throw my weight towards the Meuse.'[7] He then said the best they could hope for was to reach the river but not get over it. Afterwards von Manteuffel suggested that he should strike northward along the Meuse to trap all the Allied forces east of the river. Such a move would then help Dietrich to resume his advance. To do this and overcome Bastogne he needed all available reserves immediately. Later that night von Manteuffel spoke with Jodl again, but he was informed that Hitler had yet to make a decision. Yet more precious time was wasted.

The Germans lost Eschdorf and Ringel on Christmas Day, which were captured by the US 26th and 80th Infantry Divisions respectively. To the south of Bastogne, the Germans struggled desperately to hold at bay the US 4th Armored Division's three encroaching combat commands. On Boxing Day, Combat Command Reserve fought its way through Remichampagne to the north-west of Chaumont and towards Clochimont, which lay south-west of Bastogne. The plan was to hook to the left and through Sibret and on to the town. However, Sibret was defended by the German 26th Reconnaissance Battalion so it was decided to carry straight on up the road through Assenois directly to the south of Bastogne. By now Heilmann's battered 5th Parachute Division was in a precarious position. His men were slowly being driven from their positions, killed or captured, and their artillery was running out of ammunition.

The US 4th Armored swiftly cut through the 5th Parachute and 26th Volksgrenadiers' positions at Assenois on 26 December after a brief artillery bombardment. Both defenders and attackers were temporarily blinded by the smoke and dust. German Teller mines hastily thrown onto the road did little to obstruct five Shermans roaring right through and off towards Bastogne, though a half-track was blown up. American infantry then set about clearing the village, the woods to the north and neutralizing two 88mm guns. A lone American clambering from a half-track made the latter his own personal mission and ran forward yelling. A German soldier sheltering in a foxhole raised his head to see what all the commotion was about and was subsequently shot in the neck. The man cowering in the next foxhole was clubbed over the head with a rifle butt. Still the American ran forward shouting and the startled 88mm gun crews quickly threw up their hands to surrender.

German troops beyond the village found that the advancing Shermans were determined not to stop. The lead American tank fired 21 rounds from its 75mm gun as it passed through Assenois. The bow machine gunner then raked the tree line, catching anyone foolish enough to be on the move. German gunners inside a green concrete bunker were not spared either. Three 75mm rounds quickly smashed it to pieces, hurling debris in all directions. Amongst those captured that day was Major Frank, a 13th Parachute Regiment battalion commander. He was immensely proud of how his men had performed, remarking, 'What spirit! ... It makes your heart swell.'[8] However, when Kokott was informed by the commander of the 39th Fusilier Regiment that the Americans were in Assenois he acknowledged that, 'I knew it was all over.'[9]

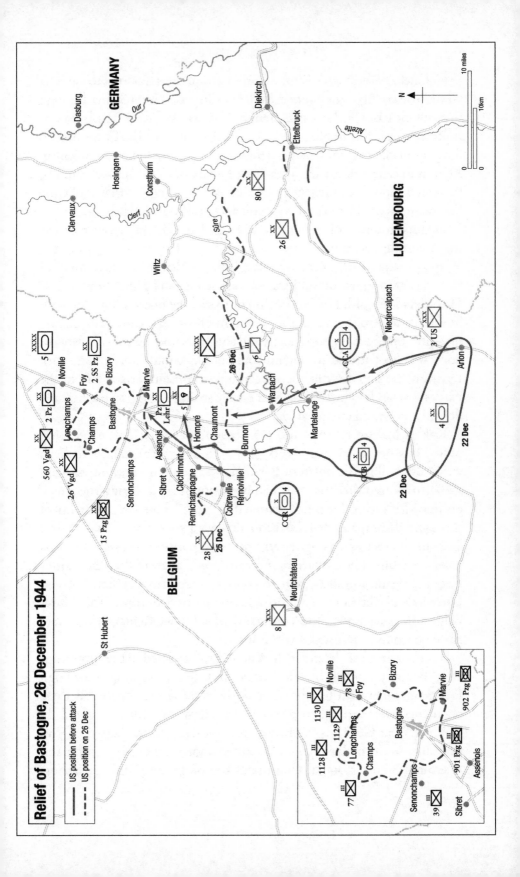

Relief of Bastogne, 26 December 1944

— US position before attack

--- US position on 26 Dec

GERMANY

LUXEMBOURG

BELGIUM

N

10 miles

10km

Dasburg

Out

Diekirch

Ettelbruck

Alzette

Hosingen

Consthum

Clervaux

Clerf

Sûre

80

26

Wiltz

Niedercalpach

3 US

Arlon

CCA 4

26 Dec

7

6

Warnach

22 Dec

4

Martelange

CCB 4

22 Dec

5

Noville

Foy

Bizory

2 SS Pz

Marvie

Pz Lehr

9

Longchamps

2 Pz

Bastogne

Champs

Hompré

Chaumont

Burnon

560 Vgd

26 Vgd

Senonchamps

Sibret

Assenois

Clochimont

Remichampagne

Cobreville

Rémoiville

CCR 4

15 Pzg

28

25 Dec

Neufchâteau

8

St Hubert

Noville

1130

Foy

78

1129

Longchamps

1128

Champs

77

Senonchamps

39

Sibret

Bizory

Marvie

902 Pzg

901 Pzg

Assenois

Colonel Zerbel at 47th Panzer Corps headquarters reported to General von Lüttwitz, 'At 1600 hours the enemy succeeded in breaking through to Bastogne past Clochimont-Assenois.'[10] When von Lüttwitz asked what units were available to plug the gap, Zerbel admitted, 'The Corps had no forces available to eliminate this danger.'[11] Lieutenant Colonel Creighton Abrams in charge of the US 37th Tank Battalion, Combat Command B, presented himself to General McAuliffe at 1710 hours. That night the first of 40 supply lorries and 70 ambulances rolled into Bastogne.

Heilmann and Kokott simply did not have the manpower to cut the American corridor. 'Officer reconnaissance troops found out in the evening hours of the 26th,' reported Kokott, 'that not a single man of the 5th Paratroopers stood between Salvacourt and Sibret anymore.'[12] He ordered his 39th Fusilier Regiment to seal the breach, 'but,' he said, 'it was obvious to them that they could not resist in the long run enemy pressure coming from both north and south around Assenois.'[13] Kokott knew that his battered command could not take much more. 'The 26th Division,' he noted, 'which had been under constant attack and in the hardest battles for eleven days, was hardly strong enough to successfully defend a powerful enemy attack.'[14]

Kokott had no reserves and his division was stretched to breaking point. His other two regiments, the 77th and 78th Volksgrenadiers, were both still to the north of Bastogne and could do nothing to help. Kokott reported that the 77th had been 'annihilated during the attack on the 25th except for a few scattered groups'.[15] Likewise, elements of the 15th Panzergrenadier Division deployed to the west and Panzer Lehr to the east of Bastogne were not in a position to assist. General von Manteuffel's headquarters informed von Lüttwitz that the Führer Begleit Brigade would be sent to counter-attack from Sibret, but von Lüttwitz and Zerbel were doubtful it would arrive in time. 'The Führer Begleit Brigade under the command of Colonel Remer always had gasoline trouble,' grumbled von Lüttwitz.[16]

Shortly after, 428 defenders in Assenois surrendered to the Americans after being pounded by air attack and heavy shelling. Although Heilmann's men had fought tenaciously to delay the enemy, his three regiments had been cut to pieces and there was nothing he could do about it. The Germans continued to be driven from their defensive positions south of Bastogne. The 4th Armored's Combat Command A secured Sibret; Combat Command B took Hompré and Salvacourt while Combat Command Reserve drove into Bastogne. To the east, German attempts to retake the high ground to the north of Ringel and the village itself failed. Nothum was lost to the US 26th Infantry Division, which pushed on the Wiltz River. The battle was far from over but the Germans' stranglehold on Bastogne had been broken.

In Hitler's headquarters there was an understandably tense atmosphere. The daily military briefings were nothing but a litany of bad news. Patton had just fought his way through to Bastogne, Battle Group Peiper's advance had ended in failure in the Amblève valley, while 2nd Panzer was being driven from Celles. The 116th Panzer had stalled near Verdenne and the enemy had refused to relinquish the Elsenborn Ridge. 'Mein Führer, we must face the facts squarely,' said General Jodl. 'We cannot force the Meuse.'[17] His staff waited for the Führer to fly into a fury.

Hitler did not want to acknowledge that his forces were either withdrawing or stalled. As far as he was concerned his offensive had only been checked temporarily. He stood scowling as he listened to the latest intelligence. 'We have had unexpected setbacks,' agreed Hitler, then looking his staff in the eye added pointedly, 'because my plan was not followed to the letter.'[18] Jodl, Keitel and the others were waiting for Hitler to authorize a halt to *Watch on the Rhine*, but such sentiments were wishful thinking. 'But all is not lost,' said Hitler with sudden unfounded optimism. 'Model can still cross the Meuse if Brandenberger's Seventh Army regains its equilibrium in the south; if Bastogne is taken; if von Manteuffel and Dietrich wipe out the great Allied force we have caught in the bend of the Meuse.'[19] It was clear to Jodl that Hitler was delusional; there were a lot of 'ifs'; furthermore, Dietrich and von Manteuffel were becoming weaker by the hour while the Allies' strength was growing.

Hitler continued to hold forth. General von Manteuffel was to swing to the north-east to outflank Hodges' US 1st Army. In the meantime, Dietrich would press on with his attacks in the Manhay-Hotton direction. What Hitler was now proposing sounded suspiciously like a version of the rejected small solution. 'I want three new divisions and at least 25,000 fresh replacements rushed to the Ardennes,' he ordered.[20] However, it was not clear where he thought these troops were going to come from. What was clear was that if Hitler could not reach the Meuse, then he was set on fighting a costly battle of attrition.

PART SEVEN
Too Late to Help

Rockets to Antwerp

Behind the scenes Hitler, in support of his Ardennes offensive, instructed that his V-1 flying bombs and V-2 rockets target the port of Antwerp. By the end of November, the Allies had cleared the majority of the docking berths and all of the cranes were functioning ready to receive the first transport ships. Just two weeks before Hitler's ground assault commenced the first 10,000 tons of supplies had been delivered. By the end of December, they were unloading 22,300 tons of supplies every day. Their greatest problem was shifting a growing backlog. During that month the Hoboken petrol facilities discharged 160,000 tons of fuel. Hitler's armies could only dream of such seemingly limitless resources.

It is unclear if Field Marshals von Rundstedt and Model were consulted about Hitler's V-weapon campaign. If they were they had much greater concerns than the long-range bombardment of Antwerp. Lieutenant General Walther von Axthelm, in charge of the Luftwaffe's flak forces, should have been informed, to ensure their anti-aircraft batteries did not accidently shoot down the V-1s. However, the need for secrecy may have been such that the Luftwaffe's 3rd Flak Corps was never notified.

Hitler optimistically hoped that his V-weapons could destroy the vital Kruisschans Lock, which controlled the water level in Antwerp docks. If this was put out of action it would prevent vessels entering from the Scheldt. If the outer and inner gates could be blown open the docks would become tidal and the quays could be damaged. He also imagined his flying bombs and rockets raining death and destruction down on any ships trapped in the docks. This was easier said than done. Nonetheless, the man to get the job done was Himmler's highly ambitious acolyte SS-Lieutenant General Hans Kammler.

The V-1 and V-2 were initially the responsibility of Lieutenant General Erich Heinemann and Major General Walther Dornberger respectively. Heinemann, though, was the man charged with coordinating operations. He and his subordinate Colonel Max Wachtel had their work cut out. Throughout the spring and summer of 1944, the Allied air forces had targeted their newly built V-1 launch and storage facilities in northern France and Belgium. In particular, the fixed launch sites had proved vulnerable to air attack. Once the Allies had broken out of their Normandy bridgehead these were soon overrun.

All was not well with the V-2 programme either. After the attempt on Hitler's life in July 1944, Himmler moved to take full control of it. Dornberger found himself answering to Kammler, who also had his eye on the V-1 programme. Kammler was a driven individual who served as the head of the SS Construction Office. In this capacity he oversaw the building of Hitler's concentration camps. Albert Speer soon became alarmed that Kammler aspired to replace him as Minister of Armaments. 'In the course of my enforced collaboration with this man,' said Speer, 'I discovered him to be a cold, ruthless schemer ...'[1]

Himmler hoped that Kammler would use his efficiency to turn the V-2 into a war-winning weapon. The rapidity of the Allied advance was thwarting such ambitions. A key V-2 site at Méry-sur-Oise in northern France had been overrun in August, forcing the crews to flee, some of whom were subsequently captured by the British at Arnhem. One of Kammler's first moves was to tighten security for the V-2 launch sites established in the Netherlands, employing SS troops. These were placed under the control of the brutal SS-Colonel Behr. Dornberger learned that Behr was using Dutch slave labourers to construct the sites and then having them shot once they were finished. 'He opened brothels for his soldiers with twenty Dutch girls,' Dornberger later reported. 'When they'd been there for two weeks they were shot and new ones brought along.'[2] Even if he wanted to, there was little he could do about the situation as Behr answered to Kammler.

Dornberger was not entirely happy with the decision to attack Antwerp with the V-2. This was really a tactical job for the Luftwaffe, but as usual it was beyond its capabilities. Albert Speer regretted backing the V-2 programme because he felt it was a terrible waste of resources. As a weapon of retaliation it simply could not deliver enough high explosives in comparison with the Allied bomber fleets. 'That was probably one of my most serious mistakes,' he admitted. 'We would have done much better to focus our efforts on manufacturing a ground-to-air defensive rocket.'[3] The V-weapons designed for strategic offence against London were now to be used for battlefield support.

Dornberger was worried that the Allies would immediately retaliate by bombing the V-weapon manufacturing, research and testing facilities at Peenemünde, Brüster Ort and Bizna. In the summer of 1943 and 1944 Peenemünde on the Baltic island of Usedom had been heavily bombed. The rocket factories at Friedrichshafen and Wiener Neustadt were also attacked. This had forced everything to go underground at Nordhausen in the Harz mountains. This secret base was supposed to produce up to 900 V-2 rockets a month using slave labour provided by Kammler. Output was actually 600 V-2s and 1,500 V-1s a month. Kammler faced an impossible task as the rockets were expensive, produced in too small quantities, inaccurate and used a highly dangerous liquid fuel.

During the winter months of 1944 Wachtel's 155th Flak Regiment in charge of launching the V-1 concentrated on hitting Antwerp, Brussels and Liège. Kammler's 444th Battery and Group North first launched V-2s against London and Paris in early September 1944. These batteries were placed under the newly created 65th Corps, which was staffed by specialist officers trained at Peenemünde. Hitler convinced himself that his V-weapons would 'convert the English to peace'.[4] Antwerp was then added to the V-2 target list. The combined V-weapon bombardment started before the port was even opened to Allied shipping. 'Hitler and Goebbels had ordered an extensive propaganda campaign to precede the first launchings of V-2,' writes Gerald Reitlinger. 'And Hitler had hypnotized himself into believing it.'[5]

The first V-2 struck Antwerp on 12 October followed by the first V-1 on the 23rd. The results were not very promising. The month after, Heinemann found himself sacked and placed on the reserve list, no doubt thanks to the machinations of Himmler and Kammler. On 12 December a V-2 fell on an Antwerp cinema, killing almost 500 military personnel and civilians and wounding another 500. At first Hitler, despite his enthusiasm for his V-weapons, did not believe the casualty figures. 'That would finally be the first successful launch,' he said to those around him. 'But it is a fairy-tale that my scepticism keeps me from believing.' Then with an uncharacteristic flash of humour he added, 'Who is the informer? Is he paid by the launch crew?'[6]

Four days later salvoes of V-1s were launched at Antwerp and Liège to herald the opening of the Ardennes offensive. A lucky strike on Liège on 17 December blew up 400,000 gallons of fuel. Many V-1s were shot down by Allied anti-aircraft guns and fighters or suffered regular systems failures. A V-1 suddenly came down in Velp in the Netherlands which was crowded with refugees, killing several people. At Breukelen fearful refugees took shelter under some trees as V-1s passed overhead, launched from the northern Dutch province of Friesland. One crashed in the woods near Chevetogne north-west of Rochefort in Belgium and exploded. On New Year's Eve another came down south of Liège, seriously injuring a British soldier who bravely shielded a Belgian child with his own body. In contrast the V-2, which was a ballistic missile, was almost impossible to detect before it reached its target. Like the V-1, however, it suffered a steady rate of failures.

The launch units for both types of V-weapon were now fully mobile and moved from site to site, making it difficult for Allied bombers to target them. The V-2s were fired from The Hague area, and by the time the Dutch Resistance had contacted London with coordinates the launchers had been relocated. The British, in order to open the approaches to Antwerp, stormed Walcheren in November, driving the Germans from the northern banks of the Scheldt Estuary. Regardless of this development, the V-2 crews were easily able to continue operating from the western Netherlands until the end of March 1945.

By then 10,300 V-weapons had hit 65 square miles of Greater Antwerp with 60 per cent landing within an eight-mile radius of the city centre.[7] This sounded impressive but accuracy blighted the campaign. In terms of denying the Allies use of the port the operation was a complete waste of time. Just over 300 V-weapons fell on the docks, causing minimal damage. These managed to sink just one ship and damaged 16 others. Although they hit the Kruisschans Lock this did not stop it functioning. A single dry dock was put out of action but this was repaired within three weeks. In all about 3,500 people were killed by this indiscriminate bombardment and thousands more were injured. Allied forces lost 682 personnel. The only real impact on the Allies' war effort was to slow ammunition shipments through the port. Liège was targeted by 3,141 flying bombs and again the results were poor.[8] Ultimately these attacks did little to help Field Marshal Model and Operation *Watch on the Rhine*. 'Those rockets, which were our pride and for a long time my favourite armaments project,' said Albert Speer, 'proved to be nothing but a mistaken investment.'[9]

Kammler had a number of other new V-weapons which he used in the winter of 1944 in support of Hitler's offensive. None of them was really ready for operational deployment. The first of these to go into action was the V-4 or aptly named Rhine Messenger, which was a solid fuel rocket. A salvo of 24 were fired at Antwerp on 24 December 1944, but they proved to be woefully inaccurate. Kammler authorized another 20 rockets to be launched at the port and then gave up with the V-4 programme. The second weapon, dubbed the V-3, was a long-range gun originally designed to bombard London from the Pas-de-Calais. By the winter the 705th Artillery Battalion under Captain Patzig was deployed in western Germany ready to shell Belgium, Luxembourg or France. The first gun targeting the city of Luxembourg opened fire on 30 December and was followed by a second. They expended a total of around 190 shells which proved to be little more than a nuisance, causing ten deaths and 35 wounded.

In a grandiose gesture Göring had boasted he would attack Antwerp with 3,000 aircraft the moment the first Allied ship entered the port. It was a hollow threat. Furthermore, the Allies ensured that the city was bristling with anti-aircraft guns. The Luftwaffe, which only conducted sporadic raids, carried out its last attempt to block the Scheldt on 23 January 1945. Some 20 Ju 88 bombers tried to drop mines, but those they did were quickly cleared up by flotillas of Allied minesweepers. The German Navy operating from the western Netherlands also attempted to hinder Allied shipping using E-boats as well as one- and two-man submarines. Although they sank a number of Allied vessels it made little difference to the volume of shipping coming into Antwerp. In response, British and American bombers pounded the German naval bases at Den Helder, IJmuiden and Rotterdam.

Hitler desperately needed to starve the Allied armies in the Ardennes of supplies. However, all his attempts to close the port of Antwerp proved dismal failures. German soldiers who watched the flying bombs pass overhead were dismayed at the results. 'Why has there been no success with the V-weapons of which so much has been said?' grumbled

Corporal Hans Hoes.[10] The irony was that they had inflicted no more damage on Antwerp than a 100-bomber raid. German troops would rather have enjoyed greater support from the Luftwaffe; instead the V-weapons wasted resources equivalent to 24,000 new fighter planes.

Kammler made two belated attempts to destroy Hoboken using V-2s. The first occurred on 19 January 1945, hitting a petrol train and three storage tanks that caused a fire lasting 48 hours. The facility, though, continued to function and the second attack on 14 February 1945 likewise failed to have the desired effect. Speer lamented the 'long-range rockets ... proved to be ... an almost total failure.'[11] Kammler, far from being castigated, had his authority extended over not only the V-1 but also the jet aircraft programmes. To their fury both Göring and Speer found themselves subordinate to Kammler.

Battle of the Airfields

At 0920 hours on 1 January 1945 Peltz's Operation *Baseplate* commenced. Every available fighter and fighter-bomber pilot was scrambled and thrown into the massed aerial attack. Nineteen-year-old Werner Molge with the 8th Squadron, 26th Fighter Group, was amazed by the sumptuous early morning breakfast served up in the pilots' mess at the Berning Hotel. The generous 'take-off' rations included the luxury of white bread, with extra butter and eggs. The white loaves made a nice change to the normal dark rye bread produced by the military field ovens. The special treat, though, was real coffee rather than the usual ersatz muck, plus chocolate enhanced with a pharmaceutical drug to help the pilots ward off fatigue.[1] The food was welcome but to some it felt like the last meal of a condemned man. They were also promised a full operations meal on their return as if it were some sort of incentive to do their duty. Molge then clambered onto a bus and was driven to an airfield at Clausheide where 50 Fw 190s were lined up and ready to go. The ground crews had worked all night to get the aircraft ready.

The Luftwaffe was tasked to hit 12 British air bases in Belgium and the Netherlands, plus four American airfields in northern France. Despite the detailed planning they ended up hitting 13 British and three American targets. This was not the grand slam against American bombers as Adolf Galland had hoped but an ambitious ground attack offensive. Pilots were instructed to shoot up the Allied air bases and in the process destroy as many enemy aircraft as possible, especially the fighter-bombers. In light of the Allies' industrial capacity the latter was a fruitless exercise as they would be rapidly replaced. What they should have done is concentrate on the infrastructure, namely control towers, barracks and ammunition dumps. For *Baseplate* to be effective they needed to kill as many Allied pilots and ground personnel as possible and to do that they needed to hit them on the ground. Engaging in dogfights would simply ensure irreplaceable losses for the Luftwaffe. It was obvious that attacking bases operating Thunderbolts, Typhoons, Spitfires and Mustangs would soon stir up a hornets' nest.

Apart from the eager young recruits, morale was not good amongst the seasoned pilots. Although confident in their abilities, the latter knew sooner or later their luck was going to run out. Prior to the operation many had been finding reasons to abort combat sorties. Common amongst these was engine, gun or undercarriage problems. In some cases, they would fly off, discharge their guns and then return to base. If they were caught doing this, they were immediately arrested for dereliction of duty. Senior officers who had once enjoyed flying with their men increasingly remained at their headquarters in order to 'supervise'. At the same time, the Luftwaffe's Commander-in-Chief in the West General Josef 'Beppo' Schmid, in an effort to save his veteran officers, tried to keep them grounded. Wing Commander Johann Kogler, commander of the 6th Fighter Group, objected to this and insisted that he be allowed to go into action with his men.

The operational orders issued by Peltz's 2nd Fighter Corps headquarters were succinct and to the point: 'Maintaining complete radio silence up to the moment of attack, all Air Wing[s] will fly low over the frontier simultaneously in the early hours of the morning to take the enemy air forces by surprise and catch them on the ground.'[2] It meant flying below 600 feet, in some cases as low as 150 feet, in order to avoid Allied radar. This required skimming the treetops.

The 1st Fighter Wing, under Group Captain Herbert Ihlefeld, with 80 planes, was to strike the three Polish Spitfire squadrons at St Denis-Westrem airfield near Ghent. Fighter ace Wing Commander Kurt Bühligen was to take 90 aircraft from his 2nd Fighter Group to pounce on St Trond airfield, north-west of Liège in Belgium. Many of his Fw 190s had only just been delivered and still lacked their tactical markings. Another fighter ace, Group Captain Heinz Bär, commander of the 3rd Fighter Group, on opening his orders found he was to rendezvous with his 70 aircraft over Lippstadt and then fly 140 miles to attack Eindhoven. Major Michalski with 68 planes from the 4th Fighter Wing would hit Le Culot. The 27th and 54th Fighter Wings were to deal with three airfields around Brussels. Wing Commander Bennemann's 53rd Fighter Group with 50 aircraft was instructed to attack Metz airfield. One squadron even found itself targeting the very airfield it had previously been stationed at.

Young Werner Molge recalled, 'Take-offs at close spacing were always dangerous due to the prop-wash which threw us about unexpectedly. Also, there were four to six inches of snow on the ground which made things even more difficult.'³ Unfortunately, to ensure complete operational secrecy no one had informed General Wolfgang Pickert's 3rd Flak Corps. His gunners naturally assumed that such large formations of aircraft passing overhead could only belong to the enemy and began to blaze away. This was especially the case with the batteries protecting the V-2 rocket sites west of Rotterdam and the flak ships operating off the coast of the Netherlands. In quick succession 16 aircraft were shot from the sky by friendly fire.

At Eindhoven in the Netherlands, Peltz's timing was perfect. His fighter-bombers swooped in just as a squadron of RAF Typhoons were taxiing to take off. Smashed aircraft quickly blocked the runway, obstructing successive squadrons. The Spitfires stationed there, thanks to a lack of space, were helpfully lined up on their runways. However, one Typhoon squadron, under Leonard Lambert, managed to avoid the destruction as it was on a mission to strafe German positions around St Vith. This was not the first time the Luftwaffe had bombed Eindhoven, as they had struck the city back in the summer shortly after it had been liberated by American and British forces. Wing Commander Stark's Arado Blitz bombers supported by Fw 190s and Me 109s disappointingly inflicted minimal damage at Gilze-Rijen.

When the fighter-bombers zoomed over Brussels at low level many pilots jettisoned their external fuel tanks. This caused confusion amongst the Allied troops stationed there as they naturally assumed the city itself was under attack. However, it soon became apparent what was happening when the 'bombs' failed to explode. British officers ran to the windows of their headquarters and saw swarms of German aircraft just above the rooftops. There was no sign of the RAF.

Spitfires at the Brussels-Evere airfield were caught trying to take off. Fighter ace Lieutenant Wilhelm Hoffmann, with his 8th Squadron,

26th Fighter Group, led the attack. Having survived this mission, he would accidently die at the hands of his wingman on 26 March 1945. At Brussels-Melsbroek the Luftwaffe caught not only Spitfires on the ground but also numerous types of bombers and spent 35 minutes shooting them up. The attack on Brussels-Grimbergen proved disappointing as the attackers only found half a dozen aircraft. To compound matters, they ran into Spitfires on the way back and suffered heavy losses. Mother Nature also took a hand in German losses. Pilot Officer Theo Nibel's Fw 190 suffered a bird strike and he was forced to make a wheels-up landing near Brussels.

One group of Me 109s and Fw 190s involved in the raids on the Brussels area was led by an officer flying a captured Mustang. On the return flight they bumped into Squadron Leader Lambert's 168 Squadron on its way back to Eindhoven. Lambert assumed the Mustang was being chased and dived to the rescue. The German commander, although his pilots were short of fuel, ordered some of the Me 109s to give battle. They made a single ineffectual pass at the British and then flew on their way. One pilot lingered, having latched onto Lambert whose aircraft had been damaged over St Vith. 'The German thought he had a sitting duck,' recalled Lambert, 'and concentrated on me and [Flight Lieutenant] Joe [Stubbs] just knocked him out the sky.'[4]

The Luftwaffe also found itself tangling with three Spitfires from the Royal Canadian Air Force's 403 Squadron. In quick succession they shot down six German aircraft consisting of three Me 109s and three Fw 190s. While this demonstrated the skill of the Canadian pilots it also showed just how inexperienced their opponents were. Lance Corporal Walther Wagner, flying just his third combat mission, was involved in the attack on St Trond airfield by the 5th Squadron, 4th Fighter Group. He came under anti-aircraft fire and his engine stalled. Lacking height from which to safely bail out he was obliged to land near his target and surrender. Wing Commander Kogler was shot down by flak while attacking Volkel airfield in the Netherlands and was also captured. Kogler's force lost a third of its strength over Volkel.

At St Trond the Me 109s and Fw 190s swooped in low and strafed everything in sight. There did not seem to be much aiming going on, with the airfield acting as the signal to open fire. Hungover American pilots and ground crew staggered from their billets and dashed for the safety of the nearby dugouts. It was not until the attackers came in for their second pass that the American anti-aircraft gunners began to fire back. They accounted for five German planes and watched another with smoke pouring from it fly off into the distance. Amongst those shot down was an Fw 190 hit near the edge of the airfield. When it caught fire the pilot bailed out and was promptly captured. An Me 109 was also brought down near one of the runways. For all their enthusiasm Kurt Bühligen's pilots achieved poor results. They destroyed just two American aircraft and slightly damaged 14 others, most of which were back flying within a couple of days.

The attack force at Metz was intercepted by American P-47 Thunderbolts. However, they caught 40 fighter-bombers on the ground, destroying half of them. The force attacking Sint-Denijs-Westrem pounced on a Polish Spitfire squadron just as it was returning from patrol. Six of them were caught on the ground and another nine as they tried to land. The air defences were slow in responding and, when they did, they accidently shot down a Polish Spitfire. Two other Polish squadrons came to the rescue and claimed 18 German aircraft as well as damaging another five.

At Asch air base, home to the Mustangs of USAAF 352nd Fighter Group, the Luftwaffe could not believe their luck as they had caught the Americans still on the ground. This included some in the process of taking off and it looked for a moment as if, just like at Eindhoven, the runway would be blocked. However, they had not taken into account the foresight of Lieutenant Colonel John C. Meyer, commander of the 487th Fighter Squadron. He had guessed that the Germans might attack the forward air bases on New Year's Day because they anticipated the ground crews and pilots would be nursing hangovers from the night before. Meyer forbade his men to hold any New Year's Eve parties. His 12 aircraft were due to conduct an early morning patrol over St Vith and were waiting for the fog to clear. He was just leading them down the runway when an Fw 190 shot over the trees towards him. For a split second, disaster loomed for the 352nd Fighter Group. Then the German pilot, spotting a bigger target, foolishly veered off to attack a stationary C-47 transport aircraft.

This decision proved to be a fatal mistake because Meyer and the rest of his squadron were able to take to the air. The distracted Fw 190 pilot now found Meyer coming up behind him with his guns blazing. The pilot's death was instantaneous when his aircraft exploded and the wreckage fell to the ground. A frenzied air battle followed with the Germans coming off worse. They lost 23 aircraft during the raid on Asch, the bulk of which were claimed by Meyer's men. He himself shot down two Fw 190s, the last of which soaked up his remaining ammunition. Elsewhere the Luftwaffe tangled with the American 357th Fighter Group operating from Leiston in Suffolk, England. In the process they lost a reported 60.5 aircraft. Another 19.5 aircraft were lost to the 20th Fighter Group and nine to the 353rd Fighter Group also operating from England. These three fighter groups were part of the US 8th Fighter Command, which was flying in support of the bombers of the US 8th Air Force busy pounding Germany.

From pilot reports of the mayhem inflicted on the Allies it looked as if *Baseplate* had been a complete success. Initially General Eisenhower's headquarters was informed that 168 aircraft had been caught on the ground, but this was not the full picture. The Allies lost 278 combat aircraft which included 150 write-offs and 111 damaged. Some 17 non-combat aircraft, that is, spotter aircraft and transports, were also lost. Amongst the latter was Field Marshal Montgomery's C-47 transport plane, which Eisenhower replaced within a matter of days. Crucially, very few Allied pilots were killed, although 100 ground crew were lost. While the damage sounded quite impressive the losses only represented 0.5 per cent of the aircraft available to the Allies.

Many of the young and inexperienced German pilots had thought they were taking part in a turkey shoot and had begun to enjoy themselves. Foolishly getting overconfident, they had lingered in the combat zone for much too long, allowing the Allies time to summon fighters from their rear bases which caught the Luftwaffe just as they began to turn for home low on fuel and ammunition. Similarly, those German pilots who had returned to conduct second attacks had been intercepted. Pickert's flak gunners had also shot at their own returning aircraft.

The Typhoons of 263 Squadron were caught on the ground by eight Fw 190s and eight Me 109s, all of which were flown by very inexperienced pilots. Flight Lieutenant Ronnie Sheward, who was acting squadron leader, had eight Typhoons poised to take off on support missions. It seemed as if all his aircraft would go up in smoke. Instead, he was appalled at the poor performance of the German pilots. Sheward noted they 'strafed a few of our aircraft but put up a very poor show and were being shot at by our AA guns'. He was amazed they took no evasive action and recalled, 'I yelled "Weave, you stupid bastards, Weave!" Recce Mustangs got two and AA claimed nine.'[5] It was like lambs to the slaughter. Nor was this an isolated incident; other reports spoke of poor shooting and tactics by German fighter pilots.

When General Koller saw the cost of *Baseplate* he knew it was impossible to consider it as anything other than an unmitigated disaster. The Luftwaffe had lost 271 aircraft plus 65 damaged. This represented about 50 per cent of the attacking force.[6] Even worse it had lost 234 pilots, consisting of 143 dead or missing, 70 captured and 21 wounded. Amongst them were 18 experienced commanders and many instructors. 'At this moment,' recalled Galland, 'I lost all spirit for the further conduct of hostilities.'[7] Many pilots had got lost and in the case of Le Culot failed to find it. The result was that many targets were attacked with weaker forces than anticipated. To make matters worse two groups had attacked a non-operational airfield. *Baseplate* was the Luftwaffe's 'death blow', concluded Galland.[8]

Furthermore, the Luftwaffe had done little to keep enemy aircraft away from the German ground troops. When the weather had cleared on 23 December American P-47 Thunderbolt fighter-bombers of the US 9th Air Force flew over 1,000 ground attack missions. In particular US fighter-bombers had conducted 250 sorties a day in support of the American garrison in Bastogne. 'German prisoners taken thereafter,' noted Eisenhower, 'invariably complained bitterly about the failure of their Luftwaffe and the terror and destruction caused by the Allied air forces.'[9] Nor had the Luftwaffe prevented Allied transport aircraft from dropping desperately needed supplies. 'Where,' asked German soldiers struggling in the snow, 'is the Luftwaffe?' Its efforts on 1 January 1945 were simply too little too late.

Nor had Hitler's new jet fighters and bombers made any discernible impact on the battle for the airfields. An Me 262 was shot down in the vicinity of Heesch air base, home to the RAF's 411 Squadron, on 25 December 1944. At the time, Flight Lieutenant Jack Boyle was escorting another Spitfire suffering from engine trouble back from the Bastogne area. He caught the jet's port engine with a burst of cannon fire. 'I scored several more hits before he clipped some treetops and then hit the ground at an almost flat angle,' said Boyle. 'His aircraft disintegrated in stages from nose to tail as it ripped the turf for several hundred yards ...'[10] At the same time an RAF Tempest hit an Ar 234 which crash-landed in the Netherlands. Six days later Lieutenant Colonel Meyer successfully shot down an Ar 234, which had been flying in support of German ground forces. These jet bombers conspicuously failed to destroy the Gilze-Rijen airfields and only managed to damage a single Mustang. This was despite delivering almost 200 fragmentation bombs.

Equally damning, the Luftwaffe failed to stop a raid by agile Mosquito light bombers of RAF 571 Squadron early in the morning on New Year's Day. They daringly attacked a series of railway tunnels being used to supply German troops in the bulge, employing massive 4,000-pound blockbuster or 'Cookie' bombs. These were dangerous to drop at low level; however, not only did 571 Squadron manage it but they even flew back to check their handiwork. German fighters spotted them but the Mosquitos, flying low over the hills of the Ardennes, gave them the slip and safely returned to their base at Oakington in Cambridgeshire.

Speer's factories might have been able to make good the Luftwaffe's aircraft losses, but the aircrew were irreplaceable. Their sacrifice had done nothing to alleviate the pressure on the ground troops still fighting the Battle of the Bulge. Neither Koller nor Christian was keen to brief Hitler on the outcome. A furious Galland held Colonel Gollob responsible for the Luftwaffe's losses over the Ardennes and confronted him. Gollob reacted by complaining to Himmler, alleging that Galland had failed the Luftwaffe. The wholly ineffective Göring made no attempt to defend Galland, who was sacked on 13 January 1945. Four days later Galland was involved in what was called the 'Fighter Pilots' Revolt'. Some of his colleagues wanted to present Göring with a list of demands. Galland was unable to accompany them as he was not permitted to fly. Key amongst these demands, as one officer put it, referring to the Reichsmarschall's corpulence, was 'Fatty must go'.[11]

Luftwaffe Colonel Günther Lützow's delegation wanted to discuss the matter with Hitler, but he refused to see them. Instead, Field Marshal Ritter von Greim and General Koller, the chief of air staff, got them in to see the Reichsmarschall. Lützow explained they wanted an end to the bombers controlling the fighters. Secondly, the Me 262 should be allocated to the fighters not the bombers. He then made the mistake of demanding that the Reichsmarschall should stop insulting the performance of the Luftwaffe. Göring was furious, declaring, 'It is mutiny. I will have you shot!'[12]

Göring and Himmler wanted Galland and the others immediately court-martialled, but Hitler intervened. Instead Galland was given an Me 262 unit to command for the rest of the war. Lützow was posted to Italy and ordered not to return to Germany. Galland was instructed to take all the mutineers with him, which he happily did. His jetfighters would claim up to 50 enemy planes by the end of the war.

In some circles it was felt that Field Marshal Milch, the Luftwaffe's Inspector General, should have replaced Göring. As early as 1943 after the Stalingrad debacle, when Göring had failed to resupply the trapped German 6th Army, Milch had advocated the Reichsmarschall's replacement. Göring now headed off such a move by sacking Milch shortly after Galland. Speer, who was a friend of Milch's, tried to get him reinstated or at least returned to active duty but Hitler was not receptive. He viewed Milch as a potential threat and decided to let the fatally weakened Luftwaffe needlessly muddle on under the inept Göring. Conducting Operation *Baseplate* over two weeks after *Watch on the Rhine* had commenced, had proved completely pointless.

Alsace Diversion

Just as the Luftwaffe were trying to obliterate Allied airfields, Himmler and General Johannes Blaskowitz launched a surprise diversionary attack far to the south in Alsace. The former was very keen on this enterprise, while the latter was simply flotsam on the tide of history. Their aim was to ease pressure on the German bulge in the Ardennes by capturing Strasbourg. Before *Watch on the Rhine* had commenced Hitler had found a convenient way to avoid Himmler being involved in that operation. He had made himself far too unpopular with the army. Field Marshal von Rundstedt as CinC West had been particularly irked by Himmler styling himself 'Supreme Commander, Westmark'. This understandably looked as if Himmler was deliberately trying to usurp von Rundstedt's authority. Instead, the Reichsführer was appointed commander-in-chief of the newly created Army Group Upper Rhine, which was independent of von Rundstedt's command and far from the action. This meant he could not meddle with the running of Sepp Dietrich's 6th Panzer Army. It also forced Himmler to commit his Replacement Army to the front; in particular, he plugged a gap in the defence of the German frontier south of Karlsruhe on the Rhine as far as the Swiss border.

Himmler's Rhine forces included the 19th Army, which previously had been part of Blaskowitz's Army Group G. Blaskowitz was left controlling just the 1st Army. Himmler's command also encompassed members of the Volkssturm, Luftwaffe anti-aircraft units, frontier guards and worker battalions. These were cobbled into the 14th SS and 18th SS Corps under police generals Heinz Reinefarth and Erich von dem Bach-Zelewski, both of whom had been involved in the extremely brutal suppression of the Warsaw uprising in the summer of 1944.

Although Blaskowitz had successfully extricated Army Group G from southern France, he was sacked following the failed counter-attack against Patton in Lorraine. He had made the fatal mistake of falling out with Himmler and Gauleiter Adolf Wagner over the preparation of German defences to his rear in the Vosges Mountains. After Blaskowitz complained to Himmler about the slow progress in fortification construction, a furious Wagner had reported the general to the Nazi Party and denounced him. A disgraced Blaskowitz was sent home to his wife in Dresden. Notably, although removed from command in September 1944, this had not been publicly acknowledged until almost the end of November. His successor, General Hermann Balck, received orders on 16 December informing him of the attack in the Ardennes and instructing him to prepare a supporting operation. However, just six days later Balck was transferred and replaced by General Hans von Obstfelder. Then, on Christmas Eve, Blaskowitz, who had been tending his cabbages, was summoned to Berlin. To his surprise Hitler asked him to take command of Army Group G once again. Von Obstfelder was put in charge of 1st Army.

For a diversionary Alsace offensive Army Group G came up with three options. The first was to strike west from the Saarbrücken area towards Metz. The second proposed easing the pressure on 19th Army by pushing south towards Strasbourg. Hitler rejected both so the planning staffs went back to the drawing board and suggested a joint operation involving 1st Army and 19th Army. This meant that Blaskowitz would have to cooperate with Himmler whom he detested. Himmler, with his first combat command, was nonetheless keen to be involved in a major attack across the Rhine. It was clear to Blaskowitz that most of the work would have to be carried out by his 1st Army. This, though, was in a poor condition, lacking artillery ammunition, self-propelled guns and tanks after having been in almost continual combat since the summer. It included such units as the 'Whipped Cream Division' officially known as the 416th Infantry that comprised men with special dietary needs. The only semi-decent unit was the 17th SS Panzergrenadier Division.

Furthermore, Blaskowitz had no reserves and knew, as always, he would get little help from the Luftwaffe.

Blaskowitz presented his revised plans to Hitler on Christmas Eve. The Führer insisted that 1st Army's operations consist of two attacks, with one to the west of the Vosges towards the Saverne Gap and the other through them. As far as Blaskowitz was concerned this would simply weaken his centre of gravity and dissipate his already meagre resources. Four days later Hitler held a meeting with Blaskowitz, Jodl, Keitel and von Rundstedt at the latter's Adlerhorst headquarters. Himmler pointedly arrived late, much to Blaskowitz's displeasure. Hitler outlined how an attack would break through the French Maginot Line defences which had been occupied by the Allies, then push south along the western edge of the Vosges to link up with the 19th Army holding the Colmar bridgehead on the west bank of the Rhine. 'With this done,' said Hitler, 'Strasbourg will fall to our troops and the destruction of the enemy in the Alsace will be complete.'[1] This was dubbed Operation *Northwind* and was to commence in the New Year, which, like *Baseplate*, was much too late to help *Watch on the Rhine*.

While *Northwind* was a strategically sound plan, the armies allocated to carry it out were simply too weak. It was to involve over a dozen divisions including the Normandy veterans 10th SS Panzer and 17th SS Panzergrenadier. The latter, under the command of SS-Colonel Hans Lingner, having been issued with 57 new assault guns, was deployed to Zweibrucken on 28 December. It was to strike either side of Bitche. The division, which had not completed its training before being sent into combat in Normandy, had been severely mauled in France. Total casualties amounted to about 8,000 men. Subsequently it struggled to reorganize and the quality of its replacements was poor, which included reluctant East European Volksdeutsche.

The 17th SS and the 36th Volksgrenadier Divisions formed the 13th SS Corps. On its left was the 80th Corps with the 559th Volksgrenadier and 257th Infantry Divisions. On the right was the 82nd Corps with the 19th Volksgrenadier, 347th Infantry and 416th Infantry Divisions. To the left of the 80th Corps were the 245th, 256th and 361st Infantry Divisions of the 89th Corps. The 21st Panzer, 25th Panzergrenadier and 606th Divisions also in the Zweibrucken area were to exploit the breakthrough. The 6th SS Mountain Division was on its way from

Denmark but was held up by delays on the railways. This unit had been combat-hardened fighting the Red Army in northern Finland. Himmler's 19th Army was to strike north using the 64th Corps comprising the 198th Infantry Division, the 108th Assault Gun Brigade and various other supporting armoured units. The 39th Panzer Corps was to join Army Group Upper Rhine in mid-January, which was to include the 10th SS and the ad hoc 7th Parachute Division. The latter was really little more than a series of battle groups formed from various Luftwaffe ground personnel and elements of the 5th and 6th Parachute Divisions.

Like so many divisions, the 10th SS, under the command of SS-Brigadier Heinz Harmel, were exhausted. They had suffered around 5,000 casualties during the battles in Normandy and had subsequently been involved in thwarting the British attempt on Arnhem. Harmel's actions gained him the Swords to his Oak Leaves on his Knight's Cross on 28 November 1944. By this stage his division was little more than a battle group and was deployed to the Aachen region with orders to refit. During December it was rebuilt to about 75 per cent of its original strength with some 15,500 men. Although earmarked as a reserve force for Army Group Upper Rhine, the division was soon in action north-east of Aachen, which delayed its redeployment.

Undoubtedly for Himmler this operation was a matter of SS prestige over the army. While the Army High Command floundered on the Ardennes battlefield, Himmler believed he could be the conqueror of Alsace if he could retake Strasbourg. Alsace had been annexed by Germany in 1940 and historically was considered German. He wanted to be the civilian who had won a victory defending Germany while the army had failed. This conveniently avoided the embarrassing truth that Sepp Dietrich's 6th Panzer Army, which included a strong SS presence, had also failed even if it was under the direction of the army.

Himmler optimistically hoped that the American and French armies would be distracted south of Strasbourg by the presence of his 19th Army in the Colmar bridgehead. Even if they were, once again the terrain was against a successful German offensive. The region, like the Ardennes, was one of mountains, snow-covered trees and icy roads. The Low Vosges mountains north of the Moder River were heavily forested, which would slow any advance on Strasbourg. Likewise, the Vosges

mountains would impede any move towards Colmar. Both Hitler and
Himmler chose to ignore the most likely French reaction to a threat to
Strasbourg. One advantage they had was that the Low Vosges formed
a ten-mile barrier between Allied forces to the west and east. While
this terrain would hamper *Northwind* it would also hamper American
counter-attacks.

German planning was flawed from the start, because the offensive
comprised three generally unrelated local attacks that could be contained
piecemeal. Himmler's SS staff dominating Army Group Upper Rhine
supported a swift advance to the Saverne Gap by the 10th SS, once
they arrived, and 21st Panzer Divisions plus the 25th Panzergrenadier
Division, supported by the 36th and 47th Volksgrenadier Divisions to
the north and the 553rd Volksgrenadier Division to the south. In theory
this would cut General Jacob Devers' US 7th Army in two, the southern
portion of which, consisting of the US 12th Armored, US 36th and US
79th Infantry Divisions, would be destroyed, allowing *Northwind* to
sweep the French 1st Army out of Strasbourg. Himmler's headquarters
was not interested in any objections by the army commanders about
the feasibility of all this.

German intelligence had a very poor opinion of the French Army;
it was ill-disciplined, ill-trained and ill-equipped. French troops had a
habit of partying in every town and village they liberated. In October
1944 the army had started incorporating hundreds of thousands of
recruits from the French Forces of the Interior (FFI) – better known
as the French Resistance. General Charles de Gaulle, head of the
provisional French government, was reliant on America to equip
his expanding armed forces. As far as he was concerned this was not
happening fast enough. He was also angry that the Allies had been
slow in recognizing his authority over France. The Germans were well
aware of this discord between the Americans and British on one side
and the French on the other.

Himmler and Blaskowitz felt they had little to fear from French
forces in Alsace. It was very notable that they had failed to deal with
the Colmar bridgehead and morale was known to be poor. Many FFI
units fighting alongside the regular French 1st Army were little more
than militia. The French were in the process of forming eight new
infantry divisions from the FFI, but only one of these was available for
operations in Alsace. The French had five regular infantry divisions in

the field, but four of those were colonial units from North Africa. They were supported by three armoured divisions, of which 2nd Armoured was undoubtedly the best. Although the colonial divisions had been combat tested in Italy, since landing in France they had rarely been out of the line due to a lack of reserves. They had also been refused leave on the grounds it was logistically too difficult. French newspapers were not concerned about the exploits of the French military and preferred to report on food shortages and the ongoing trials of collaborators. The average French citizen, having seen the well-equipped British and American armies sweeping all before them, naturally assumed that the war was as good as won.

Following Himmler's instructions Blaskowitz, in an effort to maintain a firm control over the northern portion of the coming battle against the Americans, established his army group headquarters at Massweiler along with that of the German 1st Army. Both were connected by telephone thereby avoiding unnecessary radio traffic. In order not to tip the Allies off, Blaskowitz and Himmler's forces were instructed to maintain strict radio discipline, which included not transmitting any orders. However, Allied intelligence had already advised Eisenhower and Devers to expect a German attack in northern Alsace. The result was that the US 7th Army was on alert and had permission to give ground if necessary. This included the evacuation of Strasbourg which is just what Hitler wanted.

The French, though, were not about to make life easy for Himmler and Blaskowitz. In defiance of General Devers, the commander of the French 1st Army prepared for a last-ditch defence of the city, which had only been liberated in late November. He sent the exhausted 3rd Algerian Infantry Division and the 159th Alpine Infantry Regiment to hold Strasbourg and rallied the city authorities. This meant the Americans had to protect the French left flank whether they wanted to or not. The Algerians were a tough bunch, having fought their way up from the French Riviera. They were the liberators of Toulon and Marseille and they were prepared to die holding Strasbourg. Furthermore, General Schwartz, the French Military Governor of Strasbourg, very firmly pleaded their case with Devers and contacted de Gaulle.

German planning showed a lack of foresight regarding Strasbourg. They should have appreciated that the Allies could incorporate the city in a revised defensive line anchored on the Maginot Line and the area southward where the Maginot joined the Rhine. This line was already fortified while the ground to the rear did not offer any great defensive advantages. Ultimately, aside from the political ramifications, there was little incentive for the Allies to pull back behind the city. If Himmler and Wagner seriously thought they were getting their hands on Strasbourg again, they were very much mistaken.

The French were not the only ones deploying specialists trained in mountain warfare. The mountain troops of the 6th SS were the ideal force to spearhead *Northwind*; they had proved themselves during Operation *Birch*, the successful German withdrawal from Karelia in Finland. The 6th SS had formed the rearguard and fought not only the Russians but also the Finns. They had endured appalling weather conditions, as the autumn of 1944 had been extremely cold and wet and the men had regularly slept in the open air. Unfortunately for Blaskowitz their late arrival meant that only a regimental battle group was initially available. This was assigned to the 361st Volksgrenadier Division and first went into action on 31 December. It took American troops by surprise near Pirmasens and then advanced on Wingen on the Moder.

The 17th SS Panzergrenadiers, along with the 36th Volksgrenadiers, struck the US 44th and 100th Infantry Divisions in the Rimling area on 1 January 1945. The former's objective was the Rohrbach road junction. The 44th Infantry was attacked between Sarreguemines and Rimling and the 100th Infantry between Rimling and Bitche. When the 37th SS Panzergrenadier Regiment stormed Hill 382 it suffered heavy casualties in the face of stiff American resistance. The regiment's second battalion then moved to successfully capture Frauenberg and Schlossberg. 'They won ground, but for that they lay unprotected in unprepared positions, exposed to the enemy and the inclement weather,' reported one German colonel.[2] The 17th SS's armoured forces punched three miles in the Achen area to the west of Bitche. They also took 600 prisoners. However, due to the slow advance of the units protecting their flanks, American counter-attacks managed to surround the leading battalions of the 17th SS near Achen.

The German thrust south-east of Bitche by the 256th and 361st Volksgrenadier Divisions came as a surprise as there was no preliminary artillery and mortar bombardment. This attack exposed the US 100th Infantry's right flank, but it moved to meet the threat. Task Force Hudelson in contrast was not so fortunate and was overrun.

West of Bitche at Gros-Réderching, employing captured Shermans, German troops forced French armour from the town. They beat off a subsequent American counter-attack but then disengaged. A regiment from the 6th SS Mountain Division took Wingen, which was to be their deepest penetration into the Vosges. Johann Voss, a machine gunner with the 6th SS, recalled, 'We were freezing, our hands shoved deeply in the pockets of our anoraks, caps and shoulders under the hoods of our canvas sheets for protection from the sleet that swept through the forest.'[3]

Blaskowitz was soon informing von Rundstedt that he had insufficient forces to replace combat losses and hold the ground he had taken, let alone continue the attack. In particular, he was unable to exploit the Bitche salient after the commitment of the bulk of his infantry supported by artillery and tanks. Blaskowitz was now simply not in a position to conduct a second major offensive in the Sarre Valley codenamed Operation *Dentist*. He suggested continuing the attack in the direction of Hagenau on the Moder and requested reinforcements. This was not what Hitler wanted to hear and he insisted that *Northwind* continue. Nonetheless, *Dentist* went no further than the planning stage and, apart from an attack at Rimling, the Sarre area remained relatively quiet for the rest of the month.

Within a week Blaskowitz had been thrown back and the Americans recaptured Rimling and Wingen. The 6th SS battle group holding Wingen had expected to be reinforced by armour, but this was diverted elsewhere. To make matters worse, the slow progress by German troops on the flanks had left the men of the 6th SS horribly exposed. They had no option but to fight their way out of the town, losing two-thirds of their force, though they took 400 prisoners with them. 'Our sister regiment had lost too many dead, missing and wounded,' lamented Johann Voss. 'One of them had his testicles shot off.'[4]

SS-Colonel Lingner, trying to find one of his forward units, found himself behind American lines and was captured on 10 January. That day his men retook Rimling but suffered heavy losses in the process and promptly lost it again. SS-Colonel Fritz Klingenberg was appointed to replace Lingner. Two days later American fighter-bombers pounded the 17th SS and it was expelled from the outskirts of Rimling on 13 January. The once picturesque French border town was left in ruins and its once fine church derelict.

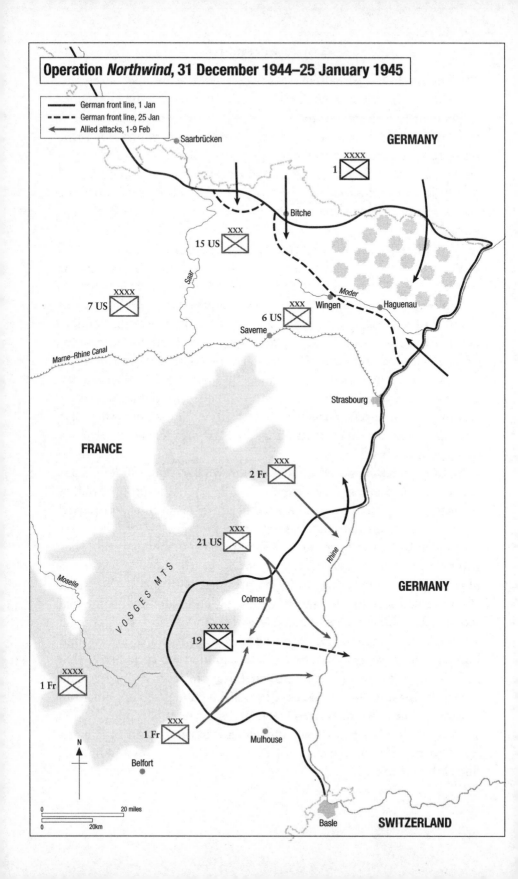

Operation *Northwind*, 31 December 1944–25 January 1945

German front line, 1 Jan
German front line, 25 Jan
Allied attacks, 1-9 Feb

GERMANY

Saarbrücken

1 XXXX

Bitche

15 US XXX

Saar

7 US XXXX

Moder

6 US XXX

Wingen

Haguenau

Saverne

Marne–Rhine Canal

Strasbourg

FRANCE

2 Fr XXX

Rhine

21 US XXX

Moselle

GERMANY

Colmar

V O S G E S   M T S

19 XXXX

1 Fr XXXX

1 Fr XXX

Mulhouse

N

Belfort

0   20 miles
0   20km

Basle

SWITZERLAND

The 17th SS Flak Battalion, which had initially moved to Hornbach, did what it could to fend off the enemy air attacks. By mid-month the much-depleted 17th SS was withdrawing towards the Siegfried Line. The flak unit was at Jagdhaus south of Hornbach, Altheim, Peppenkum, Riesweiler and Ringweilerhof, from where they tried to protect the retreating 17th SS from renewed air attack. The intensity of the fighting was such that the 3rd Battalion of the 37th SS Panzergrenadier Regiment had just 32 men remaining led by 11 non-commissioned officers. All the battalion's officers had been killed in action.

It was only after the Americans had withdrawn in good order towards the Moder south of the Forêt de Haguenau in early January that Army Group Upper Rhine launched its secondary attacks. This was Himmler's chance to shine as a military commander, as all his previous successes on the battlefield had been down to his highly competent SS-generals. Along the front stretching from Drusenheim down to Kilstett on the west bank of the Rhine there was confusion amongst American and French forces, as the latter were just in the process of taking responsibility for the area. This resulted in a chaotic and ad hoc defence by the Allies.

Himmler's attacks were carried out to the north-east of Strasbourg around Gambsheim and to the south of the city around Erstein, both on the west bank of the Rhine, on 5 January. The Germans swiftly created a bridgehead five miles long by two miles deep. This immediately threatened the eastern flank of the US 7th Army's salient in the Alsace Plain. Although an American task force, after bitter house-to-house fighting, drove the Germans from Gambsheim the following day, American units were encircled at Herrlisheim just to the north. When 29 American Sherman tanks tried to break through early on 10 January, within 30 minutes the Germans had destroyed 14 of them. However, the American troops in Herrlisheim still managed to escape. To the south, French tanks moved to contain the Erstein bridgehead which they achieved by 16 January.

Hitler hoped that if he kept the pressure up the panicked Allies would now abandon Strasbourg and declare it an open city. However, from the start General de Gaulle had made it clear to Eisenhower that he would not relinquish Strasbourg. Nonetheless, the proximity of German forces to the north and south caused great alarm on the streets amongst the civilian population. Many residents were understandably fearful of reprisals and fled westward. Hitler and Himmler considered any Alsatians who helped the Allies as traitors.

Under Hitler's rule Alsace-Lorraine had been incorporated in Germany, becoming Elsas and Lothringen. Robert Wagner, the Gauleiter of neighbouring Baden, served as the governor of Alsace. Young Alsatians and Lorrainers had been recruited into the German armed forces. French writer Guy Mouminoux (better known by his pen name Guy Sajer) from Strasbourg suffered such a fate, as his mother was Alsatian German and his father French. He was sent to fight on the Eastern Front. Wagner had not only overseen attempts to make Alsace truly German, he had also overseen the deportation of the region's Jews. When Strasbourg was liberated, Wagner escaped east of the Rhine to rally local forces. He may have helped convince Himmler that the city could be recaptured.

The loss of Strasbourg had been a double blow to Hitler as German scientists were conducting nuclear research at the university and main city hospital. Carl Friedrich von Weizsäcker escaped to Germany but many of his colleagues were not so fortunate. Nuclear physicist Professor Rudolf Fleischmann and his team, disguised as medical officers, were captured by the Americans. The resulting intelligence windfall for the Allies showed that Hitler was a long way from producing an atom bomb.

The recently arrived Panthers of the 10th SS Panzer Division did not cross the Rhine until 15 January by ferry from Freistett to the north-east of Strasbourg, two whole weeks after *Northwind* had commenced. These were painted in a distinctive winter camouflage scheme that consisted of a panzer grey base coat with a zig-zag whitewash pattern over it. Presumably the crews felt that this would best break up the outline of their tanks in the wintery Alsace terrain. They attacked the new US 12th Armored Division sent to support the US 79th Infantry Division. The 10th SS achieved some success with its operation from Offendorf north to Herrlisheim on 17 January. Although this action lost momentum, SS-Lieutenant Bachmann, adjutant of the 1st Battalion, 10th SS Panzer Regiment, commanding two Panthers remembered:

> Everything went according to plan. The two panzer crew cooperated in a first-rate fashion. Panzer 2 opened fire while Panzer 1 raced into

the junction and knocked out the first Sherman. More US tanks were knocked out, and a white flag appeared. ...

The total was twelve captured Sherman tanks and sixty prisoners. I deployed my own two Panthers forward to the edge of Herrlisheim. From there they covered in the direction of Drusenheim and knocked out two Shermans on their way to Herrlisheim. Thus my two Panthers achieved nine kills.[5]

Bachmann's tank crews were rewarded with Iron Crosses, with Bachmann gaining the Knight's Cross.

Tanks and panzergrenadiers from the 10th SS attacked from Gambsheim and Offendorf on 19 January, taking Kilstett. At Herrlisheim, German infantry supported by ten tanks attempted to cross a bridge over the local canal but American artillery claimed eight of the tanks. Then some 200 German infantry and 17 tanks crossed the Zorn River at Herrlisheim and pushed north-westward. Shortly after, 400 men and 17 tanks got over the canal. Fierce fighting went on all night but the weather was clearing, which meant impending trouble for the Germans. That evening the 39th Panzer Corps instructed, 'Stop attack, return to the line of departure!'[6] The following day American fighter-bombers flew 190 sorties, destroying 27 tanks. Despite this the 10th SS inflicted heavy damage on the Americans. The US 12th Armored, having lost 1,200 men and 70 armoured vehicles, was forced back between Weyersheim and Rohrwiller.

To the north Blaskowitz had not given up. German forces probed the US 36th Infantry Division's position on the Moder, launching a series of attacks on 21 January. Three days later the Luftwaffe finally appeared, sending at least 20 Fw 190s and Ju 88s to bomb and strafe the 36th Infantry. That night six German divisions launched a three-pronged attack against the Americans' Moder defences. German troops remained confident, fully believing that the Swastika flag would be raised over Strasbourg by 30 January – the anniversary of Hitler becoming Chancellor.

The 10th SS struck the US 36th Infantry, while the 7th Parachute and 25th Panzergrenadier Divisions conducted attacks on the US 79th Infantry. Elements of the 6th SS Mountain Division cut through the US 103rd Infantry Division and reached Schillersdorf. The 36th Volksgrenadiers also set about units of the 103rd. 'We found their remnants, signs of abundance as it seemed to us: cigarettes and candies,' recalled Johann Voss. 'It was then that my squad picked up an American heavy machine gun, ..., We reckoned that sooner or later the enemy would start a massive counterattack, and that we would need all the firepower we could get.'[7]

Elements of the 10th SS crossed the Moder on 24 January and took the high ground commanding the region between Haguenau and Kaltenhaus. Any further advances wilted in the face of determined resistance and the following day Heinz Harmel received orders transferring his division to the Eastern Front. Although the Germans got across the Moder, their attempts to surround Haguenau were soon thwarted. Early on 25 January the US 103rd Infantry cut the road between Schillersdorf and Mulhouse forcing the Germans to withdraw their attacking forces. Hitler finally recognized he was wasting his time and suspended offensive operations in the Low Vosges and Alsace. *Northwind* was over.

Although Himmler and Blaskowitz's operations caused a brief crisis amongst the Allies, they drained away Hitler's already meagre reserves. The offensive cost him 25,000 casualties, while the Americans suffered 15,600. Hitler was furious that yet another counteroffensive had failed. Himmler was sent off to the Eastern Front to take charge of Army Group Vistula, with SS-General Paul Hausser taking command of the defences on the upper Rhine. 'If Bach-Zelewski were here, I would be entirely at ease,' said Hitler to his staff. 'He would scrape up prisoners of war, convicts, everything. By the way, where is he now?'[8] To which General Jodl responded, 'The Reichsführer took him with him.'[9]

The US 36th Infantry crossed the Moder on 31 January 1945 and shortly after clashed with elements of the 10th SS at Rohrwiller. Fortunately for the Germans a sudden thaw hampered the Americans bringing up their tanks, plus they were short of artillery ammunition. It would take until 9 February for the French, supported by American forces, to liquidate Hitler's last bastion west of the Rhine at Colmar. Although the German 19th Army managed to withdraw, its two corps suffered 22,000 casualties and lost 55 armoured vehicles and 66 artillery pieces. Out of the five divisions under the command of 64th Corps just one managed to get over the river largely intact.

The three divisions of 63rd Corps were also mauled disengaging from Cernay and Mulhouse. Most of the units that got across were deployed to hold the east bank, but two divisions were sent north to bolster 1st Army, which was bracing itself for another offensive by the US 7th Army. By then Eisenhower and his generals had 85 divisions closing in on the river and there was very little left to stop them crossing.

PART EIGHT
Complete Failure

Back Where They Started

To the north of the Alsace things were not going any better for Hitler in the Ardennes. In the closing days of December 1944, the fighting around snow-covered Bastogne reached its climax. To the south everything now rested on Colonel Kokott's 26th Volksgrenadier Division. He knew it was the failure of the 5th Parachute Division to hold his flank, in the face of the American advance on 26 December, that had compromised the German grip on Bastogne. Once the US 4th Armored Division was in Assenois there was nothing to stop them reaching the beleaguered town.

General von Lüttwitz met with Bayerlein at his divisional command post in Saint-Hubert on 27 December. They both agreed that the offensive was spent. 'The attack towards the north over the Meuse was not to be continued,' observed Bayerlein. 'It was a matter of keeping what had been attained and attacking Bastogne with all forces and taking it.'[1] Kokott appreciated that the senior leadership was seeking 'to get at least a modest political gain from the "Battle of the Bulge".'[2]

Otto Remer and his Führer Begleit Brigade was supposed to have reinforced Sibret to the south-west of Bastogne, but during the night the Americans had driven the 26th Volksgrenadiers out. 'Consequently, my plans were changed,' said Remer, 'and instead we built up a flak line north of Sibret in case the American tanks attempted to move north.'[3] Kokott noted, 'On 27 December the second phase of the battle for Bastogne begins ... What a ... waste of power...'[4]

The 1st SS Panzer and the 167th Volksgrenadiers desperately attempted to sever the American lifeline into the town. To do so they had to cut their way through the US 26th and 35th Infantry Divisions. The latter had gained combat experience in Normandy and had fought to help stop Hitler's Mortain counter-attack there, so they knew what to do. The German attacks were driven back by ground fire and air attacks that claimed 55 panzers. Meanwhile the US 11th Armored and 87th Infantry Divisions to the south-west fought to widen the relief corridor. They ran headlong into Panzer Lehr and the 26th Volksgrenadiers who had launched a counter-attack. A fierce battle followed with heavy losses on both sides, but eventually the depleted German divisions were forced back to their start line. General Patton drove triumphantly into Bastogne on 30 December to congratulate McAuliffe and his brave garrison.

Although the German troops in the bulge were in an increasingly precarious position, they were told to hold their ground. The men of the 62nd Volksgrenadier Division were instructed to, 'Fight to the last bullet.'[5] The captain in charge of the 1st Battalion, 193rd Grenadier Regiment, ordered, 'The strongpoint at Trois-Ponts must be developed so elaborately that a weak attack by enemy infantry will not be able to overrun it.'[6] He also tried to reassure his men that any enemy tanks that got through their lines would 'be destroyed further to the rear'.[7]

The Battle of the Bulge, as it became known, was to have potentially serious political repercussions for the British and the Americans. It was at this point that Montgomery completely overstepped the mark with Eisenhower. He had not been impressed by the Americans' handling of the battle and made no secret of his views. Montgomery renewed his call that he should be given operational control not only over his own 21st Army Group but also the whole of Bradley's 12th Army Group.

Monty's logic was that this chain of command would make it easier to liquidate the German bulge. As always, he was thinking of the military implications and not the political ramifications of what he was insisting on. He did not appreciate that to take over at the very point a major Allied counter-attack was launched would be a slur on American military prowess. If Eisenhower agreed, it would be a vote of no confidence in General Bradley's handling of 12th Army Group. Behind the scenes it was common knowledge that, while his subordinates had shone, Bradley's leadership had been notably lacklustre.

Monty and the British press had already formed the opinion that he had saved the day. In light of American bravery, tenacity and losses this was an insult that could not be tolerated. Eisenhower, who had always shown the utmost patience and diplomacy with his British Allies through some extremely trying times, decided that this was the final straw. He drafted a signal to the Combined Chiefs of Staff saying either Monty went or he would.

Fortunately for Monty, Major General Francis de Guingand, his very able 21st Army Group chief of staff, was aware of the mounting tensions and did all he could to defuse the dangerous situation. De Guingand went to see Eisenhower and informed him Monty had no idea of the trouble he was causing and asked for a stay of execution for 24 hours. He then flew back to Monty's headquarters and warned his boss that he faced the sack. At this stage of the war the last thing Monty wanted to do was lose his command. In addition, the situation would put Prime Minister Winston Churchill in an impossible position because, if he had to sack Monty, it would cause an almighty political row in London.

There was no question of Eisenhower being replaced, which meant the war could be delayed while there was a tense stand-off between London and Washington. If that happened, it would vindicate Hitler's prediction the Allies would fall out amongst themselves before the end of the war. Fortunately, Monty agreed to sign a message drafted by de Guingand promising full cooperation with Eisenhower and asking for his signal that had caused offence to be destroyed. Eisenhower, ever the diplomat, content that Monty had been contrite, let the whole incident pass. It was lucky that Eisenhower was not a vindictive man.

In the meantime, the Allies completed their plans for a counter-attack in the Ardennes. Their intention was to cut the German salient in half at Houffalize, with Hodges' US 1st Army striking south and Patton's US 3rd Army attacking north. They would also swing eastward towards Germany and the Siegfried Line. In order to free up the US 2nd Armored and 84th Infantry Divisions for the attack, General Brian Horrocks' British 30th Corps moved to take up their positions west of the Ourthe. Supported by the British 6th Airborne Division, they were to deploy in the Marche area. The paras took over the foxholes of the frozen US 84th Infantry overlooking the German positions.

Horrocks was to move forward towards Houffalize, to the right of the US 7th Corps, with the 6th Airborne on his right and the 53rd Welsh Division to the left. Due to the transfer of the US 1st Army to Monty's command and the criticism of the US conduct of the battle in the British press, there was some grumbling in American circles that Horrocks should be assigned a greater role. Monty, though, was right to hold him back; 21st Army Group was short of reserves and to extend Horrocks' corps further east would have been foolish.

As the New Year commenced, the Luftwaffe had belatedly sprung into action with *Baseplate*. Completely undeterred, the Allied counter-attacks commenced on 3 January 1945 amidst the snow, mud and fog. The weather once again greatly hindered Allied air support. In the following days frost and heavy snow made for firmer going for American tanks, but hid German fixed positions and their minefields. In the face of very stiff resistance on the first day, 7th Corps managed to advance just two miles. The US 2nd Armored and 84th Infantry secured Beffe and 3rd Armored got to Floret and Malempré. The British 53rd Division drove the enemy towards La Roche but came up against determined counter-attacks by von Waldenburg's 116th Panzer Division.

That day the British 6th Airborne fought all afternoon against Panzer Lehr to take Bures, suffering heavy losses. Although the Germans held on to half the village, a British soldier, Sergeant Scott, bravely drove in to pick up British casualties. To his horror a massive Jagdtiger tank destroyer rumbled round the corner and parked alongside him. When the German commander emerged he looked at Scott and the stretchers on his jeep and said gallantly, 'Take the wounded away this time, but don't come back. It's not safe.'[8] The following day Panzer Lehr repeatedly counter-attacked but were unable to hold onto Bures.

'An enemy counterattack made on 3 January 1945 ... changed events,' observed von Manteuffel ruefully, '... I informed the troops of my decision to fall back by fighting delaying actions ... Lack of fuel ... forced us to destroy or leave behind considerably more armour than was put out of action by the enemy during the entire attack.'[9] He also noted a lot of their artillery fell into enemy hands because they could not move it.

SS-Major Otto Günsche, one of Hitler's military adjutants, arrived at Dietrich's headquarters with news. 'Tell Dietrich he must withdraw his divisions from the front two at a time,' Hitler had instructed Günsche. 'Tell him that I have decided to throw his entire army at the Eastern Front.'[10] Dietrich listened to his latest orders, dumbfounded. 'The Führer needs to be clear about one thing,' he warned Günsche in response. 'If my army is withdrawn, then for the British and the Americans the road is open to the Rhine.'[11] The unfortunate major shrugged, orders were orders. There was nothing he could do. Günsche stayed with Dietrich for a few days, perhaps reluctant to return to Hitler who had moved his headquarters from Bad Nauheim to Berlin.

Von Manteuffel was angered when he learned that Dietrich's 6th Panzer Army was being pulled out of the line and that his men would have to fight on alone. 'A great burden was added to the army when, during the first days of January,' he recalled, 'orders were given to withdraw the units of the Sixth Army from the fighting front.'[12] When von Manteuffel complained he was informed that they were needed elsewhere. 'On 5 January the situation was so serious,' he recalled, 'that I feared Montgomery would cut off both our Armies. Although we managed to avoid this danger, a large part of them were sacrificed.'[13]

By this stage the German armies were critically short of replacements. For January Hitler had pledged to provide 25,000 men, but they were nowhere to be seen. Kokott grumbled that his replacements comprised 'lost clumps' of rounded-up infantry.[14] SS-Captain Karl Appel, commanding the 1st Battalion, 20th SS Panzergrenadier Regiment, 9th SS Panzer, noted, 'Yesterday I received a replacement of 200 men, unfortunately practically all elderly men from the Ukraine, some of whom do not understand German.'[15] The 3rd Parachute Division could muster fewer than 1,500 men and the 3rd Panzergrenadier Division was similarly depleted. American intelligence indicated that Model had 93,000 troops, the equivalent of 12 divisions, with 290 tanks and assault guns facing Patton. These included just 1,796 reinforcements, of which 900 had gone to the 3rd Panzergrenadier Division. It also noted that the redeployment of a Volksgrenadier division from the US 7th Army front to the US 3rd Army front indicated that the Germans were struggling to come up with infantry to replace their heavy losses sustained during December.

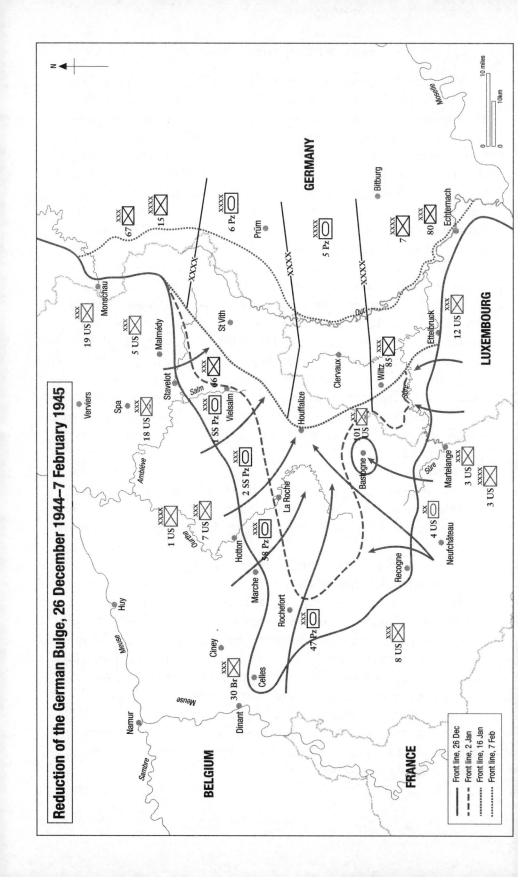

Reduction of the German Bulge, 26 December 1944–7 February 1945

N

10 miles

10 km

GERMANY

LUXEMBOURG

BELGIUM

FRANCE

Bitburg

Echternach

Prüm

80 XXX 7 XXXX

6 Pz XXXX

5 Pz XXXX

67 XXX

15 XXXX

Monschau

Malmédy

St Vith

Clervaux

Ettelbruck

12 US XXX

19 US XXX

5 US XXX

Verviers

Spa

18 US XXX

Stavelot

Salm

46 XXX

Houffalize

Wiltz

85 XXX

1 SS Pz XXX

Vielsalm

2 SS Pz XXX

Bastogne

101 US XXX

Martelange

3 US XXX

3 XXXX

Ambiève

1 US XXXX

7 US XXX

Hotton

9 SS Pz XXX

La Roche

Marche

Ourthe

Sûre

Our

Sûre

4 US XX

Neufchâteau

Recogne

Huy

Ciney

30 Br XXX

Dinant

Celles

Rochefort

47 Pz XXX

8 US XXX

Meuse

Namur

Sambre

Meuse

Clervaux

--- Front line, 26 Dec
- - - Front line, 2 Jan
····· Front line, 16 Jan
········· Front line, 7 Feb

German resistance began to wilt. Horrocks' 53rd Welsh Division captured Grimbiémont just four miles from Marche by 7 January 1945. The following day his 51st Highland Division took over the attack and by 11 January they were in La Roche. A few days later they made contact with Patton's men. By mid-month Horrocks' 30th Corps was redeploying north back to 21st Army Group ready for the battles to clear the west bank of the Rhine from the Ruhr to the Netherlands. Also, by the end of the first week of January, the US 84th Infantry had reached Marcouray and 2nd Armored had retaken Dochamps and Baraque de Fraiture. Although the Germans counter-attacked whenever they could, they found it increasingly difficult to endure Allied firepower. The defenders of the village of Samrée had 12,500 rounds fired at them by the divisional artillery of 2nd Armored. It was now that Hitler had to face up to the reality of his situation as there was little he could do to cling onto his hard-fought battlefield gains. Reluctantly on 9 January he agreed to the withdrawal of 5th Panzer Army east of the Liege-Bastogne road.

Patton commenced his main attack employing the US 4th and 6th Armored, 26th, 35th, 87th and 90th Infantry as well as the 17th and 101st Airborne Divisions. Patton, never one to mince his words, announced:

The purpose of this operation as far as the Third Army is concerned is to hit this son of a bitch – pardon me – in the flank, and we did it, with the result that he is damn well stopped and going back ...[16]

The going, though, proved to be tough against increasingly desperate German units. According to American intelligence, between 3 and 10 January those forces opposing Patton suffered 19,000 casualties and lost 70 tanks and assault guns. Panzer Lehr, 3rd and 15th Panzergrenadier, 5th Parachute and 167th Volksgrenadier Divisions struggled to hold Patton and were steadily driven back. Brandenberger's modest gains over the Our River between Diekirch and Echternach also came under pressure from Patton's forces. Meanwhile in the north, 116th Panzer along with the 12th, 560th and 32nd Volksgrenadier Divisions fought to slow the US 7th Corps' drive towards Houffalize and managed to inflict 1,600 casualties on the US 83rd Infantry Division.

On the night of 11/12 January Bayerlein began to withdraw his division from the head of the bulge. Squads of soldiers were sent back along the roads to spread sand on them to reduce accidents and to move any vehicle that broke down. Officers were posted on the junctions to keep the traffic moving at all costs. 'An almost unbroken snake of vehicles of all types, panzers and guns,' observed Major Ritgen, 'wound its way through the hilly icy roads to the east.'[17] Bayerlein had lost his armoured recovery vehicles and repair workshops to air attack so could do little to retrieve any broken-down vehicles. In total he had to abandon 53 tanks at the roadside during the retreat. 'Only occasionally were damaged panzers towed away,' noted Ritgen.[18]

Despite the presence of the 167th Volksgrenadier Division, von Manteuffel lost Wardin to the east of Bastogne after the US 6th Armored Division rolled in and linked up with the US 35th and 90th Infantry Divisions at Bras and Doncols. This trapped a pocket of German troops, including units of the 5th Parachute Division, around Harlange who were mopped up by the US 26th Infantry Division and Task Forces Fickett and Scott. North of Bastogne the US 11th Armored Division moved to the outskirts of Noville. The US 17th Airborne Division also cut the St Hubert-Houffalize highway. Shortly after, von Manteuffel's men were driven from Senonchamps by 6th Armored. The German hold around Bastogne had been completely broken. Patton was delighted, noting 'the fighting quality of American troops never reached a higher level than in this operation. Neither intolerable weather nor the best troops in the possession of the Germans were able to stop them nor prevent their supply.'[19]

Dietrich's 6th Panzer Army moved into reserve north of St Vith, though it would take it four days to comply due to Allied air attacks, blocked roads and the foul weather. German soldiers were not happy with what they saw as favouritism for the SS units; it occurred to few that they were actually destined for the Eastern Front so were hardly being done any favours by Hitler. Stalin's winter offensive commenced on 12 January 1945 and two days later Hitler ordered the exhausted 6th Panzer Army east; not to defend Prussia but rather Hungary's oilfields.

Major Bernd Freytag von Loringhoven, who served on Guderian's staff, was aghast at this plan. He and Guderian could not comprehend Hitler's logic. 'The only existing railway leading to Hungary was vulnerable to Allied air attacks,' noted von Loringhoven. 'The transfer of five divisions of the Sixth SS Panzer Army would take five or six weeks, much longer than a transport to the east where several railway lines were available.'[20]

Shortly afterwards Houffalize was lost and the US 1st and 3rd Armies linked up there when the US 2nd and 11th Armored Divisions came together. Colonel Rudolf Lanhauser's inexperienced 560th Volksgrenadiers had found themselves in the path of the US 2nd Armored. The latter took 1,742 prisoners, two-thirds of whom came from the 560th Volksgrenadiers; they also destroyed 51 tanks and self-propelled guns. When Patton entered the ruins that had once been Houffalize, he acknowledged Allied air power, remarking, 'Little town of Houffalize, here you sit on bended knees. God bless your people and keep them safe – especially from the RAF!'[21]

Around Bastogne the German position continued to deteriorate. Noville and Vaux were lost to the US 101st Airborne, while German troops were cleared from the woods to the east of Noville by the 327th Glider Infantry and 11th Armored. The survivors of Heilmann's 5th Parachute Division continued to fight on, even though Brandenberger acknowledged that it was 'completely exhausted and fantastically outnumbered'.[22] They found themselves fighting units not only of the US 4th and 11th Armored but also the 35th and 90th Infantry for over three weeks. 'For the first time in my military career,' said Heilmann, 'I started to go my own way. I intended to save human lives.'[23]

To the south-east, elements of the 352nd Volksgrenadier Division were unable to hold Hoesdorf and Battendorf on the Sauer River on 18 January. That same day Lieutenant Günther Stottmeister, commanding a company from the 352nd Volksgrenadiers, defending Diekirch was ordered to withdraw following an attack by the US 5th Infantry Division. Although his men had extensively mined the river banks, they only had machine guns and mortars with which to fend off the Americans. Furthermore, the Americans, using white phosphorus, had set many of the houses on fire. Members of the 914th Volksgrenadier Regiment did what they could to impede the American crossing. Horst Hennig and Ulrich Jonath were manning a machine gun when, in the early hours, the Americans launched their assault without a preliminary artillery bombardment. 'The group to our left also fired like mad,' recalled Jonath, 'some of our mortars also fired … There were many dead men on the slope.'[24]

In response the Americans laid down smoke and began to shell the German strongpoints in the local railway station and sawmill, forcing the defenders to flee. Jonath was wounded but successfully escaped. 'Through the binoculars I could see the Americans moving into Diekirch,' said Stottmeister. 'We were fired on but moved, guided by compass and maps, towards the German boundary, the river Our.'[25] Five days later, to the north the US 7th Armored Division retook the ruined town of St Vith. Some of the first men in were from the 48th Armored Infantry Battalion, who encountered a number of German tank destroyers on the outskirts, one of which had been waiting in an ambush position near a large brick barn.

By 28 January 1945 American front lines were back where they had started when the Ardennes offensive first commenced, thereby officially marking the end of the Battle of the Bulge. By this stage Patton's intelligence indicated that Model had 42,000 combat effectives, roughly five and a half divisions, with 95 panzers and assault guns facing his US 3rd Army. While this showed a modest increase of 1,500 men since the last estimate on 24 January, in that time the Germans had lost 95 tanks and assault guns.[26] Patton's forces had taken over 22,000 prisoners during the course of the battle.

Hitler's grand plan had all been for nothing. Nevertheless, his Ardennes offensive had proved to be a remarkable battle. He had thrown three armies at six US divisions over a 50-mile front achieving complete surprise. This resulted in an embarrassing breakthrough that brought the Americans and the British to loggerheads. Von Manteuffel and Model, though, never came close to getting to Brussels or Antwerp. Despite some American units being thrown into a state of utter confusion, their ad hoc battle groups fought with bravery and distinction on the northern shoulder, at St Vith and Bastogne. This greatly derailed Hitler's timetable.

Hitler severely underestimated the speed of the Allied response and the power of their air forces. Within the space of just four days the Allies reacted by redeploying half a million men to the Ardennes. Once the weather had cleared his forces were at the mercy of Allied fighter-bombers. His own airborne operations were ill-fated. The parachute drop during the attack ended in failure and the Luftwaffe's grand slam was too late to influence the battle. Hitler also underestimated the terrain and roads over which his armies had to fight. This slowed his advance and crucially delayed his second wave of attack forces.

The US armed forces paid a heavy price for their victory, suffering 8,407 killed, 46,170 wounded and 20,905 missing, captured or dead. Total American losses for the Ardennes-Alsace operations were estimated at 104,944. German casualties in the Ardennes were hard to gauge, but it is believed they lost 13,000 dead and 50,000 captured. Other estimates have put German losses in excess of 90,000, which including wounded is probably about right. The key point is that Hitler's armies, so carefully reconstituted and re-equipped after defeat in Normandy, had been swiftly thrown away. Some senior generals argued that they would have been much better used to defend the Rhine and Oder.

Stalin was to claim that his offensive saved the Allied armies. This of course was complete nonsense. Hitler's forces had already been fought to a standstill by then and the Americans had gone over to the counter-attack. Hitler had gambled and lost. He had thrown away the last of his armies and it was only a matter of time before his house of cards came tumbling down. The Rhine and the Oder were left horribly exposed. For Hitler there was no coming back from the brink.

24

Where Did It All Go Wrong?

What convinced Hitler to overrule his generals and launch the ill-conceived Ardennes offensive so late in World War II? It seems that one event in particular helped to shape his mindset. Certainly, following the attempt to kill him in July 1944, he believed more than ever that he was a man on a mission. 'He was convinced that he alone possessed clear perception concerning all fields of human activity,' wrote General Guderian. 'Accordingly, he condemned generals, staff officers, diplomats, government officials and towards the end even Party and SS Leaders as armchair strategists, weaklings and finally as criminals and traitors.'[1] In other words Hitler would not listen to reason. He had been intoxicated by the success of his Blitzkrieg during the early years and blindly hoped that these glory days could be recaptured. 'The will of one man and one man alone,' wrote Australian war correspondent Chester Wilmot, 'maintained a continent at war. That man was Adolf Hitler, and his resolution to fight to the end was ... fortified by the miracle of his deliverance on July 20th.'[2] Ironically, Hitler's Ardennes offensive only served to hasten that end.

Hitler remained delusional about the results of his Ardennes offensive until the very last. At the end of December, he had reluctantly conceded to Field Marshal von Rundstedt that the operation had 'not resulted in the decisive success which might have been expected'.[3] Only Hitler expected such an outcome; after the debates over the big or small solution in the West his generals knew his goals were much too ambitious. Hitler blamed his failure on the bad roads and the loss of certain bridges rather than the tenacity of the American defences. Nonetheless, he claimed the attack had bought Germany precious time until at least August 1945 or even perhaps the end of the year. 'This means a transformation in the situation,' he said, 'such as nobody would have believed a fortnight ago.'[4] It is very doubtful that von Rundstedt or anyone else actually believed him. 'It must have been obvious to the generals long before he finished,' American war correspondent William Shirer later wrote, 'that their Commander-in-Chief had become blinded to reality and lost himself in the clouds.'[5]

Hitler, realizing he had admitted defeat, tried to backtrack. 'I hasten to add, gentlemen, that,' he said, looking round at his generals, 'you are not to conclude that even remotely I envisage the loss of this war ... nothing will make the slightest change in my decision to fight on till at last the scales tip to our side.'[6] Hitler's commanders avoided eye contact. By this stage they had almost expended the last of their reserves in the West, while on the Eastern Front their defences were under enormous pressure in East Prussia, Poland and Hungary. 'Never in my life have I accepted the idea of surrender,' ranted Hitler. 'I say this only so that you can grasp why I pursue my goal with such fanaticism and why nothing can wear me down.'[7] A week later Hitler recognized the Ardennes offensive had completely failed when he had permitted his spearhead to withdraw towards Houffalize.

Hitler's generals were quick to distance themselves from the Ardennes offensive. Field Marshal von Rundstedt's prognosis was particularly damning. 'I wanted to stop the offensive at an early stage,' he said, 'but Hitler furiously insisted that it must go on. It was Stalingrad No.2.'[8] Dietrich was equally damning. 'This winter offensive, in my opinion,' he said, 'was the worst prepared German offensive of this war.'[9] Likewise, General von Manteuffel considered it as a terrible waste. 'When I saw the Ardennes offensive was blocked I wanted to carry out a general withdrawal – first to our starting line, and then to the Rhine,' he recalled, 'but Hitler would not hear of it. He chose to sacrifice the bulk of his main forces in a hopeless struggle on the West bank of the Rhine.'[10] General Brandenberger agreed with his colleagues that it had all been a waste of time. 'The Ardennes Offensive, on which the Supreme Command pinned all its hopes, completely failed,' he said, 'because the prerequisites for success were lacking from the start.'[11]

General von Manteuffel felt that his attack had been conducted on too wide a front and that his advance had been hamstrung by insufficient fuel supplies. Although his capture of St Vith was a major success, it was nonetheless 24 hours behind schedule. Furthermore, Allied air power rapidly hampered his exploitation of this vital road junction. He noted that, 'After 25 December 44, superiority of the Allied Air Force made movement on the battlefield impossible.'[12] He was also of the view that Dietrich's men had not fought with sufficient rigour. This was a little harsh in light of 6th Panzer Army suffering 37,000 casualties and losing up to 400 tanks. Von Manteuffel likewise grumbled about Brandenberger's delay before Wiltz, which obliged the 5th Parachute Division to pass through his sector.

Von Manteuffel acknowledged that his failure to take Bastogne had greatly weakened the push on the Meuse. His men had reached Bastogne at the very point that the US 101st Airborne slipped into the town to secure the vital road junction. After two wasted days of futile attacks to drive them out, von Manteuffel had no choice but to order the Panzer Lehr and 2nd Panzer to bypass Bastogne. Instead, he left the 26th Volksgrenadier Division to perform siege warfare. He admitted that 'the masking of Bastogne entailed a weakening of my strength for the forward drive, and thus diminished the chances of reaching the Meuse at Dinant.'[13] Once Patton's forces were pushing up the road from Arlon to Bastogne von Manteuffel was obliged to divert yet more troops. 'Part of the trouble,' said von Manteuffel, 'was due to the way that 7th Army had been reduced in strength, for its task was to block the roads running up from the south to Bastogne.'[14] After the war von Manteuffel became irritated by the constant focus on Bastogne. 'It's surprising to me that Bastogne has an honourable place in American military history,' he observed, 'and St Vith is hardly mentioned! The Battle of the Bulge was not fought solely at Bastogne.'[15]

'The fact that Bastogne could not be captured, was one of the main reasons for the failure of the offensive,' said General von Lüttwitz.[16] Nonetheless, even if they had taken Bastogne quickly and reached the Meuse by 22 December, von Lüttwitz knew 'Against ... [Allied] air superiority it would never have been possible ... to accomplish this mission.'[17] The outcome was that by Christmas Day von Manteuffel's advance was bogged down five miles from the Meuse starved of fuel, under air attack and with reinforcements held up at Bastogne.

General von Mellenthin also thought the operation had been a pointless exercise: 'we had suffered excessive losses in men and material and only gained a few weeks' respite. ... nothing was available to ward off the impending catastrophe in the East.'[18] He held Dietrich responsible rather than von Manteuffel. 'It was a great misfortune that Hitler placed his Schwerpunkt with the SS Army,' he said, 'whose commander was a very gallant fighter but had no real understanding of armoured warfare.'[19] This was a damning indictment of Dietrich's limitations. Notably, unlike von Mellenthin, von Manteuffel did not criticize only Dietrich: 'The junior commanders did not possess the tactical experience needed to ensure that the momentum of the attack was maintained, and fatal delays ensued.'[20]

Field Marshal von Rundstedt agreed that too much reliance had been placed on Dietrich's 6th Panzer Army. This meant that the emphasis of the attack was not in the central Ardennes, where the roads were judged to be better, but on the northern flank. 'This decision,' von Rundstedt later admitted, 'was a fundamental mistake that unbalanced the whole offensive.'[21] Hitler then made matters worse by reinforcing Dietrich and not von Manteuffel, even though the latter had created the opportunity for a breakout. The German leader placed all his faith in the SS; although he was aware of Dietrich's shortcomings, he had hoped that Krämer would be an influential hand.

Dietrich, who never wanted to command 6th Panzer Army in the first place and was opposed to the offensive from the very start, concluded, 'The whole attack was a big mistake.'[22] He tried to remove himself from any responsibility for the failure of *Watch on the Rhine*. 'I knew about the attack too late and couldn't give my best advice to my division commanders,' said Dietrich disingenuously.[23] Furthermore, he stated he was not consulted over the advisability of attacking through the Ardennes. 'If I had been asked,' he said, 'I would have been against ... A big tank attack in this terrain is impossible.'[24] Dietrich also blamed the weather: 'To use those two armies at that time of the year was the biggest mistake they made in the war.'[25]

Rather improbably, after the war Dietrich claimed that he had not heard about the plans for the Ardennes offensive until 12 December 1944. This may have been an attempt to minimize his long relationship with Hitler. When challenged by his interrogators about attending the conference in November, Dietrich claimed he was not there for the entire session. Jodl recalled, 'Dietrich was present at the meeting on 23 Nov 44. I remember it definitely. We had coffee together.'[26] It is possible that he left the room to check up on the birth of his third child as his wife had gone into labour in Karlsruhe. He also claimed that Model only told him in early December that something was going to happen, but the time and place had yet to be decided on.

None of this seems plausible. He must have known something major was brewing from the moment he took charge of 6th Panzer Army. Initially, in light of the developing situation at Aachen, this was the most likely focus of a German attack, especially once Dietrich's tanks moved to the Cologne area. Model would have had little reason not to consult him over the viability of the 'small solution'. It is hard to imagine that Dietrich did not know what was going on by late October. He saw Hitler then and the Führer's appointment of Krämer clearly shows he had a direct line into Dietrich's headquarters. The latter had received written orders on 20 November that 6th Panzer Army was to strike for Antwerp. Furthermore, Dietrich watched Model arguing in favour of the 'small solution' on 2 December. Bittrich and von Rundstedt oversaw the map exercise that day at Dietrich's headquarters which familiarized divisional commanders with the plan.

Hitler refused to acknowledge that he had been wrong and that he should have conducted a fighting withdrawal to the Rhine. Ungratefully he held von Rundstedt and Model responsible for the loss of his rebuilt armies. He felt that Model had been too narrow minded in the execution of the operation. 'Model,' grumbled Hitler, 'simply flattened me.'[27] In reality he had flattened himself. General Keitel remembered Hitler criticizing von Rundstedt and Model:

After the failure of the Ardennes offensive, Hitler told me that Rundstedt was too old. He did not have the right understanding and had insufficient influence over his generals. 'I cannot ask a man of his age to run around daily from one command post to another. We need a new and more active man.' I replied, 'Why don't you take Model? He knows the whole front and he is always on the move.' I received no reply. I was convinced that Hitler needed to have a scapegoat to avoid history shouldering him with responsibility.[28]

Pointedly Hitler eventually chose to replace von Rundstedt with Field Marshal Kesselring who was commanding German forces in Italy, not Model. The latter's fate was to die by his own hand in the closing days of the war. Eighteen-year-old Hansgeorg Model visited his father on 24 January 1945 for a few days before returning to Prussia. 'Suddenly the realization seized me,' recalled Hansgeorg as he drove away, 'I would never see my father again.'[29] Model senior knew that he had overplayed his hand with Hitler once too often. Overnight what influence he had on the German war effort evaporated.

In the wake of the Battle of the Bulge Skorzeny's concerns proved well founded, as a total of 18 commandos were captured, court-martialled and shot for masquerading as American troops. Their death sentence was in part sealed by the confession of one of Skorzeny's men who claimed he wanted to kill Eisenhower. Three commandos, Günther Billing, Manfred Pernass and Wilhelm Schmidt, taken at Aywaille, were shot on 23 December at Henri-Chappelle while the battle was still raging. A grenadier captured in American uniform was shot at Hotton three days later. Those who survived and got back to their own lines were treated as heroes.

Lieutenant General Horrocks had a grudging respect for the activities of Skorzeny's commandos. He later noted:

> Although, when the time came, only a relatively small number were able to operate behind our lines, certainly no more than fifty jeep loads – their presence had a disproportionate effect, and the atmosphere of suspicion they created greatly hampered the movements of our own personnel. I was once asked by an American sentry to establish my credentials by naming 'the second largest town in Texas'. As I did not know the answer, I had some difficulty in avoiding arrest.[30]

Horrocks also observed, 'One of the main difficulties in this battle was to find out what was happening. Rumours multiplied, particularly as regards the activities of the German commandos ... their numbers were multiplied at least twenty times.'[31]

After he was captured Skorzeny learned that a number of Americans were not as fortunate as Horrocks. A captain was held for a week after he was arrested wearing German boots, which he had picked up in France. On another occasion an American sergeant and two of his men were held as prisoners for over ten days after an incriminating German camouflage jacket was found in their jeep. One of them was German-American and spoke with an accent which aroused their captors' suspicions even more. The three Americans were put in with four of Skorzeny's men before the error was finally realized.

Horrocks acknowledged that Hitler's refusal to authorize a withdrawal until early January compounded the German defeat. He was of the opinion:

> By this time it was almost too late. Snow and biting winds added to the misery of the beaten German Armies as powerful thrusts by the 1st and 3rd US Armies struck into their flanks, while the air forces pounded them ceaselessly from above. On 11th January the two armies joined hands at Houffalize, and by the end of the month the Germans were back once more behind their Siegfried Line.[32]

'The failure of the Ardennes offensive meant that the war was over,' observed Albert Speer. 'What followed was only the occupation of Germany, delayed somewhat by a confused and impotent resistance.'[33] Everything his factories produced had been thrown away in Hitler's last throw of the dice. In the New Year out of sheer desperation Hitler's inner circle, comprising Bormann, Goebbels and Keitel, supported a *levée en masse* as the only way of saving Germany. Speer opposed total conscription on the grounds that it would paralyse their weapons factories and effectively kill the German war effort. 'Then, Herr Speer,' sneered Goebbels, 'you bear the historic guilt for the loss of the war for the lack of a few hundred thousand soldiers!'[34] Some of the blame for the failure of the operation did, though, rest on Speer's shoulders. He was responsible for the Todt Organization charged with bridge building during the offensive. However, it was not entirely his fault that the bridging equipment and the construction crews had been delayed east of the Rhine in the interminable traffic jams.

Ironically Speer's constant warnings that Germany was running out of raw materials and fuel helped to back Hitler into a strategic corner. This and the encroaching Allies had galvanized the Führer into taking action in the winter of 1944. 'Since he had nothing to lose,' wrote Major von Loringhoven in his memoirs, 'the Ardennes offensive would be his final bluff. He needed to gain time. A surprise victory over the Allies would allow him to negotiate a separate peace with them.'[35]

Speer, though, knew who the real culprit for the failure of the Ardennes was, aside from Hitler. Göring's Luftwaffe had singularly failed to support and protect the ground troops. The result was that, once the weather cleared, the Germans could only move at night and then without headlights. In contrast the Allies had complete freedom of movement both during the day and at night with the benefit of lights. One night in late December during a visit to Dietrich's headquarters near Houffalize, Speer had experienced first-hand the terrors of a low-level air attack. 'Howling and exploding bombs, clouds illuminated in red and yellow hues, droning motors,' he recalled, 'and no defense anywhere – I was stunned by this scene of military impotence which Hitler's military miscalculations had given such a grotesque setting.'[36]

Major General Freddie de Guingand, Montgomery's chief of staff, succinctly summed up the Luftwaffe's failings:

From the 22nd [December] onwards the weather improved and then our air forces taught the enemy that it is not very wise to undertake such an ambitious offensive without first having obtained air superiority. During the foggy weather the air forces attacked various railheads and rail centres feeding the Ardennes front, using instruments. After the fog cleared it was found many of these attacks had been most successful. The further back we forced the enemy railheads the more the enemy had to employ road transport to feed his offensive. And this gave our pilots unique opportunities, and the effect of their attacks was crippling.[37]

Furthermore, Speer blamed shambolic planning for the chaos on the roads which had so marred the German advance. He laid this state of affairs at the feet of Hitler:

Model offered all sorts of reasons for this confusion – lack of discipline in newly formed units, for example, or the chaos in the hinterland. But whatever the reasons, the whole scene showed that the army had lost its erstwhile famous talent for organization – surely one of the effects of Hitler's three years of command.[38]

The Luftwaffe's air attack launched on New Year's Day was too late to help the stalled ground offensive. It simply gave Allied pilots the opportunity to shoot down large numbers of German aircraft. General Koller, the Luftwaffe's chief of staff, blamed Hitler for failing to appreciate the air force's limitations. 'He had no understanding of the needs of the Luftwaffe,' Koller later complained, 'remaining an infantryman in outlook throughout his life.'[39] Another senior Luftwaffe officer felt they had been abandoned by Göring, stating, 'He hasn't any time for us.'[40]

Critically, the Luftwaffe was unable to stop the Allied air forces from pounding the German lines of communication supporting the Ardennes offensive. In the bulge, vital roads were blocked by air attack in the St Vith area. Houffalize was flattened when German troop concentrations were bombed during several night-time raids. RAF Bomber Command had targeted the railways, especially the Nippes marshalling yard in Cologne. Even when the weather was particularly bad in the week after 16 December, Bomber Command was still able to conduct raids on four nights and two days against supporting lines of communication. This greatly slowed down the Germans moving forward reinforcements and supplies.

The Luftwaffe was particularly hampered by the failure of its senior commanders to support each other. This was in part thanks to Hitler's policy of divide and rule. General Koller was placed in a hopeless position when Göring made it clear he thought their men should sacrifice themselves. He made no attempt to stand up to Göring or Hitler knowing full well that his predecessor General Kreipe had been sacked for displeasing them. General Schmid, the Luftwaffe's Commander-in-Chief in the West, was no more forceful than Koller. Galland had made clear his strategy as the chief of fighter command, but no one would support his 'Big Blow' concept. Instead, he was sacked for standing up to Göring and was sent back to do what he did best, being a fighter pilot. Major General Peltz did as instructed with the Luftwaffe's Ardennes air assault, but he knew that Operation *Baseplate* was not the best use of the Luftwaffe's dwindling resources.

A tantalizing question is, could the 'small solution' proposed by Dietrich, von Manteuffel and Brandenberger ever have worked? Taking Maastricht and Liège was a much more achievable goal than Antwerp. Mauling Simpson's US 9th Army would have been much less decisive than trapping the British 2nd, US 1st and 9th Armies and closing Antwerp to the Allies once again. However, had they taken Maastricht this would have placed them within much closer striking distance of the port than the Ardennes did. Likewise, an attack further north in the Roermond area could have posed a severe threat to Montgomery's hold on the southern Netherlands. None of these options, though, presented Hitler with a grand enough gesture, but they might have seriously slowed the Allied advance towards the Rhine. Furthermore, had the small solution trapped 15 American divisions as suggested by General von Mellenthin this could have further exacerbated America's growing manpower shortages.

General Guderian, as Chief of the General Staff, had argued since the summer of 1944 that the Eastern Front should be treated as a priority. In his view the Red Army posed the greatest menace to Germany's survival. He reasoned that the British and the Americans should be simply held on the Western Front and in Italy, while the Russians were driven back. Hitler and his other generals had not agreed. 'The whole tragedy of our military leadership was revealed once again towards the end of the war,' Guderian wrote with some bitterness, 'in this unsuccessful Ardennes Offensive.'[41] Major von Loringhoven felt sorry for Guderian, who was his boss. 'The Ardennes offensive presented Guderian with a *fait accompli*,' he noted, 'at the very time he wanted to reinforce the eastern front to block the progress of the Red Army.'[42]

Guderian was also angry that Hitler took so long to break off the attack. 'On December 24th it was plain to any perceptive soldier that the offensive had finally broken down,' he observed. 'It was necessary immediately to change direction and face east once again before it was too late.'[43] Instead two weeks were wasted. Deep down, though, he knew that it was already too late. 'The cost was so great that the offensive failed to show a profit,' acknowledged von Manteuffel. 'The last German reserves had suffered such losses that they were no longer capable of affecting the situation either on the western or eastern fronts.'[44] At the end of 1944 when Guderian had asked for help, von Rundstedt could only spare him four divisions and these Hitler instructed were to be sent to Hungary to try to save Budapest. Guderian's fears proved well founded when the Russians, not the British and the Americans, stormed into Berlin.

Appendix

DECEMBER 1944: OPERATION *WATCH ON THE RHINE*

GERMAN ORDER OF BATTLE

CinC WEST	**FIELD MARSHAL GERD VON RUNDSTEDT**
ARMY GROUP B	**FIELD MARSHAL WALTHER MODEL**

5th Panzer Army   General Hasso von Manteuffel
    19th Flak Brigade
    207th and 600th Engineer
      Battalions
    653rd Heavy Anti-Tank
      Battalion
    669th Ost (East) Battalion
    638th, 1094th and 1095th
      Heavy Artillery
      Batteries
    25th/975th Fortress
      Artillery Battery
    1099th, 1119th and
      1121st Heavy Mortar
      Batteries
    3rd Todt Brigade

47th Panzer Corps	General Heinrich von Lüttwitz
15th Volkswerfer Brigade	
182nd Flak Regiment	
766th Volks Artillery	
Corps	
2nd Panzer Division	Colonel Meinrad von Lauchert
3rd Panzer Regiment	
2nd and 304th	
Panzergrenadier	
Regiments	
74th Artillery Regiment	
2nd Reconnaissance	
Battalion	
38th Anti-Tank Battalion	
38th Engineer Battalion	
273rd Flak Battalion	
9th Panzer Division	General Harald von Elverfeldt
33rd Panzer Regiment	
10th and 11th	
Panzergrenadier	
Regiments	
102nd Artillery Regiment	
9th Reconnaissance	
Battalion	
50th Anti-Tank Battalion	
86th Engineer Battalion	
287th Flak Battalion	
301st Heavy Panzer	
Battalion (attached)	
Panzer Lehr Division	General Fritz Bayerlein
130th Panzer Regiment	
901st and 902nd	
Panzergrenadier	
Regiments	
130th Reconnaissance	
Battalion	

130th Anti-Tank Battalion
130th Engineer Battalion
311th Flak Battalion
559th Anti-Tank Battalion
(attached)
243rd Assault Gun Brigade
(attached)

26th Volksgrenadier Division   Colonel Heinz Kokott
39th Fusilier and 77th and
78th Volksgrenadier
Regiments
26th Artillery Regiment
26th Reconnaissance
Battalion
26th Anti-Tank
Battalion
26th Engineer Battalion

Führer Begleit Brigade   Colonel Otto Remer
102nd Panzer Battalion
100th Panzergrenadier
Regiment
120th Artillery Regiment
120th Reconnaissance
Battalion
120th Anti-Tank
Battalion
120th Engineer Battalion
828th Grenadier Battalion
673rd Flak Regiment

66th Corps   General Walther Lucht
16th Volkswerfer Brigade
86th and 87th Werfer
Regiments
244th Assault Gun Brigade
460th Heavy Artillery
Battalion

18th Volksgrenadier Division   Colonel Hoffmann-Schönborn
    293rd, 294th and 295th
      Volksgrenadier
      Regiments
    1818th Artillery Regiment
    1818th Anti-Tank
      Battalion
    1818th Engineer Battalion

62nd Volksgrenadier Division   Colonel Friedrich Kittel
    164th, 190th and 193rd
      Volksgrenadier
      Regiments
    162nd Artillery Regiment
    162nd Anti-Tank Battalion
    162nd Engineer Battalion

58th Panzer Corps   General Walther Krüger
    7th Volkswerfer Brigade
    84th and 85th Werfer
      Regiments
    401st Volks Artillery Corps
    1st Flak Regiment

116th Panzer Division *Greyhounds*   General Siegfried von Waldenburg
    16th Panzer Regiment
    60th and 156th
      Panzergrenadier
      Regiments
    146th Artillery Regiment
    146th Reconnaissance
      Battalion
    226th Anti-Tank
      Battalion
    675th Engineer Battalion
    281st Flak Battalion

560th Volksgrenadier Division	Colonel Rudolf Langhauser
1128th, 1129th and	
1130th Volksgrenadier	
Regiments	
1560th Artillery Regiment	
1560th Anti-Tank	
Battalion	
1560th Engineer Battalion	
29th Panzer Corps	General Karl Decker
167th Volksgrenadier Division	General Hans-Kurt Höcker
331st, 339th and 387th	
Volksgrenadier	
Regiments	
167th Artillery Regiment	
167th Anti-Tank Battalion	
167th Engineer Battalion	
6th Panzer Army	SS-General Josef 'Sepp' Dietrich
Battle Group von der	
Heydte	
506th Heavy Panzer	
Battalion	
683rd Heavy Anti-Tank	
Battalion	
217th Assault Panzer	
Battalion	
394th, 667th and 902nd	
Assault Gun Battalions	
741st Anti-Tank Battalion	
1098th, 1110th and	
1120th Heavy	
Howitzer Batteries	
428th Heavy Mortar	
Battery	

1123rd K-3 Battery
2nd Flak Division
41st and 43rd Flak
    Regiments
4th Todt Brigade

1st SS Panzer Corps   SS-Major General Hermann Priess
    4th Volkswerfer Brigade
    51st and 53rd Werfer
        Regiments
    9th Volkswerfer Brigade
    14th and 54th Werfer
        Regiments
    388th and 402nd Volks
        Artillery Corps
    501st SS Artillery
        Battalion

1st SS Panzer Division *Liebstandarte* SS-Colonel Wilhelm Mohnke
Adolf Hitler
    1st SS Panzer Regiment
    1st and 2nd SS
        Panzergrenadier
        Regiments
    1st SS Artillery Regiment
    1st SS Reconnaissance
        Battalion
    1st SS Anti-Tank
        Battalion
    1st SS Engineer Battalion
    1st SS Flak Battalion
    501st SS Heavy
        Panzer Battalion
        (attached)

1st SS Initial Assault Wave
    Route D
    Battle Group Peiper   SS-Lieutenant Colonel Jochen Peiper

1st Battalion 1st SS Panzer
Regiment
501st SS Heavy Panzer
Battalion
3rd Battalion 2nd SS
Panzergrenadier
Regiment
2nd Battalion 1st SS
Artillery Regiment
84th Flak Battalion

Battle Group Sandig   SS-Lieutenant Colonel Rudolf Sandig
1st and 2nd Battalions 2nd
SS Panzergrenadier
Regiment

Route E
Battle Group Hansen   SS-Colonel Max Hansen
1st SS Panzergrenadier
Regiment
1st SS Panzerjäger
Battalion

Battle Group Knittel   SS-Major Gustav Knittel
1st SS Reconnaissance
Battalion

3rd Parachute Division   Brigadier Walther Wadehn
5th, 8th and 9th Parachute
Regiments
3rd Artillery Regiment
3rd Reconnaissance
Battalion
3rd Anti-Tank Battalion
3rd Engineer Battalion

12th SS Panzer Division   SS-Colonel Hugo Kraas
Hitlerjugend
   12th SS Panzer Regiment
   25th and 26th SS
     Panzergrenadier
     Regiments
   12th SS Artillery Regiment
   12th SS Reconnaissance
     Battalion
   12th SS Anti-Tank Battalion
   12th SS Engineer Battalion
   12th SS Flak Battalion
   560th Heavy Anti-Tank
     Battalion (attached)

12th SS Initial Assault Wave
   Route A
     1st Battalion 25th SS
       Panzergrenadier
       Regiment
     12th SS Anti-Tank Battalion

   Route B
   Battle Group Müller   SS-Major Siegfried Müller
     25th SS Panzergrenadier
       Regiment
     Plus an artillery battalion
       and an engineer
       company

   Route C
   Battle Group Kühlmann   SS-Major Herbert Kühlmann
     12th SS Panzer Regiment
     560th Heavy Anti-Tank
       Battalion
     3rd Battalion 26th SS
       Panzergrenadier
       Regiment

Plus a self-propelled
   artillery battalion and
   an engineer company

Battle Group Bremer
   12th SS Reconnaissance
   Battalion
	SS-Major Gerhard Bremer

Battle Group Krause   SS-Lieutenant Colonel Bernhard Krause
   26th SS Panzergrenadier
      Regiment (minus its
      3rd battalion)
   Plus an artillery battalion,
      rocket battalion and
      flak and engineer units

12th Volksgrenadier Division   Brigadier Gerhard Engel
   27th Fusilier and 48th and
      89th Volksgrenadier
      Regiments
   12th Artillery Regiment
   12th Anti-Tank Battalion
   12th Fusilier Battalion
   12th Engineer Battalion

277th Volksgrenadier Division   Colonel Wilhelm Viebig
   289th, 990th and 991st
      Volksgrenadier
      Regiments
   277th Artillery Regiment
   277th Anti-tank Battalion
   277th Engineer Battalion

150th Panzer Brigade   SS-Lieutenant Colonel Otto
                                        Skorzeny

   Two panzer companies,
      two panzergrenadier
      companies and two
      anti-tank companies

A heavy mortar battalion
(two batteries)
600th SS Parachute
Battalion
Battle Group 200 (Luftwaffe
ground unit)

2nd SS Panzer Corps   SS-Lieutenant General Willi Bittrich
410th Volks Artillery Corps
502nd SS Heavy Artillery
Battalion

2nd SS Panzer Division *Das Reich*   SS-Brigadier Heinz Lammerding
2nd SS Panzer Regiment
3rd and 4th SS
Panzergrenadier
Regiments
2nd SS Artillery Regiment
2nd SS Reconnaissance
Battalion
2nd SS Engineer Battalion
2nd SS Flak Battalion

9th SS Panzer Division   SS-Colonel Sylvester Stadler
Hohenstaufen
9th SS Panzer Regiment
19th and 20th SS
Panzergrenadier
Regiments
9th SS Artillery Regiment
9th SS Reconnaissance
Battalion
9th SS Anti-Tank
Battalion
9th SS Engineer Battalion
9th SS Flak Battalion
519th Heavy Anti-Tank
Battalion (attached)

67th Corps · Major General Otto Hitzfeld
  17th Volkswerfer Brigade
  88th and 89th Werfer
    Regiments
  405th Volks Artillery
    Corps
  1001st Heavy Assault Gun
    Company

3rd Panzergrenadier Division · Brigadier Walther Denkert
  8th and 29th
    Panzergrenadier
    Regiments
  103rd Panzer Battalion
  3rd Artillery Regiment
  103rd Reconnaissance
    Battalion
  3rd Anti-Tank Battalion
  3rd Engineer Battalion
  312th Flak Battalion

246th Volksgrenadier Division · Colonel Peter Körte
  352nd, 404th and 689th
    Volksgrenadier
    Regiments
  246th Artillery Regiment
  246th Anti-Tank
    Battalion
  246th Engineer Battalion

272nd Volksgrenadier Division · Colonel Georg Kosmalla
  980th, 981st and 982nd
    Volksgrenadier
    Regiments
  272nd Artillery Regiment
  272nd Anti-Tank Battalion
  272nd Engineer Battalion

326th Volksgrenadier Division	Colonel Erwin Kaschner
751st, 752nd and 753rd Volksgrenadier Regiments	
326th Artillery Regiment	
326th Anti-Tank Battalion	
326th Engineer Battalion	
7th Army	General Erich Brandenberger
657th and 668th Heavy Anti-Tank Battalions	
501st Fortress Anti-Tank Battalion	
47th Engineer Battalion	
1092nd, 1093rd, 1124th and 1125th Heavy Howitzer Batteries	
660th Heavy Artillery Battery	
1029th, 1039th and 1122nd Heavy Mortar Batteries	
999th Penal Battalion	
44th Machine Gun Battalion	
15th Flak Regiment	
1st Todt Brigade	
53rd Corps	General Edwin von Rothkirch
9th Volksgrenadier Division	Colonel Werner Kolb
36th, 57th and 116th Volksgrenadier Regiments	
9th Artillery Regiment	
9th Anti-Tank Battalion	

15th Panzergrenadier Division   Colonel Hans-Joachim Deckert
   104th and 115th
      Panzergrenadier
      Regiments
   115th Panzer Battalion
   115th Artillery Regiment
   115th Reconnaissance
      Battalion
   33rd Anti-Tank Battalion
   33rd Engineer Battalion
   33rd Flak Battalion

Führer Grenadier Brigade   Colonel Hans-Joachim Kahler
   99th Panzergrenadier
      Regiment
   101st Panzer Battalion
   911st Assault Gun Brigade
   124th Anti-Tank Battalion
   124th Reconnaissance
      Battalion
   124th Engineer Battalion
   124th Flak Battalion

80th Corps   General Franz Beyer
   408th Volks Artillery
      Corps
   8th Volkswerfer Brigade
   2nd and Lehr Werfer
      Regiments

212th Volksgrenadier Division   Brigadier Franz Sensfuss
   316th, 320th and 423rd
      Volksgrenadier
      Regiments
   212th Artillery Regiment
   212th Anti-Tank Battalion
   212th Engineer Battalion

276th Volksgrenadier Division   General Kurt Möhring (later
                                       Colonel Hugo Dempwolff)
   986th, 987th and 988th
     Volksgrenadier
     Regiments
   276th Artillery Regiment
   276th Anti-Tank Battalion
   276th Engineer Battalion

340th Volksgrenadier Division   Colonel Theodor Tolsdorff
   694th, 695th and 696th   (committed under 1st SS Panzer
     Volksgrenadier Regiments   Corps)
   340th Artillery Regiment
   340th Anti-Tank Battalion
   340th Engineer Battalion

85th Corps   General Baptist Kniess
   406th Volks Artillery Corps
   18th Volkswerfer Brigade
   21st and 22nd Werfer
     Regiments

5th Parachute Division   Colonel Ludwig Heilmann
   13th, 14th and 15th
     Parachute Regiments
   5th Artillery Regiment
   5th Reconnaissance Battalion
   5th Engineer Battalion
   5th Flak Battalion
   11th Assault Gun Brigade

352nd Volksgrenadier Division   Colonel Erich Schmidt
   914th, 915th and 916th
     Volksgrenadier
     Regiments

352nd Artillery Regiment
352nd Anti-Tank Battalion
352nd Engineer Battalion

79th Volksgrenadier Division   Colonel Alois Weber
    208th, 212th and 226th
      Volksgrenadier
      Regiment
    179th Artillery Regiment
    179th Anti-Tank Battalion
    179th Engineer Battalion

Luftwaffe

2nd Fighter Corps   Major General Dietrich Peltz

3rd Air Division
    51st Bomber Group

3rd Fighter Division
    1st Fighter Group
    3rd Fighter Group
    6th Fighter Group
    26th Fighter Group
    27th Fighter Group
    54th Fighter Group
    77th Fighter Group

5th Fighter Division
    53rd Fighter Group

Fighter Sector Leader Middle Rhine
    2nd Fighter Group
    4th Fighter Group
    11th Fighter Group
    4th Ground Attack Group

3rd Flak Corps	Lieutenant-General Wolfgang Pickert

    2nd Flak Division
    16th Flak Division
    1st Flak Brigade
    18th Flak Brigade
    19th Flak Brigade

AMERICAN ORDER OF BATTLE

Supreme Headquarters Allied Expeditionary Force	General Dwight D. Eisenhower
12th US Army Group	Lieutenant General Omar N. Bradley
1st US Army	Lieutenant General Courtney H. Hodges
5th Corps	Major General Leonard T. Gerow

    1st Infantry Division *Big Red One*
    Brigadier General Clift Andrus

    2nd Infantry Division *Indianhead*
    Major General Walter M. Robertson

    9th Infantry Division *Octofoil*
    Major General Louis A. Craig

    78th Infantry Division *Lightning*
    Major General Edwin P. Parker

    99th Infantry Division *Checkerboard*
    Major General Walter E. Lauer

7th Corps   Major General Joseph Lawton
                                          Collins

 2nd Armored Division *Hell on Wheels*
 Major General Ernest N. Harmon

 3rd Armored Division *Spearhead*
 Major General Maurice Rose

 83rd Infantry Division *Thunderbolt*
 Major General Robert C. Macon

 84th Infantry Division *Railsplitters*
 Brigadier General Alezander R. Bolling

18th Airborne Corps   Major General Matthew B.
                                          Ridgway

 7th Armored Division *Lucky Seventh*
 Brigadier General Robert W. Hasbrouck

 30th Infantry Division *Old Hickory*
 Major General Leland S. Hobbs

 75th Infantry Division
 Major General Fay B. Prickett

 82nd Airborne Division *All American*
 Major General James M. Gavin

 106th Infantry Division *Golden Lions*
 Major General Alan W. Jones

3rd US Army   Lieutenant General George S.
                                          Patton Jr

3rd Corps   Major General John Millikin

    4th Armored Division
    Major General Hugh J. Gaffey

    6th Armored Division *Super Sixth*
    Major General Robert W. Grow

    26th Infantry Division *Yankee*
    Major General Willard S. Paul

    35th Infantry Division *Sante Fe*
    Major General Paul W. Baade

    90th Infantry Division Tough *Hombres*
    Major General James A. Van Fleet

8th Corps   Major General Troy H. Middleton

    9th Armored Division *Phantom*
    Major General John W. Leonard

    11th Armored Division *Thunderbolt*
    Brigadier General Charles S. Kilburn

    17th Airborne Division *Golden Talon*
    Major General William Miley

    28th Infantry Division *Keystone*
    Major General Norman D. Cota

    87th Infantry Division *Golden Acorn*
    Brigadier General Frank L. Culin Jr

    101st Airborne Division *Screaming Eagles*
    Brigadier General Anthony C. McAuliffe

12th Corps   Major General Manton S. Eddy

    4th Infantry Division *Ivy*
    Major General Raymond O. Barton

    5th Infantry Division *Red Diamond*
    Major General S. Leroy Irwin

    10th Armored Division *Tiger*
    Major General William H.H. Morris Jr

    80th Infantry Division *Blue Ridge*
    Major General Horace L. McBride

BRITISH ORDER OF BATTLE

21st Army Group   Field Marshal Sir Bernard L.
                                    Montgomery

30th Corps   Lieutenant General Brian G.
                                    Horrocks

    6th Airborne Division
    Major General Eric L. Bols

    51st Infantry Division *Highland*
    Major General T.G. Rennie

    53rd Infantry Division *Welsh*
    Major General R.K. Ross

    29th Armoured Brigade
    Brigadier C.B. Harvey

    33rd Armoured Brigade
    Brigadier H.B. Scott

34th Army Tank Brigade
Brigadier W.S. Clarke

Corps Reserve
Guards Armoured Division
43rd Infantry Division
50th Infantry Division *Northumbrian*

JANUARY 1945: OPERATION *NORTHWIND*

GERMAN ORDER OF BATTLE

North of Strasbourg

Army Group G	**General Johannes Blaskowitz**
1st Army	Major General Hans von Obstfelder

6th SS Mountain Division *Nord*
SS-Major General Karl-Heinrich Brenner

21st Panzer Division
Major General Edgar Feuchtinger

25th Panzergrenadier Division
Colonel Arnold Burmeister

13th SS Corps	SS-Lieutenant General Max Simon

17th SS Panzergrenadier Division *Götz Berlichingen*
SS-Colonel Hans Lingner

19th Volksgrenadier Division
Major General Walther Wissmath

36th Volksgrenadier Division
Brigadier Helmut Kleikamp

89th Corps   General Gustav Höhne

    245th Infantry Division
    Major General Edwin Sander

    256th Volksgrenadier Division
    Brigadier Gerhard Franz

    361st Volksgrenadier Division
    Brigadier Alfred Philippi

90th Corps   General Erich Petersen

    257th Volksgrenadier Division
    Brigadier Erich Seidel

    559th Volksgrenadier Division
    Major General Kurt Freiherr von Mühlen

South of Strasbourg

Army Group Upper Rhine   Reichsführer-SS Heinrich
                                        Himmler

19th Army   General Siegfried Rasp

14th SS Corps   SS-Lieutenant General Erich von
                                        dem Bach-Zelewski

    10th SS Panzer Division *Frundsberg*
    (from 15 January 1945)
    SS-Brigadier Heinz Harmel

    553rd Volksgrenadier Division
    Brigadier Gerhard Hüther

63rd Corps   General Erich Abraham

    159th Infantry Division
    Brigadier Heinrich Bürcky

    269th Infantry Division
    Major General Hans Wagner

    338th Infantry Division
    Brigadier Konrad Barde

    716th Infantry Division
    Brigadier Wolf Ewert

64th Corps   General Helmut Thumm

    189th Infantry Division
    Brigadier Eduard Zorn

    198th Infantry Division
    Brigadier Otto Schiel

    708th Volksgrenadier Division
    Brigadier Wilhelm Bleckwenn

ALLIED ORDER OF BATTLE

North of Strasbourg

6th US Army Group   Lieutenant General Jacob L.
                                        Devers

7th US Army   Lieutenant General Alexander
                                        Patch

6th Corps   Major General Edward H. Brooks

42nd Infantry Division
Major Henry Linden

45th Infantry Division
Major General Robert Frederick

70th Infantry Division
Brigadier General Thomas Herren

79th Infantry Division
Major General Ira Wyche

French 2nd Armored Division   General Philippe Leclerc de
                                     Hauteclocque

South of Strasbourg

1st French Army   Lieutenant General Jean de Lattre
                                     de Tassigny
1st Corps   General Antoine Béthouart

1st Infantry Division
General Diego Brosset

3rd Algerian Infantry Division
General Augustin Guillaume

2nd Corps   General Joseph de Goislard de
                                     Monsabert

1st Armored Division
General Aimé Sudré

1st Colonial Infantry Division
General Joseph Magnan

3rd Moroccan Division
General Marcel Carpentier

4th Moroccan Division
General Réne de Hesdin

5th Armored Division
General Henri de Vernejoul

10th Infantry Division
General Pierre Billotte

21st US Corps   Major General Frank W. Milburn

12th Armored Division
Major General Roderick R. Allen

14th Armored Division
Major General Albert Smith

36th Infantry Division
Major General John Dahlquist

20 JANUARY 1945

German Order of Battle

Colmar Bridgehead

19th Army   General Siegfried Rasp
  2nd Mountain Division
  106th Panzer Brigade

63rd Corps   General Erich Abraham
  159th Infantry Division

338th Infantry Division
716th Infantry Division

64th Corps   General Max Grimmeiss
   189th Infantry Division
   198th Infantry Division
   16th Volksgrenadier Division
   708th Volksgrenadier Division

Notes and References

PROLOGUE

1 Michael Reynolds, *The Devil's Adjutant: Jochen Peiper, Panzer Leader*, Barnsley: Pen & Sword, 2016, p.36
2 Charles Whiting, *Massacre at Malmedy: The Story of Jochen Peiper's Battle Group Ardennes, December, 1944*, London: Leo Cooper, 1971, p.30
3 Jean-Paul Pallud, *Ardennes 1944: Peiper and Skorzeny*, London: Osprey, 1987, p.15
4 Ibid.
5 Ibid., p.17
6 Ibid.
7 Whiting, *Massacre at Malmedy*, pp.30–1
8 Ibid., p.33

CHAPTER 1: SCARFACE

1 Tim Ripley, *Elite Units of the Third Reich: German Special Forces in World War II*, Miami: Lewis International, 2002, p.135
2 Ibid.
3 Otto Skorzeny, *Skorzeny's Special Missions: The Memoirs of Hitler's Most Daring Commando*. Barnsley: Frontline, 2011, p.146
4 Ibid.
5 Ibid.
6 Ibid., p.148
7 Ibid.
8 Pallud, *Ardennes 1944*, p.3
9 Skorzeny, *Skorzeny's Special Missions*, p.150
10 Ibid.

11 Ibid., p.151

12 Gerald Reitlinger, *The SS Alibi of a Nation 1922–1945*, London: Arms and Armour Press, 1981, p.395

13 Skorzeny, *Skorzeny's Special Missions*, p.157

14 Charles Whiting, *Ardennes: The Secret War*, London: Century, 1984, p.65

15 Ibid, p.126

16 Pallud, *Ardennes 1944*, p.10

17 Ibid.

18 Skorzeny, *Skorzeny's Special Missions*, p.157

19 Skorzeny simply identifies him as 'Lieutenant N' – see *Skorzeny's Special Missions*, p.160

20 Ibid.

21 Ibid., p.158

CHAPTER 2: BIG OR SMALL SOLUTION

1 Heinz Günther Guderian, *From Normandy to the Ruhr: With the 116th Panzer Division in World War II*, Bedford, PA: The Aberjona Press, 2001, p.283

2 Danny S. Parker (ed.), *Hitler's Ardennes Offensive: The German View of the Battle of the Bulge*, Barnsley: Frontline, 2016, p.251

3 Ibid., p.252

4 Ibid., p.31

5 Ibid., p.16

6 Ibid., p.37

7 Heinz Guderian, *Panzer Leader*, London: Futura, 1982, p.378

8 Ibid.

9 Guderian, *From Normandy to the Ruhr*, p.284

10 Skorzeny, *Skorzeny's Special Missions*, p.148

11 Marcel Stein, *A Flawed Genius: Field Marshal Walter Model: A Critical Biography*, Solihull: Helion, 2010, p.174

12 B.H. Liddell Hart, *The Other Side of the Hill: Germany's Generals, their Rise and Fall with their Own Account of Military Events 1939–1945*, London: Pan, 1983, p.447

13 Major General F.W. Mellenthin, *Panzer Battles*, London: Futura, 1984, p.406

14 Chester Wilmot, *The Struggle for Europe*, London: Collins, 1952, p.561

15 Guderian, *From Normandy to the Ruhr*, p.285

16 Alan Bullock, *Hitler: A Study in Tyranny*, Harmondsworth: Pelican, 1978, p.761

17 Guderian, *From Normandy to the Ruhr*, p.285
18 Charles Messenger, *The Last Prussian: A Biography of Field Marshal Gerd von Rundstedt 1875–1953*, Barnsley: Pen & Sword, 2018, p.211
19 *Late Vintage* or *Spätlese* was also the codename given to an operation conducted against Soviet partisans north of Smolensk in September 1942.
20 Parker, *Hitler's Ardennes Offensive*, p.248
21 Mellenthin, *Panzer Battles*, p.406
22 Charles Messenger, *Hitler's Gladiator: The Life and Times of Oberstgruppenführer Panzergeneral-Oberst der Waffen-SS Sepp Dietrich*, London: Brassey's, 1988, p.148
23 Ibid.
24 Ibid.
25 Albert Speer, *Inside the Third Reich*, London: Phoenix, 1995, p.559
26 Stein, *A Flawed Genius*, p.175
27 Liddell Hart, *The Other Side of the Hill*, p.451
28 Steven H. Newton, *Hitler's Commander: Field Marshal Walther Model – Hitler's Favourite General*, Cambridge, MA: Da Capo Press, 2006, p.332
29 Liddell Hart, *The Other Side of the Hill*, p.454
30 Donald E. Graves, *Blood and Steel 3: The Wehrmacht Archive: The Ardennes Offensive, December 1944 to January 1945*, Barnsley: Frontline, 2015, p.113
31 Wilmot, *The Struggle for Europe*, p.577
32 Ibid.
33 Bullock, *Hitler: A Study in Tyranny*, p.762
34 Wilmot, *The Struggle for Europe*, p.578
35 Messenger, *Hitler's Gladiator*, p.152
36 Führer Conferences, Fragment 28, 12 December 1944, cited in Wilmot, *The Struggle for Europe*, p.578
37 Ibid.
38 Ibid.
39 Joachim C. Fest, *Hitler*, London: Weidenfeld & Nicolson, 1987, p.721
40 Charles Whiting, *The Last Assault: The Battle of the Bulge Reassessed*, Barnsley: Pen & Sword, 2004, p.24
41 According to one of Hitler's secretaries, 'The expert who predicted a period of fog during December 1944, which favoured the concentration of troops before the offensive began, received a gold watch in gratitude for his correct forecast.' Christa Schroeder, *He Was My Chief: The Memoirs of Adolf Hitler's Secretary*, Barnsley: Frontline, 2012, p.125

42 Parker, *Hitler's Ardennes Offensive*, p.30
43 Ibid.
44 Messenger, *Hitler's Gladiator*, p.153
45 Liddell Hart, *The Other Side of the Hill*, p.451

CHAPTER 3: THE HOLY GRAIL

1 Red Ball was an old American term for priority cargo on the railways and the trains were marked with a red ball.
2 Major General J.L. Moulton, *Battle for Antwerp: The Liberation of the City and the Opening of the Scheldt 1944*, Hersham: Ian Allan, 1978, p.64
3 Ibid., p.88
4 For more on the German defence of Walcheren see Richard Brooks, *Walcheren 1944: Storming Hitler's Island Fortress*, Oxford: Osprey, 2011

CHAPTER 4: HOW MANY RIVERS?

1 Reynolds, *The Devil's Adjutant*, p.176
2 Parker, *Hitler's Ardennes Offensive*, p.75
3 Anthony Tucker-Jones, *The Panzer IV: Hitler's Rock*, Barnsley: Pen & Sword, 2017, pp.69–70
4 These consisted of the 207th and 600th Engineer Battalions.
5 Chris McNab, *Hitler's Armies: A History of the German War Machine 1939–45*, Oxford: Osprey, 2011, p.28
6 The German Army had a total of 92 engineer battalions, four mountain engineer battalions and nine armoured engineer regiments deployed on the Western and Italian fronts. See Nigel Thomas, *The German Army 1939–45 (5): Western Front 1943–45*, Oxford: Osprey, 2000, p.41
7 This was the 47th Engineer Brigade, see Parker, *Hitler's Ardennes Offensive*, pp.174 & 207
8 Ibid., p.183
9 Ibid.
10 Ibid., p.75
11 Ibid.
12 Gary Sterne, *The Americans and Germans at Bastogne: First-Hand Accounts from the Commanders*, Barnsley: Pen & Sword, 2020, p.28
13 Skorzeny, *Skorzeny's Special Missions*, p.171
14 Ibid., p.176
15 Ibid., p.163
16 Reynolds, *The Devil's Adjutant*, p.61
17 Skorzeny, *Skorzeny's Special Missions*, p.163

CHAPTER 5: PEOPLE'S GRENADIERS

1 Bullock, *Hitler: A Study in Tyranny*, p.757

2 Speer, *Inside the Third Reich*, p.533

3 Ibid.

4 Ibid., p.534

5 Wilmot, *The Struggle for Europe*, p.557

6 Anthony Tucker-Jones, *Stalin's Revenge: Operation Bagration and the Annihilation of Army Group Centre*, Barnsley: Pen & Sword, 2009, p.121

7 Ibid.

8 Robin Cross, *The Battle of the Bulge 1944: Hitler's Last Hope*, Staplehurst: Spellmount, 2002, pp.13–14

9 Speer, *Inside the Third Reich*, p.535

10 Some sources say he was a major general, but most of the Volksgrenadier divisions seem to have been commanded by colonels due to a shortage of senior officers.

11 Whiting, *The Last Assault*, pp.20 & 30

12 Guderian, *Panzer Leader*, p.364

13 Ibid.

14 Reitlinger, *The SS Alibi of a Nation*, p.385

15 Guderian, *Panzer Leader*, p.364

16 Reitlinger, *The SS Alibi of a Nation*, p.385

17 Ibid.

18 Charles Whiting, *'44: In Combat on the Western Front from Normandy to the Ardennes*, London: Century, 1984, p.151

19 Ibid. Whiting in both instances is citing the US 1st Army G-2 intelligence reports quoted by Milton Shulman, *Defeat in the West*, New York, E.P. Dutton & Co, 1948, pp.215–9

20 William L. Shirer, *The Rise and Fall of the Third Reich: A History of Nazi Germany*, London: Secker & Warburg, 1973, p.1088

21 Guderian, *Panzer Leader*, p.364

22 Mark Mazower, *Hitler's Empire: Nazi Rule in Occupied Europe*, London: Penguin, 2009, p.365

23 Donald E. Graves, *Blood and Steel 2: The Wehrmacht Archive: Retreat to the Reich, September to December 1944*, Barnsley: Frontline, 2015, p.18

24 Ibid.

25 Paul Roland, *The Secret Lives of the Nazis*, London: Arcturus, 2017, p.72

26 Parker, *Hitler's Ardennes Offensive*, p.27

Chapter 6: Exhausted Panzers

1 Anthony Tucker-Jones, *Falaise: The Flawed Victory – The Destruction of Panzer Gruppe West, August 1944*, Barnsley: Pen & Sword, 2008, p.188
2 Ibid.
3 Speer, *Inside the Third Reich*, p.552
4 Ibid.
5 Andrew Williams, *D-Day to Berlin*, London: Hodder & Stoughton, 2004, p.266
6 Guderian, *From Normandy to the Ruhr*, p.289
7 Graves, *Blood and Steel 3*, p.173
8 Ibid., p.174
9 Ibid.
10 Ibid.
11 Williams, *D-Day to Berlin*, p.266
12 Ibid.
13 Liddell Hart, *The Other Side of the Hill*, p.450
14 Ibid.
15 Fest, *Hitler*, p.721
16 Parker, *Hitler's Ardennes Offensive*, p.226
17 Ibid., p.225
18 Guderian, *Panzer Leader*, p.380
19 Graves, *Blood and Steel 3*, p.159
20 Ibid.
21 Liddell Hart, *The Other Side of the Hill*, p.451
22 Ibid., p.161
23 Ibid.
24 Graves, *Blood and Steel 2*, p.189
25 Ibid., pp.181–2

Chapter 7: Unleash the Tigers

1 Liddell Hart, *The Other Side of the Hill*, p.133
2 Chris Ellis & Peter Chamberlain, *The Great Tanks*, London: Hamlyn, 1975, p.103
3 Mellenthin, *Panzer Battles*, p.188
4 Liddell Hart, *The Other Side of the Hill*, p.133
5 John Nelson Rickard, *Advance and Destroy: Patton as Commander in the Bulge*, Lexington: University Press of Kentucky, 2011, p.37
6 Terry J. Gander, *PzKpfw VI Ausf E & B – Panzer VI Tiger I & II*, Hersham: Ian Allan, 2003, p.66

7 SS-Colonel Kurt Eggers served as the editor of *The Black Corps*, the newspaper of the Waffen-SS. He was killed in action in August 1943 on the Eastern Front. The SS war reporter regiment was subsequently named in his honour. Bruce Quarrie, *Hitler's Teutonic Knights: SS Panzers in Action*, London: Patrick Stephens, 1985, p.192

8 Guderian, *Panzer Leader*, p.296

9 Ibid., p.308

10 Liddell Hart, *The Other Side of the Hill*, p.134

11 Pallud, *Ardennes 1944*, p.57

12 The 'ambush scheme' was also applied to the Panther tank and Hetzer, Jagdpanther and Jagdpanzer IV tank destroyers. See Terence Wise, *D-Day to Berlin: Armour Camouflage and Markings of the United States, British and German Armies, June 1944 to May 1945*, London: Arms & Armour Press, 1979, pp.83 & 85

CHAPTER 8: FIGHTER NOT A BOMBER

1 Michael Fitzgerald, *Hitler's Secret Weapons of Mass Destruction: The Nazi Plan for Final Victory*, London: Arcturus, 2018, pp.54–5

2 Irving, *The Rise and Fall of the Luftwaffe*, p.425

3 Ibid., p.281

4 Ibid.

5 Ibid., p.289

6 Speer, *Inside the Third Reich*, p.491

7 Ibid.

8 John Weal, *Focke-Wulf Fw 190 Aces on the Eastern Front*, Oxford: Osprey, 2000, p.49

9 Irving, *The Rise and Fall of the Luftwaffe*, p.426

10 Cajus Bekker, *The Luftwaffe War Diaries*, London: Corgi, 1972, p.460

11 Speer, *Inside the Third Reich*, p.552

CHAPTER 9: THE BIG BLOW

1 Antony Beevor, *Ardennes 1944: Hitler's Last Gamble*, London: Viking, 2015, p.318

2 Ibid.

3 Irving, *The Rise and Fall of the Luftwaffe*, p.298

4 Tony Holmes (ed.), *Dogfight: The Greatest Air Duels of World War II*, Oxford: Osprey, 2013, p.266

5 Führer Conferences, Fragment 2, 6 November 1944, cited in Wilmot, *The Struggle for Europe*, p.559. American losses were actually 38 bombers and 25 fighters.

6 Patrick Delaforce, *The Battle of the Bulge: Hitler's Final Gamble*, Barnsley: Pen & Sword, 2014, pp.268–70
7 Beevor, *Ardennes 1944*, p.320
8 John Sweetman, *Schweinfurt: Disaster in the Skies*, London: Pan/Ballantine, 1971, p.154

CHAPTER 10: 'STUBBLER-HOPPERS'

1 Graves, *Blood and Steel 2*, p.87
2 Ibid.
3 Parker, *Hitler's Ardennes Offensive*, p.42
4 Newton, *Hitler's Commander*, p.334
5 Liddell Hart, *The Other Side of the Hill*, p.458
6 Beevor, *Ardennes 1944*, p.89
7 Whiting, *Ardennes: The Secret War*, pp.31–2
8 Ibid., p.29
9 Rückenpackung Zwangauslösung or rucksack packed to open.
10 Whiting, *Ardennes: The Secret War*, p.78
11 James Lucas, *Hitler's Enforcers: Leaders of the German War Machine 1933–1945*, London: Brockhampton Press, 1999, p.36
12 Whiting, *Ardennes: The Secret War*, p.78
13 Ibid., p.80
14 Ibid.
15 Ibid.
16 Messenger, *Hitler's Gladiator*, p.150
17 Ibid.
18 Many Russian parachutes tended to be square as this was more stable and gave a smoother descent. However, they opened slower and required greater height. See John Weeks, *The Airborne Soldier*, Poole: Blandford Press, 1982, p.43

CHAPTER 11: PEIPER LEADS THE CHARGE

1 Messenger, *Hitler's Gladiator*, p.153
2 John Toland, *The Battle of the Bulge*, London: Frederick Muller, 1959, p.42
3 Ibid.
4 Whiting, *Ardennes: The Secret War*, p.92
5 Parker, *Hitler's Ardennes Offensive*, p.50
6 Ibid., p.23
7 Toland, *The Battle of the Bulge*, p.65
8 Graves, *Blood and Steel 3*, p.29
9 Ibid.

10 The bodies were not discovered until 14 January 1945. The Malmedy
    Crossroads trial lasted from 16 May to 16 July 1946: 43 defendants
    were condemned to death, 23 to life in prison and eight received
    shorter sentences. Peiper was among those condemned to death,
    Dietrich was sentenced to 25 years in prison, Priess to 18 and Krämer
    to ten. The death sentences were later reduced to just six and these were
    then commuted to prison for life.

11 Whiting, '44: In Combat on the Western Front from Normandy to the
    Ardennes, p.162

12 Graves, Blood and Steel 3, p.32

13 Reynolds, The Devil's Adjutant, p.120

14 Ibid.

15 Ibid.

16 Ibid.

17 Ibid., p.121

18 Graves, Blood and Steel 3, p.32

19 Ibid.

20 Ibid.

21 Reynolds, The Devil's Adjutant, p.232

22 Toland, The Battle of the Bulge, p.232

23 Reynolds, The Devil's Adjutant, pp.232–3

24 Toland, The Battle of the Bulge, p.233

25 Ibid., p.265

26 Ibid.

27 Ibid., p.266

28 Whiting, Massacre at Malmedy, p.172

29 Ibid.

30 Graves, Blood and Steel 3, p.36

31 Whiting, Ardennes: The Secret War, p.165

32 Reynolds, The Devil's Adjutant, p.244

33 Graves, Blood and Steel 3, p.37

34 Whiting, Ardennes: The Secret War, p.166

CHAPTER 12: KRAUTS SPEAKING ENGLISH

1 Whiting, Ardennes: The Secret War, p.64

2 Ibid., p.68

3 Ibid.

4 Ibid., p.96

5 Ibid.

6 Ibid., p.106

7 To the north-east, Liège was protected by the US 49th Anti-Aircraft Brigade under the command of General Timberlake.

8 Skorzeny, *Skorzeny's Special Missions*, p.172

9 These commando exploits have to be viewed with caution. Even Skorzeny admits he had no way of verifying their claims.

10 Skorzeny, *Skorzeny's Special Missions*, p.171. Skorzeny states rather improbably that the naval officer was in German uniform at the time. Whiting, who subsequently identified him, states he was dressed as an American lieutenant.

11 Whiting, *Ardennes: The Secret War*, p.143

12 Ibid.

13 Ibid., p.125

14 Ibid., p.126

15 Anthony Tucker-Jones, 'Skorzeny's Surprise', *Military Illustrated*, April 2009, p.13; the correct answer was bandleader Harry James.

16 Ibid., p.14

17 Ibid., p.15

18 Whiting, *Ardennes: The Secret War*, p.149

19 Pallud, *Ardennes 1944*, p.14

20 Beevor, *Ardennes 1944*, p.176

21 Whiting, *Ardennes: The Secret War*, p.129

22 Beevor, *Ardennes 1944*, p.176. Whiting in *Ardennes: The Secret War* claims rather improbably that Clarke was held for five hours, p.129

23 Skorzeny, *Skorzeny's Special Missions*, p.176

24 Ibid., p.171

25 Ibid., pp.176–7

26 Whiting, *Ardennes: The Secret War*, p.151

27 Tucker-Jones, 'Skorzeny's Surprise', p.15

28 Skorzeny, *Skorzeny's Special Missions*, p.176

29 Ibid.

30 Reitlinger, *The SS Alibi of a Nation*, p.396

CHAPTER 13: THE LOSHEIM GAP

1 Liddell Hart, *The Other Side of the Hill*, p.459

2 Parker, *Hitler's Ardennes Offensive*, p.87

3 Whiting, *Last Assault*, p.90

4 Toland, *The Battle of the Bulge*, p.164

5 Beevor, *Ardennes 1944*, p.186

6 Parker, *Hitler's Ardennes Offensive*, p.105

7 Ibid., p.106

CHAPTER 14: FALCON TAKES FLIGHT

1   Charles B. MacDonald, *The Battle of the Bulge*, London: Weidenfeld & Nicolson, 1984, p.191
2   Whiting, *Ardennes: The Secret War*, p.102
3   Graves, *Blood and Steel 3*, p.96
4   Ibid., p.136
5   MacDonald, *The Battle of the Bulge*, p.370
6   Whiting, *Ardennes: The Secret War*, p.136
7   Delaforce, *The Battle of the Bulge*, p.46
8   Whiting, *Ardennes: The Secret War*, p.139
9   Delaforce, *The Battle of the Bulge*, p.46
10 Whiting, *Ardennes: The Secret War*, p.30
11 Graves, *Blood and Steel 3*, p.97
12 Bruce Quarrie, *Fallschirmjäger: German Paratrooper 1935–45*, Oxford: Osprey, 2001, p.49
13 Nigel de Lee, *Voices from the Battle of the Bulge*, Newton Abbot: David & Charles, 2004, p.270
14 Ibid.
15 Graves, *Blood and Steel 3*, p.97
16 Ibid., pp.97–8

CHAPTER 15: VICTORY AT ST VITH

1   Parker, *Hitler's Ardennes Offensive*, p.155
2   Toland, *The Battle of the Bulge*, p.161
3   Ibid.
4   Ibid.
5   Ibid.
6   Ibid.
7   Ibid.
8   Ibid.
9   Beevor, *Ardennes 1944*, p.187
10 Parker, *Hitler's Ardennes Offensive*, p.96
11 Graves, *Blood and Steel 3*, p.132
12 Parker, *Hitler's Ardennes Offensive*, pp.95–6
13 Graves, *Blood and Steel 3*, p.133
14 Ibid.
15 MacDonald, *The Battle of the Bulge*, p.475
16 Delaforce, *The Battle of the Bulge*, p.151
17 MacDonald, *The Battle of the Bulge*, p.475
18 Ibid.

19 Ibid., pp.57–8
20 Graves, *Blood and Steel 3*, p.40
21 MacDonald, *The Battle of the Bulge*, p.96

CHAPTER 16: STALLED AT BASTOGNE

1 Sterne, *The Americans and Germans at Bastogne*, p.153
2 Ibid., p.155
3 Liddell Hart, *The Other Side of the Hill*, p.460
4 Sterne, *The Americans and Germans at Bastogne*, p.156
5 Ibid., p.159
6 MacDonald, *The Battle of the Bulge*, p.511
7 Toland, *The Battle of the Bulge*, p.246
8 MacDonald, *The Battle of the Bulge*, p.512
9 Toland, *The Battle of the Bulge*, p.247
10 Russell F. Weigley, *Eisenhower's Lieutenants: The Campaign of France and Germany 1944–1945*, London: Sidgwick & Jackson, 1981, p.518
11 Ibid.
12 MacDonald, *The Battle of the Bulge*, p.513
13 Ibid.
14 Toland, *The Battle of the Bulge*, p.249
15 Delaforce, *The Battle of the Bulge*, p.239

CHAPTER 17: CLEAR SKIES

1 Delaforce, *The Battle of the Bulge*, p.319
2 Guderian, *From Normandy to the Ruhr*, p.330
3 Beevor, *Ardennes 1944*, p.251
4 de Lee, *Voices from the Battle of the Bulge*, p.116
5 Major General Sir Francis de Guingand, *Operation Victory*, London: Hodder & Stoughton, 1947, p.430
6 de Lee, *Voices from the Battle of the Bulge*, p.260
7 Will Fey, *Armor Battles of the Waffen-SS 1943–45*, Mechanicsburg, PA: Stackpole, 2003, pp.202–3
8 Ibid., p.202
9 Sterne, *The Americans and Germans at Bastogne*, p.190
10 Williams, *D-Day to Berlin*, p.282
11 Delaforce, *The Battle of the Bulge*, p.205
12 Beevor, *Ardennes 1944*, p.245
13 Guderian, *From Normandy to the Ruhr*, p.339
14 Graves, *Blood and Steel 3*, p.143
15 Ibid.

16 Wilmot, *The Struggle for Europe*, p.553
17 Duncan Rogers & Sarah Williams (ed.), *On the Bloody Road to Berlin: Frontline Accounts from North-West Europe and the Eastern Front 1944–45*, Solihull: Helion, 2005, p.145
18 Ibid.
19 Delaforce, *The Battle of the Bulge*, p.205
20 R.V. Jones, *Most Secret War: British Scientific Intelligence 1939–1945*, London: Hamish Hamilton, 1978, p.468
21 Beevor, *Ardennes 1944*, p.252
22 Sterne, *The Americans and Germans at Bastogne*, p.191
23 Beevor, *Ardennes 1944*, p.253
24 Fey, *Armor Battles of the Waffen-SS*, p.217
25 Rickard, *Advance and Destroy*, p.173
26 Sterne, *The Americans and Germans at Bastogne*, p.238
27 Max Arthur, *Forgotten Voices of the Second World War*, London: Ebury, 2004, p.376

CHAPTER 18: ALMOST TO THE MEUSE

1   Liddell Hart, *The Other Side of the Hill*, p.464
2   Ibid.
3   Fey, *Armor Battles of the Waffen-SS*, p.207
4   Ibid., p.208
5   Ibid.
6   Ibid., p.209
7   Ibid., p.212
8   Ibid.
9   Williams, *D-Day to Berlin*, p.283
10 Ibid.
11 Ibid.
12 Ibid.
13 Sterne, *The Americans and Germans at Bastogne*, p.258
14 Ibid., p.262

CHAPTER 19: AMERICAN COUNTER-ATTACK

1   Tucker-Jones, *Armoured Warfare in the Battle of the Bulge*, p.103
2   Rickard, *Advance and Destroy*, p.177
3   MacDonald, *The Battle of the Bulge*, p.521
4   Delaforce, *The Battle of the Bulge*, p.229
5   MacDonald, *The Battle of the Bulge*, p.521
6   Delaforce, *The Battle of the Bulge*, p.245

7 Liddell Hart, *The Other Side of the Hill*, p.463
8 Beevor, *Ardennes 1944*, p.293
9 Rickard, *Advance and Destroy*, p.177
10 Sterne, *The Americans and Germans at Bastogne*, p.259
11 Ibid.
12 Ibid.
13 Ibid.
14 Ibid., p.261
15 Ibid.
16 Beevor, *Ardennes 1944*, p.293
17 Toland, *The Battle of the Bulge*, p.322
18 Ibid., p.232
19 Ibid.
20 Ibid.

Chapter 20: Rockets to Antwerp

1 Speer, *Inside the Third Reich*, p.504
2 Antony Beevor, *Arnhem: The Battle for the Bridges, 1944*, London: Penguin, 2018, p.22
3 Speer, *Inside the Third Reich*, p.492
4 Liddell Hart, *The Other Side of the Hill*, p.410
5 Reitlinger, *The SS Alibi of a Nation*, p.413
6 Max Hastings, *Armageddon: The Battle for Germany 1944–45*, London: Macmillan, 2004, p.197
7 This consisted of 1,610 rockets and 8,696 flying bombs. See Jones, *Most Secret War: British Scientific Intelligence 1939–1945*, p.459.
8 Ibid.
9 Speer, *Inside the Third Reich*, p.494
10 Beevor, *Ardennes 1944*, p.25
11 Speer, *Inside the Third Reich*, p.494

Chapter 21: Battle of the Airfields

1 Whiting, *Ardennes: The Secret War*, p.167
2 Delaforce, *The Battle of the Bulge*, p.268
3 Ibid., p.271
4 Norman Franks, *Typhoon Attack*, London: Grub Street, 2003, p.191
5 Richard Townsend Bickers, *Air War Normandy*, Barnsley: Pen & Sword, 2015, p.133
6 Sources vary on the number of aircraft involved in *Baseplate*, ranging from 600 to over 1,000.

7 Bekker, *The Luftwaffe War Diaries*, p.456
8 Ibid. Also MacDonald, *The Battle of the Bulge*, p.608
9 Dwight D. Eisenhower, *Crusade in Europe*, London: William Heinemann, 1948, pp.391–2
10 Cross, *The Battle of the Bulge 1944*, p.164
11 Ripley, *Elite Units of the Third Reich*, p.168
12 Bekker, *The Luftwaffe War Diaries*, p.457

CHAPTER 22: ALSACE DIVERSION

1 Antonio Mūnoz, *Iron Fist: A Combat History of the 17th SS Panzergrenadier Division Götz von Berlichingen 1943–1945*, New York: Axis Europa Books, 1999, p.32
2 Richard Giziowski, *The Enigma of General Blaskowitz*, Barnsley: Leo Cooper, 1997, p.373
3 Rogers & Williams, *On the Bloody Road to Berlin*, p.145
4 Ibid., p.146
5 Fey, *Armor Battles of the Waffen-SS*, p.222
6 Ibid., p.223
7 Roger, & Williams, *On the Bloody Road to Berlin*, p.152
8 Reitlinger, *The SS Alibi of a Nation*, p.398
9 Ibid.

CHAPTER 23: BACK WHERE THEY STARTED

1 Sterne, *The Americans and Germans at Bastogne*, p.262
2 Ibid., p.264
3 Ibid., p.263
4 Ibid., p.264
5 Graves, *Blood and Steel 3*, p.161
6 Ibid., p.162
7 Ibid.
8 Tucker-Jones, *Armoured Warfare in the Battle of the Bulge*, p.131
9 Delaforce, *The Battle of the Bulge*, pp.301–3
10 Henrik Eberle and Mathias Uhl (ed.), *The Hitler Book: The Secret Dossier Prepared for Stalin*, London: John Murray, 2006, p.175
11 Ibid., p.176
12 Ibid., p.303
13 Liddell Hart, *The Other Side of the Hill*, p.464
14 Rickard, *Advance and Destroy*, p.319
15 Graves, *Blood and Steel 3*, p.126

16 Martin Blumenson, *Patton: The Man Behind the Legend 1885–1945*, London: Jonathan Cape, 1986, p.185
17 Williams, *D-Day to Berlin*, p.288
18 Ibid.
19 Province, *Patton's Third Army*, p.154
20 Bernd Freytag von Loringhoven with François d'Alançon, *In the Bunker with Hitler*, London: Weidenfeld & Nicolson, 2006, p.125
21 Carlo D'Este, *Patton: A Genius for War*, New York: Harper Perennial, 1996, p.696
22 Rickard, *Advance and Destroy*, p.277
23 Ibid., p.285
24 Delaforce, *The Battle of the Bulge*, p.310
25 Ibid., p.309
26 Province, *Patton's Third Army*, pp.161 & 165

CHAPTER 24: WHERE DID IT ALL GO WRONG?

1 Wilmot, *The Struggle for Europe*, p.381
2 Ibid., p.382
3 Ibid., p.605
4 Ibid., p.606
5 Shirer, *The Rise and Fall of the Third Reich*, p.1094
6 Ibid., pp.1094–5
7 Fest, *Hitler*, p.722
8 Liddell Hart, *The Other Side of the Hill*, p.464
9 Parker, *Hitler's Ardennes Offensive*, p.30
10 Liddell Hart, *The Other Side of the Hill*, p.464
11 Parker, *Hitler's Ardennes Offensive*, p.225
12 Sterne, *The Americans and Germans at Bastogne*, p.276
13 Liddell Hart, *The Other Side of the Hill*, p.460
14 Ibid., p.459
15 Martin King, *The Battle of the Bulge: Hitler's Final Gamble in Western Europe*, London: Arcturus, 2019, p.192
16 Sterne, *The Americans and Germans at Bastogne*, p.273
17 Ibid., p.274
18 Mellenthin, *Panzer Battles*, p.410
19 Ibid.
20 Messenger, *Hitler's Gladiator*, p.161
21 Wilmot, *The Struggle for Europe*, p.609
22 Parker, *Hitler's Ardennes Offensive*, p.276
23 Ibid., p.19

24 Sterne, *The Americans and Germans at Bastogne*, p.276
25 Ibid.
26 Messenger, *Hitler's Gladiator*, p.148
27 Stein, *A Flawed Genius*, p.178
28 Ibid.
29 Newton, *Hitler's Commander*, p.349
30 Sir Brian Horrocks, with Eversley Belfield & Major General H. Essame, *Corps Commander*, London: Magnum, 1979, p.140
31 Lieutenant-General Sir Brian Horrocks, *A Full Life*, London: Collins, 1960, p.240
32 Ibid., p.241
33 Speer, *Inside the Third Reich*, p.561
34 Ibid.
35 Loringhoven, *In the Bunker with Hitler*, p.119
36 Speer, *Inside the Third Reich*, p.560
37 de Guingand, *Operation Victory*, p.430
38 Speer, *Inside the Third Reich*, p.558
39 Beevor, *Ardennes 1944*, p.319
40 Ibid.
41 Guderian, *Panzer Leader*, p.381
42 Loringhoven, *In the Bunker with Hitler*, p.122
43 Ibid.
44 Horrocks, *A Full Life*, p.242

Bibliography

Biography and Memoirs

Arthur, Max, *Forgotten Voices of the Second World War*, London: Ebury, 2004

Blumenson, Martin, *Patton: The Man Behind the Legend 1885–1945*, London: Jonathan Cape, 1986

Bullock, Alan, *Hitler: A Study in Tyranny*, Harmondsworth: Pelican, 1978

de Guingand, Major General Sir Francis, *Operation Victory*, London: Hodder & Stoughton, 1947

de Lee, Nigel, *Voices from the Battle of the Bulge*, Newton Abbot: David & Charles, 2004

D'Este, Carlo, *Eisenhower*, London: Weidenfeld & Nicolson, 2002

D'Este, Carlo, *Patton: A Genius for War*, New York: Harper Perennial, 1996

Eberle, Henrik and Uhl, Mathias (ed.), *The Hitler Book: The Secret Dossier Prepared for Stalin*, London: John Murray, 2006

Eisenhower, Dwight D., *At Ease*, London: Robert Hale, 1968

Eisenhower, Dwight D., *Crusade in Europe*, London: William Heinemann, 1948

Fest, Joachim C., *Hitler*, London: Weidenfeld & Nicolson, 1987

Giziowski, Richard, *The Enigma of General Blaskowitz*, Barnsley: Leo Cooper, 1997

Guderian, Heinz Günther, *From Normandy to the Ruhr: With the 116th Panzer Division in World War II*, Bedford, PA: The Aberjona Press, 2001

Guderian, Heinz, *Panzer Leader*, London: Futura, 1982

Horrocks, Lieutenant General Sir Brian, *A Full Life*, London: Collins, 1960

Horrocks, Sir Brian, with Belfield, Eversley & Essame, Major General H., *Corps Commander*, London: Magnum, 1979

Irving, David, *The Rise and Fall of the Luftwaffe: The Life of Luftwaffe Marshal Erhard Milch*, London: Weidenfeld & Nicolson, 1973

Kempka, Erich, *I Was Hitler's Chauffeur: The Memoirs of Erich Kempka*, Barnsley: Frontline, 2012

Loringhoven, Bernd Freytag von, with d'Alançon, François, *In the Bunker with Hitler*, London: Weidenfeld & Nicolson, 2006

Matthews, Rupert, *Hitler: Military Commander*, London: Arcturus, 2003

Mellenthin, Major General F.W., *Panzer Battles*, London: Futura, 1984

Messenger, Charles, *Hitler's Gladiator: The Life and Times of Oberstgruppenführer Panzergeneral-Oberst der Waffen-SS Sepp Dietrich*, London: Brassey's, 1988

Messenger, Charles, *The Last Prussian: A Biography of Field Marshal Gerd von Rundstedt 1875–1953*, Barnsley: Pen & Sword, 2018

Newton, Steven H., *Hitler's Commander: Field Marshal Walther Model – Hitler's Favourite General*, Cambridge, MA: Da Capo Press, 2006

Reynolds, Michael, *The Devil's Adjutant: Jochen Peiper, Panzer Leader*, Barnsley: Pen & Sword, 2016

Reynolds, Michael, *Monty and Patton: Two Paths to Victory*, Stroud: Spellmount, 2005

Rickard, John Nelson, *Advance and Destroy: Patton as Commander in the Bulge*, Lexington: University Press of Kentucky, 2011

Schroeder, Christa, *He Was My Chief: The Memoirs of Adolf Hitler's Secretary*, Barnsley: Frontline, 2012

Sixsmith, E.K.G., *Eisenhower as Military Commander*, London: Batsford, 1973

Skorzeny, Otto, *Skorzeny's Special Missions: The Memoirs of Hitler's Most Daring Commando*, Barnsley: Frontline, 2011

Speer, Albert, *Inside the Third Reich*, London: Phoenix, 1995

Stein, Marcel, *A Flawed Genius: Field Marshal Walter Model: A Critical Biography*, Solihull: Helion, 2010

Weitz, John, *Hitler's Diplomat: The Life and Times of Joachim von Ribbentrop*, New York: Ticknor & Fields, 1992

Whiting, Charles, *Patton's Last Battle*, Staplehurst: Spellmount, 2002

Winters, Major Dick, *Beyond Band of Brothers*, London: Ebury, 2011

BATTLE OF THE BULGE

Beevor, Antony, *Ardennes 1944: Hitler's Last Gamble*, London: Viking, 2015

Caddick-Adams, Peter, *Snow & Steel: The Battle of the Bulge 1944–45*, London: Arrow, 2015

Cavanagh, William C.C., *The Battle East of Elsenborn and the Twin Villages*, Barnsley: Pen & Sword, 2012

Crookenden, Napier, *Battle of the Bulge 1944*, Hersham: Ian Allan, 1980

Cross, Robin, *The Battle of the Bulge 1944: Hitler's Last Hope*, Staplehurst: Spellmount, 2002

Delaforce, Patrick, *The Battle of the Bulge: Hitler's Final Gamble*, Barnsley: Pen & Sword, 2014

Graves, Donald E. *Blood and Steel 2: The Wehrmacht Archive: Retreat to the Reich, September to December 1944*. Barnsley: Frontline, 2015

Graves, Donald E., *Blood and Steel 3: The Wehrmacht Archive: The Ardennes Offensive, December 1944 to January 1945*, Barnsley: Frontline, 2015

Jordan, David, *Battle of the Bulge: Germany's Last Offensive December 1944–January 1945*, London: Amber Books, 2019

Kershaw, Alex, *The Longest Winter: The Epic Story of World War II's Most Decorated Platoon*, London: Penguin, 2006

King, Martin, *The Battle of the Bulge: Hitler's Final Gamble in Western Europe*, London: Arcturus, 2019

MacDonald, Charles B., *The Battle of the Bulge*, London: Weidenfeld & Nicolson, 1984

Pallud, Jean-Paul, *Ardennes 1944: Peiper and Skorzeny*, London: Osprey, 1987

Parker, Danny S. (ed.), *Hitler's Ardennes Offensive: The German View of the Battle of the Bulge*, Barnsley: Frontline, 2016

Pimlott, John, *Battle of the Bulge*, London: Bison, 1981

Sterne, Gary, *The Americans and Germans at Bastogne: First-Hand Accounts from the Commanders*, Barnsley: Pen & Sword, 2020

Toland, John, *The Battle of the Bulge*, London: Frederick Muller, 1959

Tucker-Jones, Anthony, *Armoured Warfare in the Battle of the Bulge 1944–1945*, Barnsley: Pen & Sword, 2018

Tucker-Jones, Anthony, 'Skorzeny's Surprise,' *Military Illustrated*, April 2009

Whiting, Charles, *Ardennes: The Secret War*, London: Century, 1984

Whiting, Charles, *The Last Assault: The Battle of the Bulge Reassessed*, Barnsley: Pen & Sword, 2004

Whiting, Charles, *Massacre at Malmedy: The Story of Jochen Peiper's Battle Group Ardennes, December 1944*, London: Leo Cooper, 1971

Whiting, Charles, *'44: In Combat on the Western Front from Normandy to the Ardennes*, London: Century, 1984

German Armour

Ellis, Chris and Chamberlain, Peter, *The Great Tanks*, London: Hamlyn, 1975

Forty, Jonathan, *PzKpfw V Ausf A, D & G: Panzer V Panther*, Hersham: Ian Allan, 2003

Forty, Jonathan, *PzKpfw IV Ausf A to J: Panzer IV*, Hersham: Ian Allan, 2002

Gander, Terry J., *JadPz IV, V, VI and Hetzer: Jagdpanzer*, Hersham: Ian Allan, 2004

Gander, Terry J., *PzKpfw VI Ausf E & B: Panzer VI Tiger I & II*, Hersham: Ian Allan, 2003

Tucker-Jones, Anthony, *German Assault Guns and Tank Destroyers 1940–1945*, Barnsley: Pen & Sword, 2016

Tucker-Jones, Anthony, *Hitler's Panzers: The Complete History 1933–1945*, Barnsley: Pen & Sword, 2020

Tucker-Jones, Anthony, *The Panther Tank: Hitler's T-34 Killer*, Barnsley: Pen & Sword, 2016

Tucker-Jones, Anthony, *The Panzer IV: Hitler's Rock*, Barnsley: Pen & Sword, 2017

Tucker-Jones, Anthony, *Tiger I & Tiger II*, Barnsley: Pen & Sword, 2012

German Army

Lucas, James, *Kommando: German Special Forces of World War Two*, London: Cassell, 2003

McNab, Chris, *Hitler's Armies: A History of the German War Machine 1939–45*, Oxford: Osprey, 2011

Ripley, Tim, *Elite Units of the Third Reich: German Special Forces in World War II*, Miami: Lewis International, 2002

Seaton, Albert, *The German Army 1933–45*, London: Weidenfeld & Nicolson, 1982

Thomas, Nigel, *The German Army 1939–45: Western Front 1943–45*, Oxford: Osprey, 2000

LUFTWAFFE/AIRBORNE

Bekker, Cajus, *The Luftwaffe War Diaries*, London: Corgi, 1972
Holmes, Tony (ed.), *Dogfight: The Greatest Air Duels of World War II*, Oxford: Osprey, 2013
Mondey, David, *The Hamlyn Concise Guide to Axis Aircraft of World War II*, London: Bounty Books, 2006
Quarrie, Bruce, *Fallschirmjäger: German Paratrooper 1935–45*, Oxford: Osprey, 2001
Quarrie, Bruce, *German Airborne Troops 1939–45*, Oxford: Osprey, 1983
Weal, John, *Focke-Wulf Fw 190 Aces on the Eastern Front*, Oxford: Osprey, 2000
Weeks, John, *The Airborne Soldier*, Poole: Blandford Press, 1982

WAFFEN-SS

Fey, Will, *Armor Battles of the Waffen-SS 1943–45*, Mechanicsburg, PA: Stackpole, 2003
McNab, Chris (ed.), *Hitler's Elite: The SS 1939–45*, Oxford: Osprey, 2013
Muñoz, Antonio, *Iron Fist: A Combat History of the 17th SS Panzergrenadier Division Götz von Berlichingen 1943–1945*, New York: Axis Europa Books, 1999
Quarrie, Bruce, *Hitler's Samurai: The Waffen-SS in Action*, London: Patrick Stephens, 1985
Quarrie, Bruce, *Hitler's Teutonic Knights: SS Panzers in Action*, London: Patrick Stephens, 1986
Quarrie, Bruce, *Weapons of the Waffen-SS: From Small Arms to Tanks*, London: Patrick Stephens, 1988
Reitlinger, Gerald, *The SS Alibi of a Nation 1922–1945*, London: Arms and Armour Press, 1981
Reynolds, Michael, *Men of Steel: I SS Panzer Corps the Ardennes and Eastern Front 1944–45*, Barnsley: Pen & Sword, 2016
Reynolds, Michael, *Sons of the Reich: II SS Panzer Corps Normandy, Arnhem, the Ardennes*, Barnsley: Pen & Sword, 2017
Tucker-Jones, Anthony, *Armoured Warfare and the Waffen-SS 1944–1945*, Barnsley: Pen & Sword, 2017

Williamson, Gordon, *The SS: Hitler's Instrument of Terror*, London:
Amber, 2002

Williamson, Gordon, *Waffen-SS Handbook 1933–1945*, Stroud: Sutton,
2003

GENERAL

Ambrose, Stephen E., *Band of Brothers: E Company, 506th Regiment,
101st Airborne from Normandy to Hitler's Eagle's Nest*, London: Simon
& Schuster, 2001/2017

Ambrose, Stephen E., *The Victors: The Men of World War II*, London:
Simon & Schuster 1997/London: Pocket Books, 2004

Bauer, Lieutenant Colonel E., *The History of World War II*, London:
Orbis, 1985

Beevor, Antony, *Arnhem: The Battle for the Bridges, 1944*, London:
Penguin, 2018

Brooks, Richard, *Walcheren 1944: Storming Hitler's Island Fortress*,
Oxford: Osprey, 2011

Chant, Christopher (ed.), *Hitler's Generals and their Battles*, London:
Purnell, 1976

Dargie, Richard, *The Plots to Kill Hitler: The Men and Women Who Tried
to Change History*, London: Arcturus, 2020

Farrington, Karen, *Victory in Europe: The Allies' Defeat of the Axis Forces*,
London: Arcturus, 2020

Fitzgerald, Michael, *Hitler's Secret Weapons of Mass Destruction: The Nazi
Plan for Final Victory*, London: Arcturus, 2018

Franks, Norman, *Typhoon Attack*, London: Grub Street, 2003

Frayn Turner, John, *Destination Berchtesgaden: The Story of the United
States Seventh Army in World War II*, Shepperton: Ian Allan, 1975

Grehan, John, *Hitler's V-weapons: The Battle Against the V-1 and V-2 in
WWII – An Official History*, Barnsley: Frontline Books, 2020

Hastings, Max, *Armageddon: The Battle for Germany 1944–45*, London:
Macmillan, 2004

Humble, Richard, *Hitler's Generals*, St Albans: Panther, 1976

Irving, David, *The War Between the Generals*, London: Allen Lane,
1981

Jones, R.V., *Most Secret War: British Scientific Intelligence 1939–1945*,
London: Hamish Hamilton, 1978

Katcher, Philip, *The US Army 1941–45*, London: Osprey, 1985

King, Martin, *Driving Back the Nazis: The Allied Liberation of Western Europe, Autumn 1944*, London: Arcturus, 2021

Liddell Hart, B.H., *History of the Second World War*, London: Cassell, 1970

Liddell Hart, B.H., *The Other Side of the Hill: Germany's Generals, their Rise and Fall with their own Account of Military Events 1939–1945*, London: Pan, 1983

Lucas, James, *Hitler's Enforcers: Leaders of the German War Machine 1933–1945*, London: Brockhampton Press, 1999

Mazower, Mark, *Hitler's Empire: Nazi Rule in Occupied Europe*, London: Penguin, 2009

Mitcham, Samuel W., *Hitler's Field Marshals and their Battles*, London: William Heinemann, 1988

Mollo, Andrew, *The Armed Forces of World War II*, London: Black Cat, 1987

Mollo, Andrew, *World Army Uniforms Since 1939*, Poole: New Orchard, 1986

Moulton, Major General J.L., *Battle for Antwerp: The Liberation of the City and the Opening of the Scheldt 1944*, Hersham: Ian Allan, 1978

Neillands, Robin, *The Battle for the Rhine 1944*, London: Weidenfeld & Nicolson, 2005

Province, Charles M., *Patton's Third Army: A Daily Combat Diary*, New York: Hippocrene, 1992

Rogers, Duncan & Williams, Sarah (ed.), *On the Bloody Road to Berlin: Frontline Accounts from North-West Europe and the Eastern Front 1944–45*, Solihull: Helion, 2005

Roland, Paul, *Life in the Third Reich: Daily Life in Nazi Germany 1933–1945*, London: Arcturus, 2019

Roland, Paul, *The Secret Lives of the Nazis*, London: Arcturus, 2017

Seaton, Albert, *The Fall of Fortress Europe 1943–1945*, London: Batsford, 1981

Shirer, William L., *The Rise and Fall of the Third Reich: A History of Nazi Germany*, London: Secker & Warburg, 1973

Shulman, Milton, *Defeat in the West*, New York: E.P. Dutton & Co, 1948

Smith, Steven, *2nd Armored Division: 'Hell on Wheels'*, Hersham: Ian Allan, 2003

Sweetman, John, *Bomber Crew: Taking on the Reich*, London: Abacus, 2005

Sweetman, John, *Schweinfurt: Disaster in the Skies*, London: Pan/
    Ballantine, 1971
Townsend Bickers, Richard, *Air War Normandy*, Barnsley: Pen & Sword,
    2015
Tucker-Jones, Anthony, *Armoured Warfare in Northwest Europe 1944–
    1945*, Barnsley: Pen & Sword, 2013
Tucker-Jones, Anthony, *Falaise: The Flawed Victory – The Destruction of
    Panzer Gruppe West, August 1944*, Barnsley: Pen & Sword, 2008
Tucker-Jones, Anthony, *Stalin's Revenge: Operation Bagration and the
    Annihilation of Army Group Centre*, Barnsley: Pen & Sword, 2009
Tucker-Jones, Anthony, *Tank Wrecks of the Western Front 1940–1945*,
    Barnsley: Pen & Sword, 2019
Weigley, Russell F., *Eisenhower's Lieutenants: The Campaign of France and
    Germany 1944–1945*, London: Sidgwick & Jackson, 1981
Westwood, John, Jennings, Patrick and Steeh, Judith, *Strategy and Tactics
    of the Great Commanders of World War II and their Battles*, Swindon:
    W.H. Smith, 1980
Whiting, Charles, *Siegfried: The Nazis' Last Stand*, London: Pan, 2003
Whiting, Charles, *West Wall: The Battle for Hitler's Siegfried Line
    September 1944–March 1945*, London: Pan, 2002
Williams, Andrew, *D-Day to Berlin*, London: Hodder & Stoughton,
    2004
Wilmot, Chester, *The Struggle for Europe*, London: Collins, 1952
Wise, Terence, *D-Day to Berlin: Armour Camouflage and Markings of
    the United States, British and German Armies, June 1944 to May 1945*,
    London: Arms and Armour Press, 1979

Index